AMERICA'S FORGOTTEN ARCHITECTURE

PANTHEON BOOKS NEW YORK

AMERICA'S FORGOTTEN ARCHITECTURE

NATIONAL TRUST FOR HISTORIC PRESERVATION, TONY P. WRENN AND ELIZABETH D. MULLOY

AMERICA'S FORGOTTEN ARCHITECTURE
by The National Trust for Historic Preservation in
the United States Copyright © 1976

Grateful acknowledgment is made to the following for
permission to reprint previously published material:
Prentice-Hall, Inc.: For an excerpt from *What You Must Know
Before You Invest* by Edgar D. Schaub. Copyright © 1968
by Prentice-Hall, Inc. Published by Prentice-Hall, Inc., Englewood
Cliffs, New Jersey. Little, Brown and Company: For the poem
"Maybe You Can't Take It With You, But Look What Happens
When You Leave It Behind," Copyright 1952 by Ogden Nash. From
The Private Dining Room and Other New Verses by Ogden Nash,
by permission of Little, Brown and Co.

New York Magazine: For an excerpt from a feature
article by Peter Blake, December 9, 1974.
Copyright © 1974 by the NYM Corporation.
Reprinted by permission of *New York* Magazine.

Acknowledgments for the photographs can be
found on pages 301–304.

Library of Congress Cataloging in Publication Data

National Trust for Historic Preservation in
the United States.
America's Forgotten Architecture.

Bibliography: pp. 297–300
Includes index.   1.   Historic buildings—United States—
Conservation and restoration.   2.   Cities
and towns—Planning—United States.   I.   Title.
E159.N356   1976a   720'.28   76-9467
ISBN 0-394-49692-2   ISBN 0-394-73228-6 pbk.

The National Trust for Historic Preservation, 740–748
Jackson Place, N.W., Washington, D.C. 20006
is the only national nonprofit organization chartered by Congress
to encourage public participation in the preservation of architecturally
and historically significant buildings and sites. Programs of
the National Trust for Historic Preservation are supported by
dues from members, contributions from donors, and matching
grants from the National Park Service, U.S. Department of the Interior,
under provisions of the National Historic Preservation Act of 1966.

ACKNOWLEDGMENTS

This book was made possible, not by a few authors or several score researchers, writers, and photographers, but by a history of concern in this country for our built environment and the need to make that environment a place of pride and sustenance for all Americans. It is a concern that is as yet shared by too few people, but our numbers are growing along with our progress toward achieving more livable surroundings that link us to the past while making room for the future. This book, then, is a synthesis of all that has been accomplished toward conserving our built resources and all the contributions of the people who have moved us closer to this goal.

Actual production of the book by the National Trust for Historic Preservation was under the direction of its Preservation Press, Terry B. Morton, Vice President and Editor—project director; and Diane Maddex, Director of Planning—project editor. It includes material and illustrations developed, collected, and written by Tony P. Wrenn and Elizabeth D. Mulloy, with assistance provided by Peter H. Smith.

The National Trust was able to provide the research facilities and support services necessary for preparation of the manuscript and purchase of the several hundred photographs with the help of matching grants-in-aid from the National Park Service, U.S. Department of the Interior, under provisions of the National Historic Preservation Act of 1966. National Trust programs and publications also are supported through contributions and dues of its members, so that the 100,000 individual and organizational members of the National Trust also must be counted among the book's contributors. This is their book too.

André Schiffrin of Pantheon Books first suggested such a book to the Preservation Press and has provided encouragement and assistance throughout its development, together with Barbara Plumb and Amy Huntoon of Pantheon and Robert D. Scudellari, Janet Odgis, and Connie Mellon of Random House.

A large number of photographs in the book have never been published before and are from the private collections of many photographers. Three of these deserve particular acknowledgment for allowing special access to their files and for sharing with us so many photographs taken because of their personal interest in preserving the built environment: Wm. Edmund Barrett, Clifton, Va.; Balthazar Korab, Troy, Mich.; and Carleton Knight III, Washington, D.C. Other photographers also offered special assistance by taking or sending photographs for review. These and others whose photographs were located in the files of the various federal, state, and local agencies and private collections are credited following the text of the book.

Members of the National Trust and Preservation Press staffs provided manuscript review and assistance with collection of photographs. Too numerous to list individually, these include those at National Trust headquarters and in its regional and field offices. Editorial research was assisted by Susan Slade.

Three programs in the U.S. Department of the Interior's National Park Service were used as primary sources for graphics and related information, and the help of the staffs of these agencies—the National Register of Historic Places, the Historic American Buildings Survey, and the Historic American Engineering Record—is particularly appreciated.

The State Historic Preservation Offices in nearly every state were extremely cooperative in enabling the National Trust to provide the most comprehensive picture possible of all that is worth preserving across the country. Space does not allow us to thank each of those who furnished photographs and information or suggestions, nor to individually recognize the staffs of the preservation groups, historical agencies, and private firms and the individuals who all together have brought this book to fruition in this important year.

This is a different Bicentennial book, however—its message being that the environment in which we live deserves our care and attention every year, not just on special occasions, and that it will take all of us working together to preserve it.

CONTENTS

IDENTIFICATION OF THE PHOTOGRAPHS THAT APPEAR WITHOUT CAPTIONS CAN BE FOUND ON PAGES 301-302 WITH THE PHOTOGRAPH CREDITS.

FOREWORD

America was built on a motto that few people ever translate from the Latin, *E Pluribus Unum:* Out of many, one. This is the melting-pot theory—that out of many nationalities, many viewpoints, and many actions emerged one homogenous nation. The year 1976 is as good a time as any to face the fact that in so many aspects of American life, including our architecture, this isn't exactly true. The pot has not all melted, mixing the wealth of tastes and colors and textures into one stew. Consciously or not, 200 years after the beginning of the nation Americans still retain strong ties to their multi-faceted heritage of social customs, political views, language, even culinary habits. Diversity, not sameness, is also the keystone of our architectural heritage. Out of many needs for shelter, many climates, many kinds of topography, many nationalities, and many tastes and abilities have come many types and styles and qualities of structures in which we carry on our activities. As the following pages show so clearly, there is no one type of structure or style of architecture that epitomizes America's built environment, that part of our surroundings shaped more by people than by nature. This environment is composed in turn of Indian pueblos and New England saltboxes, eighteenth-century Georgian colonial mansions and twentieth-century bungalows, austere Shaker meetinghouses and Baroque Spanish cathedrals, bracket-eaved Main Street stores and Chicago School skyscrapers, rural and urban, old and new, paving materials, public sculpture, and street lights as well as the structures themselves. It is this variety that makes our built environment as culturally rich as the nation itself, and as worth preserving.

Architecture is one of the "necessary" arts, always with the capacity to reach the peak of creative impulses, but always tempered by the need to function. Built structures play a significant role in giving character, good and bad, to every inch of inhabited land in this country. They physically define an area, making it different from any other. Through their historical or cultural associations and stylistic ambience (or lack of it), they affect the ways in which people regard their environment. But because buildings are so necessary, the built environment, like air and water and the land, has been overlooked until its loss of quality or viability is almost inescapable.

No matter how belatedly they have come to realize it, there are not many people who any longer deny that there is an inherent right to a healthful natural environment. It is obvious, as one looks at the blight of urban slums, abandoned cities, leveled acres lost to urban renewal or commercial pressures, suburban sprawl, and the dehumanizing new buildings going up around us, that the same right to a decent built environment has hardly even been recognized, much less accepted or implemented. Perhaps the time has come, after two centuries of gradually acknowledging the rights of all the animate and inanimate elements that together make us a nation, to approve a bill of rights for our total environment, the built along with the natural. There are many of us who believe that the public welfare demands this. The United States Supreme Court, for one, has recognized the right of cities to be beautiful for their inhabitants. In a 1954 opinion written by then Associate Justice William O. Douglas, the Court asserted that the concept of public welfare represents values that are "spiritual as well as physical, aesthetic as well as monetary. It is within the power of the legislature," said the Court, "to determine that the community should be beautiful as well as healthy, spacious as well as clean, well-balanced as well as carefully patrolled. . . . there is nothing in the Fifth Amendment that stands in the way."

There is nothing that stands in the way except the fact that this part of the environment has remained almost totally forgotten. It is difficult to believe that something as necessary and as pervasive as buildings, or at least their quality, can be forgotten. But it is indisputable that buildings are the forgotten environment. When they are remembered, it is too often piecemeal, in terms of major landmarks but not the interstices, the background buildings and street furniture and other elements that hold the built environment together. It is to all the overlooked architecture that this book is dedicated, both the landmarks whose value is not questioned—only the means to save them—and those that have not yet crossed the threshold of proving their worth. America's forgotten architecture is any structure or group of structures that could be used and deserves to be used again, from a townhouse in New York to a barn in Iowa or a pueblo community in Arizona.

Of course, not everyone has forgotten. This year, in fact, marks a decade of unprecedented growth in the number and scope of preservation efforts nationwide, due in great part to passage of the National Historic Preservation Act of 1966, with its consequent upsurge in state preservation and planning efforts. The National Trust for Historic Preservation, the only Congressionally chartered national preservation organization, has strived for more than a quarter century to awaken Americans to the need for conserving their built resources along with the natural.

Since its inception, the National Trust has used a variety of means to carry out its mandate. One of the most effective has been communication through the written word and, because what we're talking about is significantly a visual thing, through pictures. The Trust publishing program only last year was expanded to a full-fledged press, undertaking a wide range of books in addition to the monthly newspaper and quarterly magazine and other publications that the Trust has traditionally published. In our publishing, as in all our preservation efforts, the concern is to produce works of lasting value, things that are a pleasure to use and behold. It is thus especially appropriate for the Trust to have been able to cooperate with Pantheon Books in this effort at furthering preservation on paper.

And what does the word "preservation" mean? It also is not one thing, but many. In a sense, it is indeed the right of our cities, or any other place where people are, to be beautiful. This does not mean an ephemeral, effete beauty; where the only other choice is a new but sprawling, inhuman tenement that nobody wants to maintain, beauty can be a clean and humanly scaled, rehabilitated old row house. There is preservation that moves a threatened house out of the way of a highway, and the kind that gets residents out to fix up and take pride in a whole neighborhood. There is also the preservation that makes museums of antebellum plantations, and the kind that turns abandoned nineteenth-century factories into thriving commercial enterprises. There is just plain maintenance and renovation, as well as concern about designing new buildings to fit peaceably into old areas. There is preservation that maintains the setting, the natural environment, as well as the built. Preservation means basically conserving irreplaceable resources.

This book can show only a few of the things worth saving in our country and a few of the ways people are already going about it. But if it does nothing else, it should put to rest forever that arbitrary habit of singling out environmentalists and preservationists as "them"— the other side. There is only one environment out there, and what happens to it is not up to any vague or far-removed "them," but to *us*.

James Biddle, President
National Trust for Historic Preservation

AUTHOR'S PREFACE

In the past, books about historic preservation written for general readers tended to be one of two types. Either they were coffee-table volumes, lavishly illustrated with artful photographs of famous and historic houses, complete with interior views of antique wood and silver gleaming in candlelight, or they were tales of lament, full of speckled documentary photos or stark mugshots of venerable old buildings pictured in mid-demolition, their insides hanging out after the onslaught of a wrecking ball. Both approaches serve a purpose: the first, to inspire appreciation of major landmarks of beauty and historical importance; the second, to anger building-lovers to the point of taking action to save them.

Because such books have been successful, people in many parts of the country have been encouraged to join in evaluating and preserving their architectural heritage. The federal, state, and local governments have played a significant role in these activities. But now that a number of programs are under way, many people think that all those things that should be saved are, in fact, *being* saved. In actuality a vast wealth of structures that deserve to be saved and can be saved stand overlooked, some still in use, some abandoned and in jeopardy.

In historic cities such as Charleston, S.C., New Orleans, and San Francisco, where preservationists cut their teeth on programs to save major landmarks, many have moved on to fostering appreciation of the so-called background buildings, structures, and sites—those elements of the built environment that provide a setting for the more outstanding structures. Many other towns have discovered their own uniqueness and have saved their architectural identities from pressures to forfeit character for modernity. But in too many places the vernacular and background architecture that gives an urban or a rural community a personality of its own has not been recognized for the valuable resource it is. Because it is familiar, many communities fail to see the importance of what is around them.

It is primarily to such communities and the people who live in them that this book is addressed. And these communities are everywhere—in the heartland of the country, even in the hearts of cities.

The buildings and places in the following pages have been hidden by a number of factors, not the least of which is a lack of knowledge of architecture itself. In the second chapter, beginning on page 35, we have suggested some ways of looking at both the insides and outsides of buildings and have briefly outlined basic American architectural styles to help readers classify what they see. Other exercises are included that will, we hope, introduce new ways of experiencing the built environment.

The structures and sites pictured in this book have been hidden not only by misconceptions of what is beautiful or valuable but also by the very fact that they are not set apart but are to be found everywhere—in downtown areas, in housing developments, in the midst of pedestrians and traffic, behind commercial signs and telephone poles and lines, in shopping centers surrounded by cars, around animals and machinery. Some of the photographs show them in these settings, in the context in which they exist. All photographs are intended to serve as guides to making new discoveries, for there is no area where needs have not produced changes in the built environment, changes that created places worth noting, understanding, studying, and perhaps saving.

Because many of the things shown here are not yet universally recognized as valuable, there have been few systematic efforts to record them with photographs and historical information. The national and state collections on which this book is partially based have documented only a fraction of this resource. Inadequate funding and small staffs have hampered many efforts at more widespread recording, so that often only the cream is skimmed off. Many interesting and usable older structures receive little attention until (a) they are in imminent danger of being torn down and photographs are taken for documentary purposes, (b) they are eventually included in a national program such as the Historic American Buildings Survey or the Historic American Engineering Record, or (c) they are photographed by professional or amateur photographers who take the initiative and the time for sheer personal pleasure. We have sought out all of these sources.

Although our desire was to picture only standing structures or sites that can still be seen and saved, without doubt some are being destroyed (just as some are being saved) as these words are being read. We have tried, however, to avoid nostalgia for the lost, concentrating instead on pointing out successful preservation programs in communities of every size across the country so that these examples might be applied in others.

Most of all, we have tried to pique curiosity so that readers will go exploring in their own communities, see what's there, show it to others, and, working together, save it.

January 1976

OUR HIDDEN INHERITANCE

OUR HIDDEN INHERITANCE

An American family decides to combine education with vacation. To soak up some history, they set out for Colonial Williamsburg, Va., probably the most famous re-created village in America.

To get there, they travel an interstate highway, grateful that they don't have to drive through all of those little, out-of-the-way towns as they once did. Never mind that the little towns may be filled with historic sites or delightful buildings.

So impressed are they by the colonial style of building they see in Williamsburg—and on many gas stations en route—that, returning home, they add a white clapboard façade and a cupola to their split-level home. *Voilà.* Instant colonial.

If you want to see beautiful or historic buildings, you can always go to Williamsburg, or build copies of it.

Last year, 1.5 million people went to Williamsburg. And while they were gone, historic buildings in their own home towns and all the little towns en route were being demolished. Williamsburg played host to 1.5 million people, while the national organization chartered by Congress to help Americans preserve old buildings throughout the country was happy to reach a membership of 100,000. By a vote of 10½ to 1, Americans favored Williamsburg over all other historic buildings.

Although making such a comparison is somewhat of a game, the figures cannot deny attitudes common enough today to be a real threat to the quality of the built environment—that portion of our surroundings constructed by people. And even though the growth rate of the National Trust for Historic Preservation was 50 percent in one year, compared with Williamsburg's 12 percent, the total figures nonetheless illustrate that America's architectural inheritance is a hidden one, literally and figuratively.

It is hidden in one way by the American definition of progress: the idea that something has to be the biggest to be valuable and especially that the new is to be preferred over the old. A related notion is that the cost of something in dollars and cents is its real and complete cost. The importance of America's built environment is hidden, too, by a collective failure to know what is architecturally or historically valuable in a community. A reliance on a single well-known standard develops, and the limits of appreciation remain narrow, leaving only certain styles or historical periods to be viewed readily as

Dallas, Tex., seen from above through a fisheye lens, shows what highways do to the cityscapes and landscapes of America.

insult and grievance to provoke a revolution. A bicentennial commemorates 200 years—not just the years on either side of a hyphen. History, then, is minutes, days, months—a continuum that is still going on, making yesterday and today potentially just as historic as 1776 or 1865.

Another criterion limits many people's thinking about "important" architecture. A structure is significant, they believe, only if it has been designed and constructed under the supervision of an important architect. Vernacular or folk architecture is not considered of major importance. The problem with such a view is that most of the American architectural heritage has been given to us by unnamed people who left traces only in ethnic building techniques or decoration. Our ancestors signed

Worker housing in the shadow of a factory, such as this late-nineteenth-century building at the Richard Borden Manufacturing Company in Fall River, Mass., is as much a part of America's architectural heritage as more readily acknowledged landmarks.

Despite "modernizing" efforts that hide Victorian-era storefronts under neon, many Main Street rows can still be appreciated by those who look up to the cornice lines. These Monroe, Mich., buildings retain much of their original dignity.

truly "American" and therefore worth saving—places like Williamsburg and Mount Vernon.

To many, "historic" means the site of a single event involving notable people, a place such as Kitty Hawk, N.C., where the Wright brothers made their first flight, or Independence Hall. Some narrow the definition even further and insist that a historic event is something that happened before a certain date.

If we take an honest look, however, we find that the stuff of history is not made up of single events alone. Events are only punctuation marks; the process itself is history. It takes days and days of irritation and heat and

In rural settings and urban, buildings, streets, and whole towns of vernacular origins are the "real thing" people are leaving home to find. In Clifton, Va., houses from several eras (the eighteenth century through the twentieth), trees, different types of fencing, the ebb and flow of sidewalks, even power poles, form a unique townscape. In San Francisco, a Victorian row waits to be discovered.

their names with the craftsmanship they put into their buildings, just as anonymous medieval stonemasons did on the great cathedrals of Europe.

The results of such an outlook are manifold. A community overspends on new construction while failing to see that the old is priceless. The reproduction is preferred over the original, which is lost. The Disney World version of a Victorian main street is a crowd-pleaser, yet a town full of Victorian-era houses and commercial buildings is altered beyond recognition—in a nation that spends billions for "the real thing" in a soft drink.

Anonymous buildings may be harder to save, but not necessarily to enjoy. The careful brickwork of this nineteenth-century Italianate building in Saginaw, Mich., can be seen in the window lintels and stringcourses, even through spalling brick.

Government policies often recognize that preservation of historic buildings is next to motherhood and apple pie. Yet, despite these policy declarations, government actions and regulations are often more likely to inhibit than encourage preservation. Highways are allowed to plow through towns of architectural integrity, charm, and character, obliterating them. Ironically, highways make it possible for people to travel somewhere else to see the very things that may be left at home.

In the cities, owners of old properties who maintain or improve them are penalized by the tax system for their increased value. Zoning and other building regulations are almost always designed to encourage, if not subsidize, new development and construction. Landmark buildings are under a constant threat because, being smaller generally than modern skyscrapers, they usually do not produce the revenue of tall buildings. It is not always easy, even if it is possible, to convince a banker to lend money to restore or renovate an old building. It is often difficult to find someone, architect or carpenter, who can deal with an old building in a sympathetic way. Building codes, often geared to modern construction techniques, frustrate those who are fixing up old buildings. High-rise office buildings are routinely approved for construction in the midst of late-nineteenth-century residential areas. The inner cores of cities, where the oldest and most historic structures are often found, are abandoned, gutted, vandalized, and then finished off by arson. Other buildings topple to neglect or to bulldozers. Empty spots then eat away at the fabric of a community and parking lots mushroom in the gaping holes of the townscape.

As a town's original character becomes obliterated, clues to scale and harmony of design and color are lost and the holes are plugged seemingly without rhyme or reason. Sensitive design is replaced by insensitive, visual pollution blights the community, and housing developments spring up with no consideration for the natural environment. Amenities once provided by trees, spacious verandas, and walkways are abandoned for the sake of economy. And along with what has worked go examples of what has not worked—without anyone's

New buildings sympathetic to old are rare. A 1964 wing joined to San Francisco's Mutual Bank Building (1902) on the site of an old five-story structure has been called both "a beautiful tribute" and "an enlarged fire escape."

A 1924 Riggs Bank branch in Washington, D.C., fell to make way for a new Federal Home Loan Bank Board office, but not before the bank's ornamental Italian Renaissance Revival stonework momentarily framed a preview of the typical replacement building.

asking why. Thus, the same mistakes continue to be made.

Most tragic of all is that with the loss of this inheritance comes a loss of sense of place. London Bridge is transplanted to Arizona, a Wild West saloon springs up in New England, a New England waterfront village grows in Los Angeles. Meanwhile, farm museums, assembled piecemeal (albeit after research for authenticity), are considered the last word in education, but historic farm buildings in their original conditions and in their original locations are never safe from financial pressures that dictate destruction. Like Rip van Winkle, Americans wake up to find the anchors of their memories gone; they can't go home again because home is now a Dairy Whiz doing business in the middle of a sea of asphalt and after the fad for Dairy Whiz fizzles, it, too, is replaced. The disorientation caused by a constantly changing landscape rules out pride of place as well and

Although South Pass City, Wyo., and its Sherlock Hotel (1868) and Grecian Bend Saloon (1889) are being restored by the state to their gold rush boom town era, America's genuine ghost towns are too often forsaken for the fake, and real mountains that bring people west, such as these along Arizona's Black Canyon Highway, sometimes cannot be seen for the billboards.

gives rise to psychological woes appropriately called root-lessness. Being surrounded by an environment without beauty or a past, an environment that is ugly, takes a toll, reducing people's sense of well-being and productivity.

It's all a vicious circle. How can people learn to appreciate what they've already destroyed? This litany of dire results is the logical end of a failure to practice preservation.

PRACTICING PRESERVATION

But is preservation the answer? Increasingly, people are

Industrial archaeology—studying and saving landmarks of American engineering such as the nineteenth-century factory town of Lawrence, Mass.—is one facet of the broadened scope of preservation efforts.

finding it is at least part of the answer. Not only historians and architects but planners, government officials, business people, and realtors also are waking up to the benefits of preservation. Unfortunately, others have not considered it a possibility in their communities. The reason seems to lie in the fact that there is also a narrow understanding of what preservation is all about.

Mention the word "preservation" and there may be a vague recognition of the term, a vague agreement that yes, there are some landmarks around. If asked to name one, a surprising number will respond: "Mount Vernon," or some other Revolutionary War–era structure or site. If asked to name an example of something of architectural significance, they will probably name a seventeenth- or

A plan to convert this gasworks in Seattle, Wash., to a public park is an outgrowth of the realization that where open space and usable structures are at a premium, almost anything can be recycled for continued use.

In the days before the health of the national economy depended on planned obsolescence, preservation was not a movement but was synonymous with conservation: necessary maintenance and a stewardship of resources. It meant patching or remaking worn-out clothing and handing it down from person to person until it could be used no more. Preservation meant literally preserving foods such as berries or cucumbers, or preparing staple foods in a variety of ways and using them in different forms to feed both humans and animals. Architectural preservation meant keeping houses, barns and outbuildings, meetinghouses, town halls, and churches in repair, painting them regularly and replacing window sashes when necessary. Preservation was making sure that fence lines held and that streets were at least passable. When things were preserved, it was because saving was necessary to surviving, and continued maintenance meant saving. "Waste not, want not" was not merely a quaint legend to be cross-stitched on a sampler.

Preservation can still mean keeping buildings in good repair, so that they can continue to serve the uses for which they were built. This late-nineteenth-century church in King George, Va., has been maintained with the same care that went into its individualistic design.

eighteenth-century building, usually a house, and usually located in New England, certainly east of the Mississippi.

Even within the ranks of professional preservationists—architects, architectural historians, curators, people engaged in building crafts, government officials—limited ideas of what is worth saving predominate. This myopia has been loudly decried among them, but the viewpoint persists.

These answers reflect some regrettable misconceptions. One is that a structure or site, to be considered worth saving (in other words, to be a landmark), should be a product of the earliest possible century, or at the very least separated from today by a hundred years or so. Another is that "landmarks" are only those sites where notable deeds were done or those places with which notable persons can be readily associated: here the President was born, there the general won the battle, here the war ended. A third is that a structure is respectable only if it has some lineal connection with the Pilgrims or with Thanksgiving Day.

Where did these ideas come from? Some of them are to be found in the origins of the preservation movement.

A preservation movement did, however, develop early in the country's history, for patriotic rather than economic purposes. In *Presence of the Past,* a history of preservation in America up to 1926, Charles B. Hosmer, Jr., points out that America's need to establish a national identity manifested itself long before the Civil War in efforts to commemorate the nation's origins by preserving its historic sites. Appropriately enough, considering that George Washington was the object of the most intense veneration, almost deification, his memory prompted the first widespread activity. One of the first of a host of places saved for the reason that Washington slept there was the Hasbrouck House, Washington's one-time headquarters in Newburgh, N.Y. In 1850 the New York state legislature, hoping to kindle patriotism, voted to spend enough money (less than $2,400) to save the building as a shrine to the hero. It also voted an additional $6,000 to purchase the surrounding land for protection.

Old farm buildings often have a longevity surpassing that of other structures, at least where farming methods have not changed radically. Even in their well-worn state, it is obvious that this springhouse, corncrib, and barn in Gerrardstown, W. Va., continue to function well.

The Virginia legislature, however, showed less of this kind of enthusiasm. Even though Washington's home, Mount Vernon, had already become a "mecca for patriots," the legislators failed to respond to plans to turn it into a hotel, refusing to appropriate the $200,000 necessary to save it from that fate. One of Washington's worshippers, however, a frail South Carolinian named Ann Pamela Cunningham, could not tolerate the thought of such a desecration. In 1853, galvanized by the federal government's subsequent refusal to save the Potomac estate, she began to enlist an army of like-minded lieutenants in the South. That army, the Mount Vernon Ladies' Association, became a nationwide preservation machine par excellence and an exemplary fund-raising

network. Within five years Cunningham raised enough money to purchase the property; she also personally saw to it that a capable staff captained the estate through the Civil War, even though its location made it vulnerable to forays by Union and Confederate soldiers alike.

Cunningham's crusade was based on her view that the historic plantation, being a three-dimensional piece of history, could teach its visitors as no book or lecture could hope to do, not only giving them a sense of a past way of life but also inspiring the same kind of patriotism and the same noble character and deeds as it had once witnessed. Other groups followed the same reasoning. The Tennessee legislature bought Andrew Jackson's home, The Hermitage, near Nashville, in 1856. At the same time Carpenters' Hall in Philadelphia, where the First Continental Congress convened in 1774, was renovated by the Carpenters' Company and opened to the public. Washington's headquarters were preserved in Morristown, N.J., and Valley Forge, Pa., in 1873 and 1878, respectively.

As the basis for the first formal preservation activity in America, the patriotic motive has remained lodged in the popular consciousness. But it did not remain the sole motive for preservation.

By the turn of the century an aesthetic argument—preservation for architecture's sake—had been established almost singlehanded by William Sumner Appleton, a Bostonian who in 1910 founded one of the most influential private preservation organizations, the Society for the Preservation of New England Antiquities. Appleton was educated and traveled enough to appreciate the value of the structures erected in America in the two earlier centuries. He also was foresighted enough to see that such enterprises as the private development that destroyed John Hancock's Boston home in 1863 constituted a major threat to many other landmarks in the country. Appleton devoted his life to saving these landmarks.

From the work of people like Cunningham and Appleton—the classic stories of preservation—seem to have come not only limited ideas of what is valuable but also persistent misconceptions and stereotypes about the kinds of people and methods involved in preservation.

One popular idea, for example, is that the only noteworthy preservation has been done in New England or the South. True, New England has harbored the preponderance of historical societies concerned with the preservation of their ancestors' homes, and many groups long have been active in the South (including the Ladies' Hermitage Association and the Association for the Preservation of Virginia Antiquities, which in the 1890s saved Jamestown Island). Yet, midwestern groups early on recognized the need to preserve historic sites. In 1883

Lincoln's homestead in Springfield, Ill., was opened as a museum and later the nearby historic town of Salem, Ill., was reconstructed according to the recollections of Lincoln's contemporaries as to how it looked during his days as a young lawyer. In the Far West, efforts were made to rescue the San Luis Obispo de Tolosa Mission buildings in 1876, and societies such as the Native Sons of the Golden West and the Landmarks Club of Southern California were active in the 1890s and the early twentieth century. In the Southwest, the old Spanish Governors' Palace (c. 1611) was requested by the Historical Society of New Mexico for its headquarters in Santa Fe in 1881 and was opened as a museum shortly after 1900.

Another popular image seems to be that preservation is an activity of the rich, the superpatriotic, the dilettante, or "the little old lady in tennis shoes." Patriotic groups such as the Daughters of the American Revolution and the Sons of the American Revolution and the Colonial Dames and the United Daughters of the Confederacy, to be sure, have been involved in preservation, but they have never been the only people involved. Hosmer notes that from lists of donors it is obvious that many early preservationists were generally middle-class citizens, not the socially elite nor the very rich, and that more buildings were saved by small contributions than by dramatic, large gifts. (The sale of ten-cent certificates was part of a fund-raising campaign to save the Betsy Ross House in Philadelphia.) And, in fact, even at the beginning of the Mount Vernon fight, men were active in the crusade, and not just patriotic or military groups, but businessmen as well. Edward Everett, former Massachusetts Senator, mastered the art of stump-speaking in his travels to save Mount Vernon; the $500 lecture fee he averaged for each of his 139 appearances was given to the cause. The priests at San Juan Capistrano also were active in the mission's preservation, doing much of the restoration work themselves. Although amateurs played a large part in the early preservation movement, there also were professionals, curators and antiquarians like Appleton. Chapters of the American Institute of Architects in Philadelphia and Boston were active in preservation before the turn of the century and in New Orleans in the first quarter of this century.

It is true that most of the plans for restored buildings called for the creation of monuments, shrines, or museums, but not all. In 1867 the city of Philadelphia saved an area of eighteenth- and nineteenth-century houses built on the banks of the Schuylkill River. These structures and grounds were incorporated as Fairmount Park—not as an outdoor museum of architecture, but as a city park and public recreation area.

What is left of the historic built environment has been preserved pretty much unconsciously. As Grady

A lone remnant of the great plantations that once bordered the Ashley River near Charleston, S. C., Drayton Hall (1738–42) has survived without plumbing, heating, gas, or electricity, its dependencies gone. Called one of the finest Georgian houses in America, Drayton Hall is being preserved, much as it looked here in the 1930s, by the National Trust as the focus of a river conservation effort.

Clay, editor of *Landscape Architecture* magazine, suggested in the National Trust magazine, *Historic Preservation*:

> The great historical preservatives in America have been poverty, plutocracy and privacy. It was poverty that protected . . . the great architectural treasures of Charleston and Beaufort, S.C., and Savannah, where nothing, literally nothing, had happened since the Civil War to change the framework or alter the old structures built before and after the Revolution . . . nobody had the money to fix up, paint up—or even to tear down. . . . it was plutocracy that created, maintained and preserved the Newports, the Bar Harbors, the Tuxedo Parks

and the wealthy suburbs of such cities as Baltimore. . . . the third great preservative—privacy and isolation . . . remarkable townscapes and landscapes that are still memorable and visitable today, many are so because they are isolated from the juggernaut of progress. . . . They are everywhere: the great clusters of stone house-barn-outbuildings-fences scattered along the U.S. 40 axis of central Kansas; the gingerbread carpentecture of bypassed Victorian districts from San Francisco to Macon, Ga.; the slowly disintegrating mountain villages of ancient Mexican and Indian cultures within a day's drive of Santa Fe, N.M.; the towering and echoing blocks of semi-abandoned commercial buildings in Lower Manhattan, east and west. . . .

With active efforts based almost solely on historical and cultural associations and passive efforts based on such things as poverty, plutocracy, and privacy, the preservation impact remained limited. Thousands of structures have been saved through these means, but this is only a very small percentage of the old buildings and unique areas in the country that can be saved and used. "Preserve one building," adds Grady Clay, "and you preserve one building."

It is an all too common occurrence that once a historic building has been turned into a museum it ceases to be a contributing part of the community. The building is removed from the tax rolls, is used only on special occasions, and usually does not generate enough revenue to meet operating expenses. The result is that the building

Now "isolated from the juggernaut of progress," Norton, Kans., is typical of the midwestern settlements that grew up around grain elevators and the railroads that carried grain to markets to be processed into cereals, bread, and other products. Here the grain elevators dwarf the single-line railroad track and combined railroad station and stationmaster's dwelling.

Decaying buildings in Lower Manhattan's Schermerhorn Row (1811–12) await rehabilitation as part of the South Street Seaport effort to reclaim and study the physical vestiges of a way of life that built New York. The mercantile row is the last in the city to retain its original features. Plans call for turning it into the New York State Maritime Museum.

begins to suffer an agonizing decline as deferred maintenance begins to take its toll. The past becomes ossified.

Richard Candee, a researcher in architecture at Old Sturbridge Village, Sturbridge, Mass., wrote recently about preservation in *Historic Preservation:*

Today this movement is undergoing widespread redefinition, quite properly expanding the boundaries of the umbrella term "preservation." More than at any time in the past, those actively engaged in this aspect of environmental conservation have been forced to question their basic assumptions, asking what should be preserved and (just as important) why. Simultaneously, they are seeking new methods to preserve those portions of the built environment that meet the ever-shifting criteria for preservation.

CHANGE MANAGEMENT

The realization is coming, in fits and starts, that buildings are a part of our total environmental resources and that old buildings are nonrenewable resources. Preservation today is being seen as a means of change management. Because the world is constantly changing, preservation is viewed as a method of controlling the rate and effects of change by advocating, for instance, the importance of human scale in the environment—accommodating the pedestrian in the city as well as recycling buildings that contribute to this livable scale and create a sense of place. The "historic" part of preservation is being sidestepped in favor of an approach that is geared to conserving the resources of the built environment in ways that make them consistent with contemporary needs and demands.

The new preservation calls for viewing buildings in the context of their total environment, saving the built with the natural. The confluence of the Potomac and Shenandoah rivers at Harpers Ferry, W. Va., has provided an isolated opportunity for preservation.

In addition to the old "cultural memory" and "antique texture" bases, three new arguments for preservation have been pinpointed by Pierce Lewis, a professor of geography at Pennsylvania State University: successful proxemics, environmental diversity, and economic gain. As past preservation efforts showed, cultural memory is the argument that we must have reminders, physical reminders of our past, suggests Lewis. Antique texture he defines as people's reactions to old things, things with patina such as a well-worn newel post. The preservationist's new argument for successful proxemics, says Lewis, concerns the very livability of cities, the relationships between people and things such as buildings that create a space and a society that work. The argument for environmental diversity is that everything need not and perhaps should not be alike, that preservation of elements of the past can create environments that offer alternatives to much of modern society. Finally, the argument of economic gain is used by preservationists to convince skeptics that preservation of old buildings can be a profitable venture.

To save old buildings, preservationists in the last decade have been learning and adopting the developers' skills and methods. They have assembled land to thwart unwanted new construction and embarked on ambitious financing plans. They have also learned to use the ballot box effectively and to engage in effective litigation. Preservationists have learned to talk so that others will understand. They have learned to persuade of the necessity, to explain the methods, and to teach the techniques for preserving old buildings. They are able to show that in

its many forms, preservation is a respect for the built environment, that is, a respect for the accomplishments and thoughts of other human beings.

Preservation's new breed is less concerned about the differentiation between subgroups of an architectural style or the buildings by a specific architect. For them, historical or architectural connotations and connections are not as important as evaluating each structure for what it contributes to the community fabric. They ask whether it can be used productively, giving a broad and flexible definition of "productively." Other questions likely to be asked today are, What is the condition of the structure? What is the current zoning? What rate of return on investment can be expected?

Preservationists have had to become increasingly litigious to assure that buildings worth saving get their day in court. One of the most fought over because of its real estate value is New York City's Grand Central Terminal (1913).

It is certainly undeniable that preservation is popular. In virtually every corner of the United States conscious efforts to save and recycle old buildings can be found. It is the continual subject of magazine articles, especially in decorating magazines that extol the aesthetic advantages of restoring or recycling old buildings, and in books that tell the prospective restorer how to buy an old building and fix it up. There is even a monthly publication called the *Old-House Journal* that tells people how to fix up their new old homes. For some it is the "in" thing to do. One leading midwestern preservationist who does a lot of traveling is constantly astonished at the extent of preservation activity, especially the "restoration" of houses, and remarked that one way of gauging the extent and upsurge of this activity might be to compare the amount of paint stripper sold before preservation became so popular, about fifteen years ago, with the amount sold today.

The activities that now fall under the rubric of preservation are just as varied as before they were narrow. In San Francisco four young men produce bronze and cast-iron hardware, ornamental woodwork, glass, wood, and plaster work to enable people to restore Victorian homes at a reasonable cost. In Boston a florist prevented construction of a parking lot by building a greenhouse in the gap left by the demolition of two Back Bay row houses (a

location, incidentally, that he finds ideal for growing plants). In Wilmington, Del., Baltimore, Washington, D.C., Philadelphia, Newark, and Rockford, Ill., modern pioneers are practicing urban homesteading: buying abandoned houses from the city for a little money and a promise to rehabilitate and live in them.

In 1973 voters in the mayoral elections in Detroit, Pittsburgh, and Seattle put avowed preservationists into power. Others, in order to save bridges, canals, mining structures, and mills, organized letter-writing campaigns and formed citizens' lobbies in support of protective legislation. In Seattle "Friends of the Market" mounted a campaign to save the 1907 Pike Place Market and placed on the ballot a measure establishing the market area as a

Grand Central's interior is a reason the city and preservationists have fought to prevent loss of its landmark designation and construction of a 55-story tower overhead. The Beaux-Arts station also is a uniquely conceived transportation center.

historic district. The referendum was passed by a substantial margin, succeeding in listing seven acres in the National Register of Historic Places. In Maryland preservationists fought to protect a lighthouse. Growing numbers in many communities organize to see that consideration of historic areas is a major factor in civic land-use decisions.

An architectural firm has taken this proud survivor of a downtown Detroit block and rehabilitated it for offices, with room for a restaurant and an artist's studio.

Four-H Clubs aid in conducting surveys of historic buildings and sites in their home towns and in rural districts, compiling histories from interviews with older residents. Eleventh-grade students in New Canaan, Conn., have raised three times the money needed to save an eighteenth-century schoolhouse and are now using the building as an object lesson in their study of local history. College students in a sociology course, working in a Lexington, Ky., program called "Adopt-a-House," are rehabilitating substandard housing in a troubled area of that city, in the process becoming familiar with community problems and establishing relations with the families who occupy the houses.

One of the fastest-growing and most challenging preservation activities is finding new uses for old structures that seem to have outlived their original purposes and rehabilitating them to fit new needs. Basically, adaptive use means recycling resources. The opportunities are almost unlimited. A high school in Ithaca, N.Y., has been converted into usable and desirable residential-commercial space, with a variety of shops and offices combined with forty-nine apartment units. A bank and warehouse now host theatergoers in Louisville, Ky. Railroad stations are being employed for a variety of creative uses. In Baltimore, Waterbury and New London, Conn., Ann Arbor, Mich., North Easton, Mass., San Diego, Duluth, Indianapolis, Natchez, and, of course, Chattanooga, old terminals are now centers of community activity—with

An important engineering landmark, the 1830s Monocacy Aqueduct of the Chesapeake and Ohio Canal at Dickerson, Md., has been saved for recreational use as part of a national park.

museums, arts-and-crafts studios, meeting rooms, and gymnasiums—or commercial ventures such as restaurants and shops. Some even renew life as railroad stations.

Places other than single structures or sites are also being saved. Under the auspices of the U.S. Department of Housing and Urban Development, a piece of land on California's Marin Peninsula is protected, partly for its historical value, but also for its rare indigenous flowers. The commercial Waterfront Historic District in the whaling country of New Bedford, Mass., is the object of

In Louisville, Ky., a warehouse (c. 1870) and the Bank of Louisville (1834) have been adapted as the Actors Theatre of Louisville. The French Chateau-style Union Depot in Duluth, Minn. (1892), is now the St. Louis County Heritage and Arts Center.

Threatened by urban renewal in the 1960s, Victorian buildings such as this in Denver, Colo., were converted into a profit-making commercial complex, Larimer Square.

preservation through a combination of funding programs. The Indianapolis Motor Speedway, the scene of the 500-mile Memorial Day race, is listed in the National Register of Historic Places, officially recognized as a historic site.

Rehabilitation of substandard neighborhoods, another aspect of historic preservation, is being carried on with government, commercial, and private funds in urban centers such as Manhattan and other boroughs of New York City as well as in Allentown, Pa., Medford, Ore., Beaumont, Tex., and Norfolk, Va. Some cities have established housing service agencies to assure that rehabilitated housing is available to people of low and moderate income levels, thus preventing the "pricing-out" that sometimes occurs when neighborhoods are restored.

Along with the houses, the street furniture (benches, telephone booths, light standards, paving, bus stops, mailboxes) is being refurbished; landscaping efforts range from setting out window boxes to planting trees along major thoroughfares. Related programs have been established to counsel homeowners about such things as maintenance responsibilities and to secure low-cost financing for those who need it.

When this Wilmington, Del., house was being built in 1862, the U.S. government was offering land to willing settlers on the western frontier. In 1973 this house was given to an urban homesteader as part of a new movement to revive abandoned city properties.

Old West Side in Ann Arbor, Mich., found itself worth saving for its nineteenth-century character and vernacular design. Swiss Avenue, a neighborhood of early twentieth-century houses in Dallas, has done the same. Recognized historic districts in Mobile, Ala., St. Louis, Mo., Santa Fe, N.M., Charleston, S.C., Providence, R.I., Cape May, N.J., and areas of Cincinnati and New Orleans and Boston are being protected through special zoning and legal devices, including covenants and ordinances that control alterations or prevent incompatible new construction. Even whole towns such as Harrisville, N.H., have been brought back to life.

From such projects people are discovering numerous benefits—some obvious, some unexpected but nonetheless welcome. The "fixing up" done on one street generates pride so that others are caught by the spirit, and restoration activity spreads spontaneously. Neighbors begin to pool resources for landscaping and repairs and find a new sense of neighborhood.

As the preservation movement has grown and spread across the nation, institutions have grown up with it. A wide variety of groups, organizations, and individuals come together, often disperse, and then come together again as the need arises to save parts of the built environment. There are advocacy groups or spokespeople for virtually every facet of the built environment, groups that concentrate on a place, a particular building style, a construction technique, or a certain period: Save the Fox Theater, Don't Tear It Down, Pioneer America Society, the Victorian Society, Society for Industrial Archeology, Association for Preservation Technology, Friends of Cast Iron Architecture, Council on Abandoned Military Posts, Small Towns Institute, Back to the City, Inc.,

A major influence on the increasing concern for conservation not just of buildings but of whole neighborhoods, the Pittsburgh History & Landmarks Foundation's Birmingham restoration program has helped to promote a focus on preservation for people.

The Cooper-Molera Adobe (1829) in Monterey, Calif., is one of the westernmost properties of the National Trust. Under a special agreement with the state, it is being restored to interpret the Mexican-American period and the Yankee-trader influence in the Pacific.

Brownstone Revival Committee, Landmarks, Inc., as well as groups supporting railroads, canals, covered bridges, ships, and more. There are bureaus in every state and in many county and city governments that are charged with encouraging preservation. At last count there were well over 200 separate programs in the federal government that deal in some way or another with preservation. There are also a number of private national groups that promote preservation.

With more than 100,000 members, the National Trust for Historic Preservation is the largest. Under a Congressional charter issued in 1949, it serves as a clearinghouse of information for preservation groups through its advisory and educational services and its publications. Headquartered in Washington, the National Trust reaches the rest of the country through regional offices serving New England, the Midwest, the West, the Southeast, the Southwest, and the Mid-Atlantic States, all of which provide professional services in preservation-related areas such as restoration, property management, financing, urban planning, preservation law, architecture, history, publications, and public relations. The Trust, which operates more than a dozen historic properties and jointly maintains several others, also pioneers methods of protecting, administering, and interpreting buildings and their settings and shares its experience with other groups through nationwide seminars. To encourage the development of professional standards in preservation, the Trust awards grants to educational institutions. It also gives financial assistance to organizations in the form of grants and loans.

Other programs in the private sector are carried out by national historical and preservation societies such as the American Association for State and Local History and the Society of Architectural Historians, as well as professional groups such as the American Association of Museums, the American Institute of Architects, the American Institute of Planners, the American Society of Landscape Architects, and the American Society of Interior Designers. Some national groups that used to confine themselves to the natural environment also are beginning to recognize that proper management of our structural surroundings is an integral part of managing the natural environment.

PUBLIC RESOURCES

That such a variety of preservation activity is going on is due in part to the impetus given by the 1966 "Preservation Congress," which passed several laws of significance to the quality of the total environment. Although the act was preceded by national legislation such as the Antiquities Act of 1906 and other policies and programs indirectly benefitting preservation, activities dramatically accelerated after the mid-1960s.

The legislation most significant to preservation in 1966 was the National Historic Preservation Act (P.L. 89-665), which provided mechanisms for implementing what had been articulated as national policy as early as 1935 in the Historic Sites Act. Specifically, it expanded the National Register of Historic Places to make it a nationwide inventory of districts, sites, structures, and objects of state and local as well as national importance maintained by the National Park Service, U.S. Department of the Interior. Prior to 1966, the Park Service, in addition to administering sites, properties, and monuments, maintained a National Historic Landmarks registry; this schedule, however, included only sites on the order of Mount Vernon—places judged nationally important to America's development. By creating a list encompassing places of state and local value as well (the National Historic Landmarks program has continued), the federal government expanded its official recognition of what was worth preserving. Today the Register includes more than 15,000 properties.

The National Historic Preservation Act also created a review agency, the Advisory Council on Historic Preservation, made up of federal officials and private citizens to advise the President and Congress on historic preservation. More important, the council is authorized to comment on plans for such federally funded or licensed projects as highways and utility construction—whatever projects are likely to have an effect on structures and sites in or eligible for the National Register. Although the Advisory Council has no police power, it can wield some influence when interests conflict, as they did when the U.S. Department of Health, Education, and Welfare proposed to transfer the Old U.S. Mint (1874) in San Francisco to the State of California, a move that would have resulted in its demolition. A National Historic Landmark, the structure had survived the earthquake and fire of 1906. Because of the Advisory Council's recommendations it also survived the demolition proposal, and HEW returned the building to the custody of the U.S. General Services Administration, which, at the urging of Mint Director Mary Brooks, gave it to the Department of the Treasury for use by the Bureau of the Mint as a numismatic museum and offices.

Most significant, the 1966 act authorized the Interior Department to distribute matching grants to aid the states and the National Trust in carrying on preservation programs. Since its first grants in 1968, the program has allocated more than $72 million for preservation. Initially, the funds were used in the states to conduct statewide surveys and to draw up plans for preservation. "Brick and mortar" grants have in recent years been appropriated for use by the states in actually acquiring and restoring structures and sites. Grants to the National Trust are used to support its ongoing educational and property programs. One portion of its grant was used to conduct a study to determine if the Willard Hotel on Pennsylvania Avenue in Washington, D.C., could be recycled and once again become an asset to the city. The study enumerated several potentially profitable uses for the building; efforts are currently under way to revitalize the structure.

To implement the surveying, Register nomination, and grant-in-aid programs in the states, state historic preservation officers were appointed and in many cases new agencies were created to supervise the programs. This comprehensive network of preservation in all the states and territories has been a keystone in the growth of state and local preservation efforts since 1966.

The National Park Service also conducts research and salvage programs in archaeological areas as well as historic site surveys for the National Historic Landmarks program. The Historic American Buildings Survey, a documentation program that began in the 1930s, collects measured drawings, photographs, and historical and architectural data with the help of teams of architects and architectural students and deposits them for public use at the Library of Congress. Lamentably, the archives are all that remains of about a fourth of the buildings. Since 1969, the Historic American Engineering Record, a collection of the same nature, has kept information on engineering landmarks such as bridges, mills, factories, foundries, subways, and tunnels.

The Department of Transportation Act of 1966 (P.L. 89-670) was also of benefit to preservation because it placed restrictions on the use of federal funds for highway construction. In this law it was declared national policy that the natural beauty of public parks, recreation areas, wildlife and waterfowl refuges, and historic sites be protected. No federal transportation program or project adversely affecting a historic site or natural area can be approved by the Secretary of Transportation unless it is demonstrated that there are no feasible and prudent alternatives and that all possible planning has been done to minimize harm. As with listing in the National Register, this law does not provide protection from state and locally funded construction projects, but it helps to establish some limits to their encroachment. For example, Wyoming planned to widen and improve a road between Fort Casper Historic Site and Zonta Park in Casper. The State Highway Department, after review by the U.S. Department of Transportation, minimized damage to surrounding property by taking appropriate measures: landscaping, removing all traces of the existing road, and transferring land no longer needed to the park.

The 1966 Congress passed other legislation of benefit to preservation. The Demonstration Cities and Metropolitan Development Act (P.L. 89-754), also called the Model Cities Act, set up urban renewal demonstration grants to make it possible for communities to identify, acquire, and restore historic structures and sites, and allocated funds to assist those people who were relocated because of urban renewal activity. From then until their termination in 1973, the act's Open Space Land and Urban Beautification programs, besides making loan insurance available, funded approximately $37 million worth of historic preservation projects.

Since 1966, however, there have been many changes in the HUD programs. Revenue sharing, initiated in the early 1970s, made funds available for community improvement in the form of categorical grants for services such as improved law enforcement, schools, and waste disposal. Seattle, Wash., used this funding to establish a $600,000 revolving fund for the purchase and preservation of buildings in its downtown historic area.

The latest change has come in the Housing and Community Development Act of 1974 (P.L. 93-383), which gives federal support to states and cities in the form of block grants. They enable local governments to set priorities for their particular communities. Preservation programs can, theoretically, be given even more money than before. However, because programs are now overseen by local officials and not by federal representatives, it is the responsibility of local citizens to initiate preservation programs, to make sure such projects are given high priority, and to take advantage of opportuni-

One landmark that succumbed before preservation came of age was New York City's Pennsylvania Station (1906–10), seen here near its opening. It lost to the marketplace in 1963.

ties for public review and comment. Among many to do so is the Heritage Hill Foundation, a preservation organization in Grand Rapids, Mich., which received a $6,000 grant for streetscape improvements from the city's $4.7 million allotment. New Bedford, Mass., has allotted $1.3 million of its $10 million block grant for neighborhood housing preservation and improvements.

In nature, landmarks, such as Arches National Park near Moab, Utah, tend to attract more attention than the everyday elements, and the same has been true in the built environment.

One of the federal government's most active preservation funding programs is the Architecture + Environmental Arts Program of the National Endowment for the Arts. Through this program, whose "primary aim is the improvement of our built environment," some $9 million has been channeled into studies to meet this objective. One of the projects funded was an inventory of urban potentials in ten cities. Urban potential was defined as "the countless buildings, spaces and neighborhoods in U.S. cities with great potential for imaginative use and recycling instead of being destroyed for inferior replacements." In Nashville, Tenn., NEA funded a plan for reuse of three waterfront blocks that include "the largest uninterrupted assembly of Victorian commercial buildings in the United States." Under an NEA grant another group developed an audiovisual presentation on the reuse potential of industrial and manufacturing struc-

tures that is receiving wide distribution. The Humanities Endowment also aids preservation research efforts.

The U.S. Department of Health, Education, and Welfare's Social Rehabilitation Service has awarded grants to the Newark, Del., Optimist Club to renovate the Old City Water Works Building for use as a senior citizens' center; in Lincoln, Neb., the City Recreation Department transformed an old fire station into a center for both old and young people. The U.S. Department of Commerce, through its Economic Development Administration, gives loans and assistance based on the economic impact a preservation project can have on economically depressed areas, such as the number of jobs that can be produced. A $120,000 matching grant was given to residents of Lawrence County, Ark., to restore the former county courthouse (1888) in Powhatan. It is now open as part of a state park.

Under its surplus-property regulations, the U.S. General Services Administration, which oversees the occupancy and operation of more than 10,000 federally owned buildings, can transfer "excess" public buildings to cities for museums and for revenue-producing purposes. The Old Federal Courts Building in St. Paul, Minn., a National Register property, was conveyed to the city for renovation to house restaurants, shops, city and county agencies, the Minnesota Museum of Art, the St. Paul Arts and Science Council, and the Minnesota Metropolitan State College. The U.S. Department of the Treasury has initiated a "Historic Customhouse Program" in which it designates present and former facilities of historical or architectural significance to encourage their preservation. One example is the Yorktown Customhouse, Yorktown, Va. (1706), said to be the oldest customhouse in the original thirteen colonies.

Under the President's Executive Order 11593 for the "Protection and Enhancement of the Cultural Environment," issued in 1971, federal agencies were directed to locate, inventory, and nominate their historic properties to the National Register. Hundreds of "found" government properties have since been added to the Register, and others determined eligible but not yet in the Register receive the same protections from adverse federal actions as registered sites.

Recently, it has been proposed in Congress that space in federal buildings be opened up for commercial, cultural, educational, and recreational purposes (a system used in Canada), in order to create multiple uses of the buildings and to eliminate the "dead" time before and after working hours. GSA also is being encouraged to consider purchasing and rehabilitating older buildings for federal use rather than always initiating new construction.

For all the progress of federal law and agency programming, however, there would be little real preservation without the interest and initiative of citizens on state and local levels. Many states, California and Oregon, for example, have pioneered tax incentives for preservation, developed sophisticated recognition programs, and conducted extensive statewide architectural surveys. Many local governments are also becoming increasingly involved in preservation. A National Trust survey in 1975 found that there were more than 400 local public commissions directly involved in historic preservation, a figure that represents many more hundreds of private preservationists.

THE TOTAL ENVIRONMENT

In the years since 1966, as more historic preservation programs have developed, the federal government and the private sector have made inroads into educating the public about America's cultural heritage. There has been a parallel and even stronger awareness of and concern for the natural environment, a realization on the part of the American people that the elements of the environment—air, water, even the earth itself—are finite and that these resources demand wise stewardship. Americans are coming to see that the environment is a complex and fragile system, vulnerable to complete destruction by the abuse of a single element.

Responding to national demands, the federal government has given some degree of protection to these elements. The National Environmental Policy Act of 1969, for example, set up the Council on Environmental Quality to assure consideration for environmental factors, including historic preservation, in federal project planning. In particular, federal agencies are required by that law to prepare environmental impact statements for projects that would significantly affect the quality of "the human environment," a phrase that links the historic heritage with the natural. According to the findings of the Task Force on Land Use set up by the Rockefeller Brothers Fund in 1973, the proliferation of consumer interest groups indicates growing public concern for the quality of the total environment. Americans today realize that conservation is not only the protection of the so-called wonders of nature—the Grand Canyons—but also includes the protection and wise use of streams and wetlands necessary to our survival.

Unfortunately, the analogy between the need for saving the natural environment and saving the cultural or built environment does not seem to have fully become a part of the public consciousness. The "everyday" elements of the built environment—what air and water and land are to the natural environment—are only beginning to receive some of the same attention. While some mansions are saved, outbuildings and surroundings are still being lost. Citizens may rally to save single struc-

The Swan Mercantile Store (c. 1875) in Chugwater, Wyo., was once part of the Swan Land and Cattle Company ranch complex, the hub of an operation handling several thousand cattle. Now the environment is encroaching, slowly obliterating a piece of America's past.

tures and sites, but open space and townscapes, vital elements in the community fabric, disappear. In the 1954 case *Berman* v. *Parker*, United States Supreme Court Justice William O. Douglas asserted that a city has the right to be beautiful as well as safe and sanitary for its citizens. Yet in terms of what has been done to their architecture, most cities' rights have been violated. The toll on inhabitants of ugliness and pastlessness and rootlessness is only beginning to be measured, and communities that continually erase themselves have little chance to feel pride.

But places can be made to have beauty. Continuity and character can be preserved and enhanced—if the past is built upon rather than in place of. The only requirement is that people look around, find what is worth saving, and make the effort to claim it as their own. To claim an inheritance, it must be seen and understood. That is one of the purposes of this book: to show America its hidden inheritance.

THE BUILT ENVIRONMENT

How does one go about finding structures, sites, and objects—things worth saving? Recognizing the ways they are hidden is a good start. Some are located on back roads and in small towns where progress (in the form of airports and highways) has passed them by, and some in inner cities where a lot of us do not dare or care to look. Some are covered up by the addition of inappropriate materials. Most frequently, though, they are hidden by our own blindness: our familiarity with their presence and our unfamiliarity with their value.

Once upon a time, everyone in a community was involved in its architecture, because everyone's labor was needed for sewing tepee skins or raising barns. Today, building is left to specialists—to architects, engineers, construction workers, developers, and bankers. In school we learn the primary colors and we paint; we learn to beat drums and play tambourines; we have to memorize poetry, if not write some now and then. But we have little chance to build except with toys. Thus most people do not know the terms or the rules of the art of building and have lost the skill even to see the built environment and what is happening to it. Perhaps because architecture seems so functional many do not think of it as an art form at all. Why else do we feel shock at attacks on Michelangelo's *Pietà* but watch placidly as New York City's Pennsylvania Station bites the dust?

Many terms have been used in recent years to describe those parts of our surroundings that have been conceived and created by people—the built, the man-made, the cultural, the architectural environment—but they all encompass the same part of our world. They signify townscape in contrast to landscape, people's impact in contrast to nature's. It is the buildings, the structures and places that we have made, that can remind us continually of the great human capacity to have an impact on our surroundings and to adapt them to our needs. Just as each successive occupant leaves an imprint on a house, people, responding to their personal needs and to society's demands, apply layer upon layer to the fabric of the built environment.

To fully appreciate this environment, we need to know its language. Many of us know only that a certain building or structure is capable of making us feel a certain way: nostalgic, uneasy, alienated, significant, forgotten. Words like "vermiculated" and "quoin," "mullion" and "mansard," "lintel," "balustrade," "fenestration," and "setback" are almost a foreign language, although these things affect our moods and attitudes every day. A familiarity with the basic terminology of the components of the built environment provides a common language with which to share the experiences and translate our feelings about these structures. When the images and reactions are broken down into verbal terms, a new-

The Gothic-arched corridors and vaulted ceiling of the U.S. Post Office (1897–1901) in Buffalo, N.Y., provide a sense of expansive space.

found vocabulary enables us to communicate feelings and concerns about the built environment, including the importance of preserving it.

Begin looking at the environment as a collection of landmarks in the literal geographical sense of the term. Wherever people live, in cities or in rural communities, in towns or suburbs, there are landmarks, things that have been around long enough to be common reference points. They tell us how to get from one place to another and serve as marks on the collective memory and on the actual landscape. It may be the old gas station on the corner that marks the place to turn, a motel on the top of a rise, or a clock on a bank building. But most important, landmarks are those structures which tell us where we've been as a community and thus help us decide where we should be heading.

Alison Owings, the founder of a Washington, D.C.,

preservation group named Don't Tear It Down, said it rather well in 1972 when she wrote: "Don't Tear It Down was born of anger. . . . [What were] distressing were the buildings one couldn't quite remember as architectural statements, but as city moods; something fat and turreted on 13th and Massachusetts; and blocks and blocks of individual yet cohesive 19th century rowhouses-shops on Pennsylvania above the White House. . . . There was also a converse frustration: being able to picture a favorite building, but not remember exactly where it had been."

In preservation, the beginning is to look about at the world. Look up, look down. Buildings, especially older buildings, are often different above the first floor. Roadways and sidewalks can yield interesting forms, textures, and clues to the past. Perspective is different when you are on foot, on a bus, on a train, or in a car. Each vantage point offers a world tailored to its own perspective. The way to understand the built environment is what may be called the Holmesian method: looking at the elements—closely, inquisitively, suspiciously, thoroughly.

What follow are some elementary aids to looking, including some vocabulary excursions; some exercises with which to try various points of view; and some questions—not so much for answering as for inspiring further questions. Finally, the photographs provide a sample on which to practice looking, a taste of the unique architectural heritage to be claimed wherever people can and will look.

Finding a sense of place can begin where you are at this moment, with the elements that are around you.

SEEING FROM A VARIETY OF POINTS OF VIEW

SEEING FROM THE INSIDE

SPACE AND MASS

The relationship of open areas to mass—windows to walls, for example—creates a feeling of expansiveness or close quarters; high ceilings may give a sense of leisure and plenty; small cubicles may produce just the opposite effect.

TEXTURE

The textures of interior building materials create a wide variety of effects, from the coldness of marble and the warmth of wood to the roughness of concrete and the coolness of glass. Materials also can translate a sense of richness or plainness through cultural associations such as the difference between velvet and muslin.

Right above: Warmth is imparted through the use of wood for this coffered ceiling in the new Federal Building (1975) in Seattle, Wash.

The conservatory of the Irwin Union Bank & Trust Company (1974), Columbus, Ind., allows the sunlight to create almost a *trompe l'oeil* painting.

LIGHT

Light is the most variable of elements and can be one of the most powerful. It can expand a space or reduce mass. It can change textures and colors. Natural light changes with the time of day, weather conditions, the direction of a building, even the geographical location—near bodies of water, on the beach or desert. Artificial light can be used to complement or to counteract the effects of natural light.

The curve of wood in the stairway of Philadelphia's Metropolitan Opera House (1908) creates rhythms for the eye and patterns for the feet.

PATTERN AND RHYTHM

Pattern and rhythm are created by the juxtaposition of repetitive elements in a design. The spacing of doors, windows, and wall decorations all work like notes of music on a staff. The intervals, either short or long, even or uneven, can give a static or moving effect. They can lead the eye to something, such as a door or a sign, or away.

SMELL

Smells are ingrained in a building, just as sights and textures are, and are part of experiencing the built environment. Smells are forever associated with public buildings: gyms and chalky classrooms and sulfurous chemical laboratories in schools; musty libraries and old churches; cabbage and Airwick-filled halls in apartment buildings; popcorn in movie theaters.

Smells are ingrained in all buildings, most pungently where food is found, such as Eastern Market (1873), still actively serving Washington, D.C.

DETAILS

Decorations on elevator doors, mailboxes, woodwork, and moldings can be elements of communication between the maker and the viewer. They are expressions of an owner's and builder's attitude or craftsmanship. The condition of a building, how it is cared for physically, tells much about the way its occupant or owner feels about it, and this is transmitted to those who see it.

Art Deco designers lived for the detail. This metallic frieze is at New York City's 60 Wall Tower, Cities Service Building (1932).

Left, above: At Olana (1874), Church Hill, N.Y., even the furnaces show the artisan's skill. Below: Nashville's Grand Ole Opry (1892) reverberates with the sounds of its past.

SOUND

Sound is a surprisingly important element of architecture, more for the decisions it prompts than for its actual presence. Selection of floor and wall coverings, window treatments, and ceiling materials is related in some way to the desire to channel or reduce sound. Partitions are used in offices to make sound travel less and in concert halls to make it travel more. The science of acoustics is in fact a vital part of architecture. The echoing taps of footsteps in old banks, the clamor of banging lockers in school hallways, the drone of libraries in summer, the clattering and ringing of bells in a department store, the carpeted nonsounds of funeral homes, the vast echoes of an empty parking garage are all part of the acoustical properties of every structure. Sounds can tell us what a building is used for and whether it is in use.

In addition to affecting moods, color can create patterns of its own, as in this stairway at the Powers Building (1869–70), Rochester, N.Y.

COLOR

Color in the built environment generally has a more subtle effect on people than other elements. Cool colors such as greens and blues are thought to be restful; thus, they have been used extensively in hospitals and in schoolrooms, where green boards replaced the traditional blackboards for a few years. So-called warm colors—yellow, orange, and red, especially red—excite, so they are used in restaurants to make people eat faster and consequently consume more and leave more quickly, making room for new customers.

SEEING FROM THE OUTSIDE

The same basic elements operate on the outside of a building as on the inside, but they assume a larger and bolder scale outside. Theoretically, besides enclosing shelter, the outside of a building can convey what is inside.

SCALE AND PROPORTION

How structural elements relate to each other and to their human viewers determines our sense of a building's scale and the correctness of its proportions. Based on the human measure, buildings can be monumental or intimate in size or scale, compatible or inharmonious. Visual and aesthetic perceptions also create rules of proportion whereby various portions of a structure relate or do not relate harmoniously as part of the whole. The size of a Roman column, for example, determined the sizes of all other building elements.

TEXTURE

Exterior building materials are essentially limited to durable materials such as stone, brick, wood, concrete, steel, and glass. Glass can partially reflect the outdoors, mirror it totally, or bring it inside through transparency. Concrete used naturally or dressed creates a solid, enduring effect. Stone can be used smooth or polished, grooved or rough-hewn. Wood can organically relate a structure to the natural surroundings.

Left: The setback of the now demolished Kansas City, Mo., Board of Trade Building (1886) relieved its sense of mass. Above: The cobblestone of this Childs, N.Y., schoolhouse (1849), more commonly used in streets, gives a unique wall texture when coursed in mortar. Below: The rhythm of this undulating façade was lost when the Poland Spring House (1875–76), Poland Spring, Maine, was burned.

PATTERN AND RHYTHM

On the outside of a building the placement of windows and doors, curtain walls, carvings and balconies, columns, arches, and horizontal slabs creates patterns, for any break in a plane catches light and creates shadow. Rhythm is created by the shapes of roofs and towers. Patterns created by the exterior of buildings probably affect mood more boldly than interior work, for outside the eye can be more influenced by form than by color and small detail.

Color can be pure white as in this Greek Revival church, Dingman's Ferry, Pa. (above), or polychromatic, as in the post office (1879) in Evansville, Ind. (right, above).

COLOR

Color is also used to create desired exterior effects. The whiteness of Greek Revival structures may symbolize purity; the terra-cotta color of unadorned brick bares the earthiness of the clay from which it was formed. During the post–Civil War era architects strove to attain ideals of truth and character, even in building materials. Applied paint in single colors was eschewed in favor of integral polychrome materials—"constructional color-ation" created through contrasting stones and tiles and natural decorative touches. Today, architects call for the same honesty, but the result—the slabs of gray concrete that characterize many modern buildings, for example— is quite different.

Below: A buffalo for Buffalo, N.Y., this rough-hewn gargoylelike figure on the U.S. Post Office (1897–1901) shows the presence of concerned craftsmanship.

DETAILS

Building exteriors can suggest personal elements beyond those designed into them. The craftsmanship of the brickwork or stone masonry gives evidence of individual skills, as do window frames and moldings over entrances. Carvings are clues to the fact that human beings have been involved in construction: arrogant cornerstones, artistic carvings, even the graffiti engraved in freshly poured cement give character to the built environment.

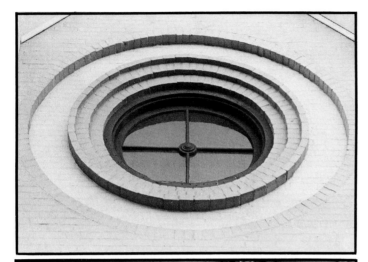

Seeing a building requires looking at the whole, as well as at the details. Opposite page: Wood weathers even when painted, allowing comparison of the varied textures of the old and the new at St. Paul's Episcopal Church (1785), Woodbury, Conn. The variety of nails and the design of the molded sill and sash give further clues to changes in building technology. Left and left, above: Italianate rhythms in brick catch and reflect light and shadow and relieve the monotony of flat walls and rectangular forms in the Gobin Guards Armory (1881), Carlisle, Pa. Above: Building exteriors indicate interior spaces and uses. The small window on the left of this house in Carlisle, Pa., may illuminate a stair; those to the right may lead to a second-floor stair and a dining room below.

Above: The streetscape of Seattle's Pioneer Square is enriched by its paving, light standards, fireplugs, and cast-iron pergola, a symbolic focus of the area's restoration.
Right, above: Dormers against roofs, tiles against brick, and tall chimneys in Harpers Ferry, W. Va., create townscape rhythms visible from above.
Right, below: "Hoop" benches around the fountain of New York City's Bowling Green Park provide a place to rest as well as a link with the past century.

SEEING THE WHOLE,
STREETSCAPE AND TOWNSCAPE

"One building is architecture," suggests British planner Gordon Cullen, "but two buildings is townscape." Buildings in combination with one another create a sum that is greater than their parts. A structure can echo its neighbor's color or contrast its massiveness with delicacy, absorbing its partner's best characteristics or lending some of its own. Building groups in combination with other constructed elements, landscaping, and the street furniture—paving, fences, benches, lampposts, mailboxes, utility poles, chute covers, transit shelters, kiosks, street signs, and commercial signs—create a streetscape. Added to the natural environment, these give us townscapes, the unique ensembles that mark an identity for every place where humans have put their hands.

Some of the elements that operate to form a streetscape are: building height, the average and violations of that average; proportion of the façades (height to width and variations); rhythm of solids to voids, that is, the relation of one building to another and the patterns on each; space to mass (all together as in row houses or detached); and spacing on the street and continuity (walls, fences, landscaping, and the repetition of certain elements such as building materials, colors, and textures).

In evaluating a streetscape these questions can be asked: Does it invite human interaction? Are buildings set too far back from the street to be readily experienced? Are they set at a distance that permits comfortable walking? Are there surprising and interesting vistas that appear as the pedestrian passes? Are there gaps caused by poor design or by demolition? Do the things that help tie buildings together into a total environmental unit—landscaping (trees, shrubbery, parks, open green areas) and street furniture—add or detract? Do they, in other words, pull everything together or apart?

The silhouette of a townscape, its skyline, may present distinguishing landmarks, both natural and built: church steeples, university spires, grain elevators, skyscrapers, water towers, a courthouse cupola, a capitol dome; rolling hills, craggy mountains, valleys, streams, woods. To be appreciated visually, some townscapes are best approached by boat, by bridge, or by air. Most in fact are seen from superhighways or train tracks. From any vantage point, it becomes clear whether town and environment are unified or whether town looks incidental to setting, failing the human need to come to terms with the environment.

Above: Granite fanned in arcs, brick laid in common bond or in herringbone, cobblestone—all are part of the built environment, the furniture of the street. This rich variety from the nineteenth century is found in the Georgetown Historic District, Washington, D.C. Right, above: Installed about 1875 as part of a major park and street improvement program, these cast-iron posts with chain barriers survive in several places in Washington, D.C. Right: Salt Lake City's ornamental iron-base "Indian-head lights" are being recycled with new bulbs, but the old poles and globes remain.

LEARNING TO IDENTIFY
ARCHITECTURAL STYLES

The vocabulary of the built environment also includes standard names for types of building designs, terms that are used in textbooks and guidebooks and that are recognized in most regions of the country. In the opinion of one well-known categorizer of architectural styles, Marcus Whiffen, such vocabulary building is an attempt to do for American architecture what Roger Tory Peterson did for American birds in his popular field guides. But while bird species may not mate, architectural styles do. Thus, a standard style description may leave out the fringes, the combinations and adaptations, that at times may be the most interesting. Many of the structures pictured in this book fit into this nonstandard category because many are vernacular and eclectic, built in a combination of styles and not according to academically correct standards. Yet all have sprung from some common heritage. They echo prototypes—if only because there are limited materials with which to build and standard geometric forms that have proved to function best in accordance with physical laws and human needs.

Before the advent of building codes—and, some would argue, even now—many structures took shape without the firm guidance of an architect. The designer hovering in the background of these structures was often only a pattern book; with its examples, drawings, and directions on how to reproduce currently popular styles, such a book served as many builders' closest architectural "companion." In other cases, traditional building concepts passed from generation to generation were used. By adapting architectural idioms to given tastes, budgets, available materials, climates, and building skills, these efforts produced hybrid, handmade styles outside the textbook vocabularies and often even outside current fashions in the national architectural centers. This is true even today.

Although such vernacular structures seldom contain all elements of a formal style, they often present sufficient clues to indicate a building's derivation from a particular style or styles. These indicators include scale, proportion, massing, height, shape and floor plan, roof lines, types of construction materials and finishes, textures, color, porches and entrances, columns, towers, chimneys, windows and doors, moldings around doors, windows, and cornices, decoration, even landscaping. Interior clues are found in wainscoting and paneling, flooring, color, decorative elements, moldings, mantels, doors, stair balustrades. Construction methods—bonding of brick, use of timber or steel frames, joining of logs—are other guides. Some elements of the built environment nonetheless almost defy stylistic description.

While one can find textbook examples of privies in the Federal or Greek Revival modes, many structures elude pigeonholing into formal styles.

Assigning dates to indicate when styles were most popular is as tricky a task as breaking down America's vast architectural heritage into categories, for each time frame, just like each stylistic description, seems to challenge someone to think of an exception. Dates given in the following section do not indicate the only years during which buildings in particular styles were constructed; rather, they reflect the era of the style's American inception and height of popularity. Most have earlier and especially later examples. Structures using Greek Revival elements, for example, were built as early as the 1790s, but the style did not become prevalent until about 1820; its widest use in the East had peaked by 1840, but Greek Revival buildings were still being built across the country during the Civil War era and into the 1870s in California. This pattern held true for most major nineteenth-century styles as they moved westward with the settlers. During the late nineteenth and early twentieth centuries, the Midwest and West began to produce uniquely American styles that moved eastward, as a new architecture—the Chicago School—rose from the ashes of the 1871 Chicago fire and as architects found the meeting place of East and West in California fertile land for innovation during the twentieth century. Changes in style also often occurred earlier in urban centers and later in outlying sections, another factor contributing to different dates of usage.

Houses and other structures were not built in a day, either. Construction often stretched over a period of years, with rooms in houses finished as needed or as funds were available. When additions or alterations were made to structures continuously occupied or used over a long period of time, they often reflected a currently popular style.

How it was done, in the Holmesian scheme of things, has a lot to do with when it was done, and this is true also of determining the age of buildings. The style clues are helpful for placing structures in their design eras, but a knowledge of the technology that produced the buildings (and particularly the materials that went into them) is another method of getting to the facts. Prefabricated cast iron, for example, was not prevalent prior to 1850; it proliferated after mid-century, when the technology for wide-scale production and distribution developed. The technologies of manufacturing brick, stone aggregates, and concrete also fit into chronological eras and can be used in dating structures.

Thus there are three major indicators that can be used in dating buildings: the design itself—what stylistic elements are present in a structure; technology—the materials and how they are used; and research—information on the history of the building, its land and community. Whatever the style of a building, it cannot have been built before that style was used and known, before the technology developed, or before the land came into the possession of the person reputed to be the owner and builder (unless it was later moved to the site).

Perhaps the most important point to remember, however, is that being a certain style and having style are two different things entirely. Everything that exists, for better or worse, has style.

SOME ARCHITECTURAL STYLES IN THE UNITED STATES

The Indian village of Abo, N.M., its dry stone walls now in ruins, was occupied from the late prehistoric through the early Spanish Colonial period.

INDIGENOUS

To 1600. The native American architectural styles range from the wigwams and longhouses of the Indians in forested areas, raised shelters of the southeastern Indians, and tepees of the Plains Indians to the igloos of the Eskimos and the sophisticated communal pueblo cities carved out of mountainsides or built of stone or adobe in what is now New Mexico. Some of these briefly served as models for the European colonists before they began to build permanent structures in styles adapted to the climate but derived from their own native traditions.

COLONIAL

1600–1780. The term "colonial" is often used to refer to seventeenth- and early-eighteenth-century buildings erected in English settlements on the East Coast, but it is applicable to any buildings in America where exploration and colonization were taking place.

Spanish colonists built simple pueblo churches as well as Baroque: San José de Gracia (1760–76), Las Trampas, N.M. (top), and San Xavier del Bac (1797), Tucson, Ariz. (below).

SPANISH

Although Spanish colonists possessed superior masonry and timber building techniques backed by the wealth of the Spanish state and Catholic church, their architectural achievements were lost to the westward conquests of the northern colonists. A century after the first Spanish settlement at St. Augustine, Fla., in 1565, construction of the stone Castillo de San Marcos gave America its first major example of military architecture. Missions and provincial government buildings built from 1600 to 1800 in the Southwest reflected the Spanish Baroque style, sometimes elaborate but often simplified because of the adobe and wood materials and the limited skills of the native Indian workers. The twenty-one-mission chain begun in 1769 by Father Junipero Serra had left a trail of Spanish design along California's El Camino Real by 1823.

Left: Saltboxes such as the Dole-Little House (c. 1720–30), Newbury, Mass., evolved with the English colonists. Above: The David Demarest House, River Edge, N.J. (top), is typical of simple 1700s Dutch houses. The gambrel-roofed Downing House (c. 1730), East Caen, Pa. (below), combines English and Dutch forms.

ENGLISH

In 1607 and 1620, respectively, English colonists brought their provincial building techniques to the South and the Northeast, adapting them to the different climates. They used the traditional materials, plaster and framing, adding exposed wood clapboard siding to keep out the elements. Brick also became popular in the South. In the North, houses were usually one-and-a-half- or two-story symmetrical wood-frame structures with steep gable roofs. In the "saltbox," a single story in the rear swooped up to a two-story front elevation, a product of lean-to additions that evolved into a formal style. A central chimney gave warmth to rooms located around it. In the South, chimneys were often moved to the ends of the house to provide a breezeway through a central hall. Southern houses were generally one-and-a-half stories with high ceilings to provide ventilation. The gable or ridge roof was popular in both regions.

DUTCH

The Dutch were in undisputed control of the Hudson River area for only forty years, but their influence on building in the Middle Colonies lasted from 1625 to 1820. Especially noteworthy were their skills in the manufacture and laying of brick and in the structural framing that made possible characteristic Dutch or gambrel roofs and parapeted gable ends that projected above the roof level. Parapets were frequently stepped or treated with decorative stone or tile cresting.

FRENCH

There were few French settlements along the Mississippi and St. Lawrence rivers and Great Lakes waterways, but the French built various timber forts, trading posts, and dwellings from about 1665 to 1803; Duluth's fort was erected in 1679 and New Orleans was founded in 1718. Little remains in the North other than restored portions

The galleries of Madame John's Legacy (1788), a raised cottage town house in New Orleans, show French and West Indian influences.

or artifacts of the fortifications at Old Fort Niagara, N.Y. (1726), and Fort Michilimackinac, Mich. (1715). The town of Ste. Genevieve, Mo. (1735), also survives. French plantations left in the southern half of the Mississippi river area show West Indian influences, most often seen in the combination of raised upper floors and hipped roofs projecting to cover a piazza or porch.

CLASSICAL DERIVATIONS

Cliveden (1763–67) in Philadelphia's Germantown section bears the Georgian imprint in its pedimented pavilion, massive chimneys, and classical detailing.

GEORGIAN

1700–1780. Named for Kings George I, II, and III of England, this style was prevalent in residential and public buildings by 1720. Based on English versions of Roman classicism laced with Dutch Renaissance, typical Geor-

gian structures are symmetrical with gable roofs, often including dormers, although pyramidal and other roof forms were used. Materials varied widely from wood to brick and stone. Entrances were emphasized and ornately decorated, with transoms or fanlights over the door and columns or pilasters (piers made to look like columns) frequently taking the form of one- or two-story pedimented porticoes (porches). Classical details around windows and doors and in cornices, columns, pilasters, and quoins (outside corners) became more lavish in late Georgian structures. Unlike the provincial designs brought by unskilled colonists, this style was transmitted through the immigration of building tradesmen, professionals such as masons and a few trained and amateur architects, and by architectural pattern books.

Transitional between the elaborateness of the Georgian and the simplicity of the Federal, Wheat Row (1794–95), Washington, D.C., blends four units into one.

FEDERAL

1780–1820. Named for the new republic, this style appropriately rejected much of the English-inspired Georgian decoration but retained its symmetry and such details as pilaster-framed entrances, fanlights, and side lights. Windows were simply framed and quoins abandoned. Roofs were often low, sometimes hipped, with dormers. Row houses became prevalent. Much Federal architecture, especially interiors, was patterned after the work of the Adam brothers in England, characterized by delicate detail in cornices, entrances, and interior features. Thomas Jefferson popularized a French-inspired Jeffersonian classicism, more Roman than Adamesque, which is noted for massive white-columned pedimented porticoes, often two stories high, against red brick or boxlike hipped structures with flanking wings joined by pavilions.

Andalusia (1794, 1834), the Nicholas Biddle estate near Philadelphia, is the Greek Revival in its most classical temple form.

GREEK REVIVAL

1820–60. One of the most popular and long-lived styles in America, especially for public buildings, because Greek forms were thought to embody the ideals of democracy. To create the effect of a Greek temple, architectural emphasis changed to columns and pilasters supporting a prominent triangular, gabled pediment, a focal point of the façade and an extension of the roof. Freestanding columns often formed a portico on the building's front or sides. Highly symmetrical, Greek Revival structures exhibit unadorned simplicity and purity, often emphasized by white or neutral painted exteriors.

GOTHIC REVIVALS

Early Gothic Revival buildings like those at the Allegheny Cemetery (1848, 1868), Pittsburgh, Pa., reproduced the battlements and pinnacles of the medieval period.

EARLY GOTHIC REVIVAL

1830–80. A romantic style traceable to the remodeling of Sir Horace Walpole's estate Strawberry Hill near Twickenham, England, in 1747. Distinguished by verticality—pointed arches and steep, complex gable roofs with finials—and medieval decorative motifs, including battlements, pinnacles, and delicate window tracery, it was popular for public buildings. At first a secular style, the Gothic Revival later took on religious connotations and was favored over the allegedly "pagan" classical designs for use in ecclesiastical buildings. Grand country houses featured wide verandas and square or octagonal towers or turrets.

A Picturesque Gothic Revival cottage built for a polygamous family, the Watkins-Coleman House (1869), Midway, Utah, displays the typical lacelike barge boards.

COTTAGE RESIDENCES

1840–90. A type of smaller Gothic country house popularized in the twelve editions of *Cottage Residences*, a builders' handbook published by horticulturist Andrew Jackson Downing based on designs of architect Alexander Jackson Davis. Quintessentially Picturesque, residences in this style featured the pointed gables and arched windows of the academic Gothic, but decorative elements tended to stand up (finials) or hang down (barge boards, the so-called gingerbread scrollwork under eaves). Houses were built of wood and brick with stucco, often using elaborate sawn "Carpenter Gothic" details.

The complex rooflines, Gothic forms, and polychromatic detailing of New York's Jefferson Market Courthouse (1877) are characteristic of the High Victorian Gothic.

HIGH VICTORIAN GOTHIC

1865–80. The epitome of "Victorian" architecture in its eclectic colors, complex roof lines, and solidity of character. Gothic forms were relied on, but were distinguished by the addition of constructional color, heavier detailing, and varied roof shapes, including dormers and towers. The use of "honest" built-in colors instead of applied color was urged by critic John Ruskin, and the resultant contrasting bands of brickwork, varying stone facings between wall surfaces, and variation in window arches or friezes have caused this to be called "Ruskinian Gothic." Exposed woodwork, when used on gable ends, for example, also followed the quest for honesty and is more structural than ornamental.

ROMAN AND ITALIANATE STYLES

While tending toward later Richardsonian massiveness, the University of Texas Medical School (1888–91), Galveston, uses Romanesque Revival round arches.

ROMANESQUE REVIVAL

1845–75. Sometimes called the Lombard or Round style for its distinguishing feature, the semicircular Roman arch. Favored for churches and public buildings, these structures were often asymmetrical, with towers of differing forms and heights, frequently with pyramidal roofs. Wall surfaces were of smooth stone.

ITALIAN VILLA

1845–75. A popular residential and public-building style that continued a Picturesque, asymmetrical massing but coupled it with low gable or hipped roofs, sometimes barely visible, and wide eaves supported by decorative brackets. Based on vernacular Italian farmhouses, features also included square or octagonal towers, cupolas or glass belvederes (for the "beautiful view"), round-arch windows in groups of two or three, bay windows, verandas (or piazzas), balustraded balconies, and ornamental brick.

Above: Belvedere (1857) in Galena, Ill., was no doubt named after its Italian Villa-style central tower. Below: Cast iron, used for New York's Haughwout Building (1857), proved a malleable medium for the ornamental North Italian Renaissance Revival.

RENAISSANCE REVIVAL

1845–80. Based on two Italian precedents and characterized by symmetrically formal straight-fronted buildings crowned with massive cornices. Wall surfaces in the Romano-Tuscan derivation were usually smooth with rusticated quoins. Second-story windows were often emphasized, and balustraded balconies were sometimes used. Instead of smooth walls, North Italian examples featured rich sculptural ornament in classical orders around regular arched windows.

With its variegated wave, diagonal, scalloped, and geometric patterns, this Columbus, Ind., house shows how ornate the Stick Style could be.

ITALIANATE

1870–90. A style used predominantly in commercial buildings to carry the sculptural qualities of the North Italian Renaissance one Victorian step further. Exaggerated brackets and cornices of the villa style joined the classical, symmetrical window treatment and decoration of the Renaissance to produce lavishly wrought store and office building fronts. Straight-sided, flat-topped, and other distinctive arches were used in contrast to the earlier rounded Italian derivations. The newly efficient cast iron proved a perfect material for mass production of stylized classical ornament, often in whole façades.

Designed by H. H. Richardson, the Cheney Building (1875–76), Hartford, Conn., is quintessentially Richardsonian in its massing and rough masonry.

RICHARDSONIAN ROMANESQUE

1870–95. Named for Henry Hobson Richardson and characterized by a massive, heavy appearance, simplicity of form, and rough-faced masonry. An innovative and highly personal style, the Richardsonian Romanesque elongated the round Spanish or Syrian arch and emphasized it by contrasting masonry over arches and other structural features. Windows were deeply recessed to stress weight, and the spacing and shape of doors and windows often were irregular. The style was widely copied in residential, public and commercial buildings.

RESIDENTIAL "VICTORIAN" STYLES

With its variegated waves, diagonal, scalloped, and geometric patterns, this Columbus, Ind., house shows how ornate the Stick Style could be.

STICK STYLE

1855–1900. An almost purely American nineteenth-century residential style characterized by use of exposed framing overlaid on clapboard in horizontal, vertical, or diagonal patterns to suggest structural supports. Its irregular silhouette and extensive verandas echoed elements of earlier Gothic cottages and Swiss chalets. Beginning in the 1890s and lasting well into the twentieth century, a western adaptation of the style emerged in works by Greene and Greene and Bernard Maybeck, among others. Heralded by some as "modern" architecture, this is characterized by horizontality, structuralistic timber framing, and often Japanese influences.

Eclectic in form, this Port Townsend, Wash., Victorian shows Stick Style inflences in its horizontal framing and porch and cornice detailing.

QUEEN ANNE

1875–90. Vies with High Victorian Gothic as the most exuberant and eclectic style in texture, color, forms, and massing, and thus as the most "Victorian." Based on Elizabethan and Jacobean precedents, brick and stone were often employed on the first story to contrast with shingle or clapboard above. Colors were combined in bold contrast, and tall, thin chimneys and multiple gables created complex roof shapes and irregular silhouettes. Round turrets, octagonal towers, and bay windows also were common. Unlike that of Victorian Gothic, detailing was small in scale.

The Shingle Style reached its apotheosis in houses such as McKim, Mead and White's Southside (1882–83) in Newport, R.I.

Above: Even with its multiplicity of forms and materials, this Woodbury, Conn., house (c. 1910) is a restrained essay in the Queen Anne style. Below: Eastlakian woodwork can be seen in this house along the East Battery of Charleston, S.C.

SHINGLE STYLE

1880–95. A modern adaptation of seventeenth-century New England forms in reaction to the structuralism of the Victorian era. Rather than suggesting structural skeletons as in the Stick Style, shingled buildings de-emphasized structure by opening floor plans and covering surfaces usually in monochromatic shingles. Rambling and horizontal, houses featured wide verandas, hipped or gambrel roofs, and occasionally turrets. Rarely used for anything but houses, this weather-resistant style was especially popular and suitable at the shore.

EASTLAKE

1875–90. A residential style similar to Stick Style and Queen Anne except for its distinctive three-dimensional scrollwork and gingerbread. Loosely based on the designs of English architect Charles L. Eastlake, the style was extremely popular in California and other western areas and is noted for its knoblike decorations, especially on porches.

FRENCH SECOND EMPIRE

1860–75. Variously called "Mansard" for its characteristic roof and "General Grant" for its period of greatest popularity, but based on styles of the reign of Napoleon III and especially the New Louvre in Paris. Height was emphasized with elaborate chimneys, dormer windows, and circular windows protruding from the roof. Projecting pavilions, undulating façades, and classical ornament produced an unqualifiedly three-dimensional effect. In residences, frequently of wood, the style often became asymmetrical and included porches and towers.

Opposite page: The Old State, War and Navy Building (1871–88) in Washington, D.C. (right, below), is an unparalleled example of the French Second Empire style. Below: Built for Philadelphia's 1876 Centennial Exposition, Memorial Hall (1875–76) was a precursor of the return to symmetrical Beaux-Arts classicism.

NEOCLASSICAL REVIVALS
BEAUX-ARTS

1890–1915. A strictly symmetrical classical style that ushered in an era of academic architectural revivals. Although popularized by students of the Ecole des Beaux-Arts in Paris, the style came into its own in America following the 1893 Columbian Exposition in Chicago and was used principally in public buildings. Characterized by columns grouped in twos and threes and sculptural figures, it is also noted for monumental flights of steps.

OTHER REVIVAL STYLES

1880–1940. The rise of Beaux-Arts classicism was accompanied by a host of revivals of earlier styles (often revivals themselves) for residences and public buildings: Neo-Renaissance Revival, Neo-Colonial Revival, Georgian Revival, Tudor Revival, Jacobean Revival, Late Gothic Revival, Spanish Colonial Revival, Mission Style, Pueblo Style.

THE CHICAGO SCHOOL

The large plate-glass windows of Cleveland's Perry-Payne Building (1888) have been bricked in, reducing its original Commercial Style impact.

COMMERCIAL STYLE

1880–1915. The skeletal, rectangular style of the first five- to sixteen-story skyscrapers. Brought to full form in Chicago, although its origins can be found in earlier structures in New York, Philadelphia, and other eastern cities, the Commercial Style is characterized by flat roofs and little ornament, except slight variations in spacing of windows and frequent use of "Chicago" windows (large plates flanked by smaller windows). The extensive use of glass was made possible by steel-frame walls that could bear structural loads masonry could not.

SULLIVANESQUE

1890–1910. Named for Louis H. Sullivan and noted as much for his stylized geometrical ornament as for simple multistory forms ending in bold cornices. Sullivan's skyscrapers were designed as if they were classical columns; to emphasize the tall form, he used vertical rows of windows separated by ornamented bands, much in the manner of fluting on classical columns, and massive cornices that resembled capitals.

The Frederick C. Robie House (1907–09) in Chicago shows Frank Lloyd Wright's mastery of the Prairie Style's horizontal and organic forms.

Above: Sullivanesque detail extended even to the flat side of a stoop in the architect's A. W. Sullivan House (1890), in Chicago, since demolished. Below: Adler & Sullivan's Wainwright Building (1890–91) in St. Louis carried out Sullivan's classical "column" concept: fluted, with a base and a capital.

PRAIRIE STYLE

1900–1915. A low, horizontal house style associated with the work of Frank Lloyd Wright, who designed these homes to fit naturally into their flat midwestern settings. Horizontal elements were emphasized with single-story wings, horizontal strips of dark wood, projecting hipped main roofs, and shelf roofs between stories. With open interior spaces and prominent verandas, the style greatly influenced twentieth-century residential architecture.

In the Greene brothers' Gamble House (1908) in Pasadena, Calif., bungalow, Oriental, Prairie, and Stick styles are blended.

BUNGALOWS

1895–1930. A small, usually single-story house style given the Hindu name "bangla," meaning traveler's rest house. Popularized in the West, a basic type featured two gables, one over a front porch and another slightly to the side on the body of the house. The porch overhang was often supported by columns on piers. Decorative exposed rafter ends and massive chimneys also were used.

The double gables, exposed rafters, and porch supported on flaring piers easily identify this San Diego house as a bungalow.

"MODERN" ARCHITECTURE

Featuring automotive motifs and exposed metal, New York's Chrysler Building (1929) is exuberantly Art Deco in its geometrical polychromatic designs.

MODERNISTIC

1920–40. Predominantly a mode of ornamentation combining rectilinear patterns, including zigzags, with geometric curves in the form of polychrome low-relief frames. Known through the years as Art Deco, Art Moderne, and Depression Modern, its ornamentation around doors and windows and on panels stresses the verticality of the skyscrapers for which the style was popular. Stepped setbacks are common, giving the buildings the appearance of having been chopped out of blocks.

Above: Indianapolis's former Coca Cola Company (1931) celebrates the Art Deco with stylized relief on glazed white tile. Below: The uninterrupted walls of the Cleveland Museum of Art's education wing (1970) recall the International Style.

INTERNATIONAL STYLE

1920 to present. Noted for the lack of applied ornament and smooth, uniform wall spaces often cantilevered over lower floors. Used for houses and commercial and public buildings after the work of architects Ludwig Mies van der Rohe, Walter Gropius, and Le Corbusier, the style's effect of mass and weight was minimized by white or neutral colors, cantilevers, and treatment of windows as continuous wall surfaces. The result is almost a work of abstract or cubist art.

Right: The Neo-Formalistic National Geographic Society headquarters (1964) in Washington, D.C., reinterprets the classical form of base, column, and capital. Below: Embodying the sweeping motions of flight, Dulles International Airport (1963) near Washington, D.C., is Neo-Expressionistic.

Above: Even the rivets in the concrete are Brutalistically exposed in Boston's Logan Airport control tower (1974). Right: Mies van der Rohe's Farnsworth House (1950), Plano, Ill., is typically Miesian: modular, with a steel frame and glass walls.

POST–WORLD WAR II

1945 to present. A range of postwar styles for public, commercial, and apartment buildings and single-family residences made possible by developments in building technology allowing wider use of steel and precast concrete. *Miesian* structures are modular buildings of steel frame with great expanses of glass; in high-rise buildings, lower stories are generally set back beneath projecting upper stories. *Neo-Expressionist* structures are characterized by continuity of form and by sweeping curves instead of rectangular forms, but with occasional sharp breaks in movement. *Wrightian,* the later work of Frank Lloyd Wright and his students and followers, is characterized by horizontality but takes either rectangular, polygonal, or circular forms, usually based on natural materials and details. *Neo-Formalism* combines classical symmetrical forms and smooth wall surfaces with arches of precast concrete and decorative metal grilles, often excessively delicate in appearance. *Brutalism* is distinctive in its weight, texture, and massiveness, created by the use of exposed rough or patterned concrete. Windows tend to be tiny holes, and the combination of voids and solids may give walls an egg-carton appearance; inside, conduits and plumbing are often left exposed.

GETTING TO KNOW THE BUILT ENVIRONMENT: MISCELLANEOUS EXERCISES

1. Touch a building.
2. Think of places as being historic – your home, for example. What would it tell an archaeologist if it were unearthed a few centuries from now?
3. Think of all the things you can remember from childhood about your neighborhood: the best trees for climbing, the paths through backyards where fences blocked a fast getaway; or about your bedroom: the windows, lighting, materials, patterns in the wallpaper. Now, without looking, name the number of windows in the room you're in.
4. Assess your total environment. What influence does it have on you? Can it be improved by saving or by changing parts of it?
5. Find a building that repels you and ask yourself why.
6. Spend the day as an architectural photographer would, preparing to photograph a building, looking at the play of light on it, seeing it from every angle. How many pictures will it take to sum up the essence of the building? What should they show?
7. Sketch a streetscape and note all the similarities and differences between the buildings, as well as the variety of street furniture and landscaping.
8. Design an infill structure or use for a gap between buildings. What elements could you use to tie one to another and both to the street?
9. Watch faces at a demolition site and eavesdrop on comments.
10. As you look at the following photographs, think of their counterparts in your community.

LIVING SPACES

Human needs for shelter are fairly basic. People need protection from certain climatic conditions and space for such basic activities as eating, sleeping, and working. It would seem that these universal needs coupled with standardized technologies and common geographical factors would create in a given community a homogenized group of structures. Yet, most American communities contain a great variety of building types and styles bearing the imprint of the people who built them and use them. For the main influences on what a building "says," besides its materials, site, and intended use, are still the builder and the owner and user.

Living spaces are, above all, a home or a home away from home, an oasis wherever one can find it. Preceding pages: The primacy of the porch as a vantage point to the outside, seen here (left) put to good use by a family summering at Montauk on New York's Long Island around 1904, has given way to the backyard. Pipe Spring, a real oasis in the desert near Fredonia, Ariz., was settled by Mormons who in 1871 built this fort and ranchhouse (right). Opposite page: The continuous evolution of a house is seen in this Greek Revival Nantucket, Mass., home (c. 1845). The railing may date from about 1900 and the picket fence from even later. Left: This temple-form Beaufort, N.C., house (c. 1850) was doubled in size so skillfully early this century that the addition is difficult to detect. Below: Stepping down with the land, the fence of the pre-1850 Coburn Tyler House, Rockport, Maine, encloses a private space with arrowhead-shaped pickets and ball finials.

Nowhere is the imprint of individuality more obvious than in housing. Besides being shelter, living spaces can also be messages to a community about the inhabitants and their financial resources or social aspirations, their taste, their cultural background.

Housing includes a multitude of types: survival structures based on indigenous forms; single residences, attached dwellings, and row houses; apartments; buildings designed by architects, vernacular adaptations of academic styles by community craftsmen, and oddities built by eccentrics; and also commercial housing—the taverns, inns, hotels, and other structures that provide a home away from home.

As in most coastal areas, builders on Kent Island near the Chesapeake Bay favored wood. The gambrel roof of this early-nineteenth-century house in Stevensville, Md., shows the area's Dutch and Quaker influences.

Few social practices have challenged the architectural mind as much as polygamy and the need to build houses for separate families living under one roof. Sometimes called the "architecture of equal comforts," it has produced structures such as the Samuel Pierce Hoyt House (1863), Hoytsville, Utah, which is T-shaped and features symmetrical parlors and two seventeen-foot-wide bedrooms.

In the country's earliest houses one of the biggest influences on form was location. It determined the extent of shelter needed and the materials available for construction. Some settlers borrowed indigenous forms from natives who had already faced these requirements. In New England, where the temperature ranged forty degrees above and below that of their homeland, colonists built longhouses of thatch and bent trees. Only when tools arrived from England and sawmills were constructed could the settlers build in their native style, sometimes putting clapboard over wattle-and-daub structures (mud-plastered twigs woven between poles) to keep out the elements. In the Southwest, where little lumber was available, adobe made from desert clay provided shelter to the Spaniards as it had to the pueblo dwellers. Along the Mississippi River and in the Southeast, the French departed from their native forms, borrowing the West Indian style; raised first floors protected the open foundation from rot caused by dampness, and verandas took advantage of breezes.

Other methods of construction and design were brought by settlers from their native lands. The famous "American" log cabin had at least one antecedent in Swedish construction. The Dutch, expert brickmakers, tried consciously to reproduce their homeland in America and were successful in doing so in the Middle Colonies, especially in New Amsterdam (New York). Although taken over by the British in 1664, the city retained mostly Dutch structures until 1776, when a fire wiped out the core of buildings; remaining Dutch houses are now found mainly in the Hudson River Valley and northern New Jersey. Spanish Baroque styles were seen in the forts of Florida and in the missions of New Mexico, California, Arizona, and Texas. Germans influenced areas from Wisconsin to southern Texas. Scandinavians built communities in the Great Lakes country and the Dakotas. West Indian architecture was echoed in Florida, the Carolinas, and Louisiana. The Chinese brought Oriental influences to the West.

The adaptation of imported techniques to indigenous materials and climates continued as long as new frontiers were opened and new forms of shelter had to be found. During the rush for land following the passage of the Homestead Act in 1862, for example, homesteaders in the plains found no trees and no clay to build the "twelve-foot-square dwelling with a door and window" necessary to establish ownership. Settlers copied the grass huts of the Indians and built "soddies" out of bricks of damp prairie sod. Although they sometimes dissolved in storms, these bricks would not burn and they provided relatively cool quarters in summer and

Above: Built by Belgian immigrant Isadore Haumont in Nebraska's "French Table" area, this house (1887) transformed common sod into a vision of the settlers' homeland. Below: Two houses in the Virginia countryside almost mirror each other in their utilitarian designs, conceding only sawn woodwork on the porches. The house at left is in Lewinsville, Va. (c. 1890); at right is Bodmer's store (c. 1858), Sterling Va., whose business died with the railroad.

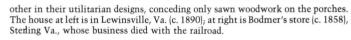

warmth in winter. The melting-pot phenomenon was perhaps nowhere as evident as in the mixture of skills and building techniques that made American architecture what it is.

Even before the Revolution some housing was influenced by pattern books and scholarly works such as William Kent's *Designs of Inigo Jones* (1727). These were imported from England and Europe and gave examples, patterns, drawings, and directions on how to reproduce successful designs. Available at first only to wealthy families, these styles eventually influenced other housing to varying degrees. All it took was a book. One of the most influential was Batty Langley's *The City and Country Builder's and Workman's Treasury of Designs* (1740), which contained plates showing more than 400 details for all portions of the house. Books of equally widespread influence, if not more, were Asher Benjamin's *The Country Builder's Assistant* (1797), which gave plans for Federal houses and other buildings, and the 1827 edition of his *The American Builder's Companion*, which included plans for the Greek Revival style so popular with the new republicans.

Spurred by builders' handbooks, the Greek Revival captured the American imagination. Now headquarters for a Mobile, Ala., preservation group, Oakleigh (1831–32) is a Southern version in a raised T-plan with exterior spiral stair.

One of the most influential books, one that established architectural and landscape styles from coast to coast for those who could afford to build or remodel their own homes, was *Cottage Residences* (1842), by landscape architect Andrew Jackson Downing. The book's basic offerings were cottages designed by Downing's friend, architect Alexander Jackson Davis—houses with steep gable roofs and large verandas, fulfilling the

Picturesque element promoted for the architecture of the day. Downing also included plans for indoor water closets, which he considered indispensable. The book was so popular that it went through five editions and thirteen printings between 1842 and 1887.

One of the most singular of the many other building books was Orson Squire Fowler's *A Home for All: or, the Gravel Wall and Octagon Mode of Building* (1848). Fowler, a phrenologist and inventor, argued persuasively that the octagon, being a prevalent form in nature, was the most healthy and most efficient form of building for providing ventilation and light to interior rooms. Fowler also experimented with the use of glass roofs and storage vats for rainwater. His book went through six printings and a revised edition by 1853.

Above: East Templeton, Mass., did not miss the fad for octagonal houses, promoted by pattern books. Opposite page: The home as part of the community was interpreted in Aspen, Colo. (above), with a rustic bandstand and Queen Anne house. The home as castle is epitomized by the Henry Townsend House (1887), Germantown, Pa. (below).

The important element of popular styles was that they seldom remained static; fleshed out in brick and mortar, they became individual statements. As folk ballads change to suit the singer and listener, so architecture changed to suit the builder and owner. If a local craftsman had a pattern book or his own collection of drawings, the prospective homeowner could pick out what was most appealing: a roof from this plan, a porch from another, a newel post or cornice, this color or that. Some "statements" resulted in the construction of castles and oddities, often called "So-and-So's Folly."

What made such idiosyncrasies possible were developments in building technology. Mass production of timber and nails, for instance, opened the way for so-called

By the mid-nineteenth century, the columned front portico or porch became a familiar sight in all types of houses. Left: Built about 1870, this modest house near the Garden District of New Orleans is what is known as a "shotgun" house: one room wide, with no central hallway, the house supposedly could take a shot from a gun straight through without receiving a bullet in any wall. Below: Deceptively resembling stone, the Stone House in Linton, Ga., used wood instead of the classic marble as the building material more appropriate to the region's resources and its setting flanked by red cedars.

balloon-frame construction; instead of having to rely on heavy timbers assembled on site, buildings could be prefabricated from thin timber, nailed together, packed, and then sent or carried across country. Already in use in Chicago in the 1830s, prefabricated balloon-frame units by the thousands were shipped west by 1850 to relieve the need for housing in boom towns. There they were covered with clapboard, decorated, and made into houses as well as churches and hotels because the interior spaces could be opened wide. With new power-driven jigsaws, decorative woodwork peaked in fantasies of "Carpenter Gothic" trim (which also could be purchased through catalogues by the less creative). The expanding production of new materials also made possible a post–Civil War industry of speculative housing, tract houses for rent that were often rigidly repetitive.

Some people's privies reached heights of fancy unequaled in others' houses. This late-nineteenth-century necessary in Georgetown, Colo., with its machine-made decorative cupola, cornice, and entrance, may be the star in its class.

The mid-nineteenth-century population boom in the United States, caused by natural growth and by the vast immigrations from Ireland, Germany, and eastern Europe, swelled the large cities. By 1890, Philadelphia, New York, and Chicago each passed the million mark, and by 1900, New York City was second only to London in population. Tenement apartments (houses with tenants) rose along trolley lines built to serve those without carriages. The influx of non-English-speaking peoples

who were jobless turned already substandard tenements into slums where people were stifled by inadequate facilities, air, and light, and plagued by rodents. Attempts were made to provide sanitary, low-cost nonprofit housing, but that generally left children with no place to play except the streets and adults with no place to meet and socialize. In the 1860s Frederick Law Olmsted and other pioneers in landscape architecture and city planning began to design green parks in such cities as New York and Chicago, and plan whole towns such as Riverside, Ill., to provide recreational land for the physical and mental health of the urban dwellers, a new direction that was to have a major influence on civic architecture. Other designers produced experiments in worker housing, such as Pullman, Ill., begun by the sleeping-car manufacturer in 1880 as a model industrial community.

During the mid-nineteenth-century population boom and influx of immigrants, workers' quarters rose to fill the housing need. Few were as well-designed as these frame and porticoed houses (c. 1830) in Mobile, Ala., now rarer than grand mansions.

Housing for travelers followed the same general evolutionary pattern as residential housing—from the primitive, often rude accommodations of the frontiers to the lavish accommodations of modern urban centers. Spaced by the distance of a day's travel on horseback, the first inns ranged from log cabins inside fortified settlements in the wilderness of Tennessee and Kentucky to unpretentious frame structures on the prairie. Later, with the coming of the railroad, hotels became lavish complexes with restaurants and shops; great resorts grew up around places where people could "take the waters," such as Hot Springs, Ark., and Saratoga Springs, N.Y. The design amenities often were matched by specialties in cuisine or by proximity to vacation amusements. Hotels have since become centers of community activity with special rooms for civic and fraternal meetings, wedding receptions, and other social affairs.

LIVING SPACES

On two separate coasts, linked mainly by their tropical-like foliage, living spaces catered to those who communed with nature in their varying ways. Below: Designed by Eastern architects Carrère and Hastings, St. Augustine's Hotel Ponce de Leon (1888) was built during Florida's boom era, helping to change the landscape of the state's sleepy Spanish days to that of a string of resort communities now home to millions. Opposite page: John Muir, the conservationist and naturalist, lived in this Italianate frame house in Martinez, Calif., between 1890 and 1914. It was Muir who, in writing about forests, suggested that "our government . . . like a rich and foolish spendthrift, has allowed its heritage to be sold and plundered and wasted at will."

Picturesque cottages and summer residences multiplied during the Victorian era with the mass manufacture of building components; the power-driven jigsaw also allowed quick and inexpensive creations of elaborate sawn woodwork. Clockwise, from bottom left: Villa Montezuma (1887), the Jesse Shepard House in San Diego, Calif., mixed Moorish and Gothic details in a Queen Anne framework. Sunnyside (c. 1780) in Tarrytown, N.Y., was purchased by author Washington Irving in 1835 as his country retreat and remodeled to the Victorian taste, including a massive wisteria vine at the entrance. The Watkins-Coleman House (1869), Midway, Utah, was built by a Mormon missionary to house his two wives. Noted for its lacy sawn decoration the Pink House (c. 1882), in the once popular coastal resort of Cape May, N.J., is now part of the town's historic district. A local newspaper owner saved the house from urban renewal by purchasing and moving it. Opposite page: Built as a testimonial to the possibilities of wood, the Carson Mansion (1889), Eureka, Calif., epitomizes Victorian elegance with a paint scheme outlining its obvious charms.

Multiple dwelling units—row houses, apartments, hotels—were built from the 1700s on and continue to offer urban streetscapes unified in materials and styles. Clockwise, from bottom left: The Idanha Hotel (1901), Boise, Idaho, an object of community pride almost too late. Riley Row (1884), St. Paul, Minn., a Richardsonian Romanesque row with varied rooflines. Town houses on Capitol Hill, Washington, D.C., showing architectural changes from 1850 to 1895. Lansdowne Apartment House (c. 1890), a target for graffiti artists. Opposite page: A long-gone row in New York City's Yorkville area, rising in stepped Dutch gables.

The rising standard of living since the turn of the century, together with various government loan programs, has made it possible for many to own their own homes. Builders and developers have relied heavily on the designs of such architects as Frank Lloyd Wright in the Midwest and the Greene brothers and Irving Gill in the Far West. The bungalow style that took hold in the West in the early twentieth century was spread across the country by popular magazines and became one prototype of the "middle-class home." Small in scale and open or semi-open in plan, the best of these houses provided the viewer and dweller with a simplified direct statement of utilitarian housing for the single family. Materials, concrete or stucco enhanced by natural wood inside and out, were as much a part of the decoration, or nondecoration, as of the construction. Although this style did not continue much beyond the 1920s, the general form and function of the bungalow were the basis for mass housing developments of later decades. Methods of mass production and on-site assembly used by these innovative early-twentieth-century architects and by the federal government in creating greenbelt towns and slum-clearance housing during the Depression-recovery era provided the basis for construction methods incorporated into the Levittowns of the 1950s and 1960s and the New Towns of the 1970s—as well as the sprawl of suburbia.

Given modern technology, it may seem ironic that today the tendency of many developers and builders is to think first of tearing down the genuine old only to imitate their styles—the clapboard Cape Cod, the adobe

Called a monument to the Craftsman aesthetic after the magazine that published early 1900s California designs, the Greene brothers' Gamble House (1908) in Pasadena shows the style's emphasis on natural wood and its use of historical influences—Mission, Oriental, Tudor, Prairie—to transform rustic bungalows.

pueblo, the Georgian Colonial, the mission style—in inappropriate materials, scales, and locations. Although the past has always been a favorite building block, what is missing in such neo-old houses is the touch of the vernacular, the personal signature and adaptation to local environments that once kept patterns from becoming molds. As many people find it less and less possible to have a distinctive new home designed and built, some are taking an alternative route: rehabilitating the real thing—an old house whose style matches its technology. Individual private efforts, neighborhood programs, even federally funded urban homesteading are reclaiming part of the country's older housing stock now threatened by changing tastes and life-styles. Some old living spaces do

Leading exponents of the naturalistic Arts and Crafts movement, Charles and Henry Greene designed California bungalows such as the Van Rossem–Neill House (1903) in Pasadena that became prototypes of the twentieth-century house.

Contemporary artist Georgia O'Keeffe's adaptation of the traditional adobe form for her home in New Mexico shows the influence of the Southwest on her living place as well as on her work.

not easily bridge the generation gap. Lavish homes built for large families with servants are daily becoming more out of reach of the average single family's size and means. But where the will exists, mansions are being converted to condominium and other multifamily uses, and row houses, detached houses, and apartments continue to serve their original uses.

Built at the time that the San Diego area boom town of National City, Calif., was being incorporated, the Kimball Block Row House (1887–88) is an Eastern-style row transplanted to the West. Stick Style porches unify the long Italianate group.

Since the advent of automobile travel and the demand for parking at the door, older hotels also find themselves white elephants, losing the competition to slick motels and trailer parks. Farsighted communities are applying some of the same native ingenuity that built these stopping places to see that they are returned to their former use as centers of community activity. And innkeepers are proving to interstate travelers weary of "motel modern" that old hotels can still be grand.

The porticoed Grand Hotel (1887) on Mackinac Island, Mich., built by a leading resort developer, has continued in use for almost a century, first for Midwestern magnates, later including politicians. Enlarged in 1897, 1912, and 1919, the hotel is part of a complex of staff housing, stables, and power plants.

Seldom ever merely utilitarian, residential stairways—whether simple risers, cantilevered from a circular wall, or paired to ascend and descend—add a rhythmic sense to living spaces. Opposite page: Although part of the house dates to 1807, the great hall of Ringwood Manor in Hewitt, N.J., now a state park, received its Gothic character in an 1877–78 redecoration. Above: In simple and egalitarian Shaker style, the stairs of the Centre Family Dwelling House (1824–34), Shakertown, Ky., are paired. Below: While rising in a spiral, the stairway at Shakertown's Centre Family Guest House (1839–41) also is part of a pair. Right: Thomas Day, a free black craftsman, left his signature in the newels of simple stairways, like that in the Bartlett Yancey House (above), Yanceyville, N.C., and the one in the Wm. Long House (below), Semora, N.C., which possibly incorporates Day's initials.

After their modest and often rustic beginnings, hotels by the late nineteenth century displayed an opulence in detail and architectural eclecticism sufficient to compete for travelers' attention. Clockwise, from bottom left: The gateway to a private world of leisure, the Lake Mohonk Gate and Gatehouse in New Paltz, N.Y., is a fortresslike Richardsonian Romanesque. With interior styles ranging from Pompeian to Louis XVI, the Jefferson Hotel (1895), Richmond, Va., still receives visitors. A letter box at the Bellevue Stratford Hotel (1904), Philadelphia, Pa. features a figurehead said to be Buffalo Bill. Opposite page: An early landmark amid its wooden false-front neighbors, the Grand Hotel (1887) in San Diego, Calif. (above), continues in use as the Hotel Horton. Shown in 1897, the Hotel del Coronado (1888) in Coronado, Calif. (below), was built during San Diego's boom era with semiskilled labor and was meant, said its developers, to be the "talk of the Western world" and "a place where people will come long after we are gone."

By the middle and late nineteenth century, many living spaces had come a long way from the basic human need for shelter. Above: Side by side in all their similarities, two Monroe, Mich., houses built about 1880 still retain their Victorian individuality, the Italianate house at left with a cast-iron railed deck on a hip roof, its brick neighbor with a mansard roof and iron roof cresting. Right: Patterns popularized by Andrew Jackson Downing were adapted for this arched window in the now demolished James Winslow Gatehouse, Poughkeepsie, N.Y., which from the interior presents an unusual optical illusion. Opposite page: Anchored at its ends by pergolalike enclosures, the porch of this sea captain's house not far from the ocean in Frankford, Del., adds a touch of the Steamboat Gothic to the eclectic Italianate and Victorian Gothic house.

AGRICULTURE

Long before the European colonists found the fertile lands of the New World, there was agriculture in America. The Indians hunted and fished and tilled the land in limited pursuits from forest to desert and plain. Essentially nomadic, they have left only a few relics of their cultivation: the slatted corncrib on posts, the husking peg, some say even the scarecrow. While the Plains Indians kept herds of horses, the eastern tribes did not, and neither has left examples of barns. But their legacy is imbedded in many of the crops and processes that have been the mainstays of American agriculture: corn, tobacco, beans, squash. Succeeding generations of farmers have left their own imprints on the cultivation of the land, meeting specific demands of growing a certain crop or raising livestock as well as meeting the dictates of nature. Now agrarian structures constitute probably the most diverse elements of the built environment.

Agrarian structures weather like the land. Preceding pages: Treated posts and three strands of barbed wire above a woven base in this fence (left) near Casper and Glenrock, Wyo., are said to make it sheep-proof. In Monroe County, Mich. (right), barns, silos, and outbuildings echo each other across a landscape of cultivated fields. Opposite page: Even after years of neglect, this Greek Revival farmhouse in Dundee, Mich., still indicates the farmer's cultural awareness and the importance of farming to his life. Left: This Utica, N.Y., farm seems to be an organic part of the landscape. Above, left: W. A. Graham's circular barn (c. 1900) in Forest Home, N.C., is thought to have been built as part of an experimental farming effort. Above, right: Rev. J. E. Biehler's round barn (1914) in Easton, Kans. Below: Often repaired but in continuous use since it was built in 1826, the Melvin Thompson Icehouse in South Bristol, Maine, is the only natural ice business still in operation in Maine, a state that produced more than three million tons of ice in 1890.

Places where the land is cultivated—farms, plantations, ranches—have been and often remain nearly self-sufficient communities. Besides a springhouse for keeping water supplies uncontaminated and food cool, and a summerhouse for cooking and laundering, a typical agrarian homestead may include a smokehouse, a bake oven, corncribs, a lime kiln, pigpens, a woodshed, a wagon shed, chicken coops, a dairy, a root cellar and a pumphouse, as well as the main house, several barns, and a necessary (privy).

America's built agrarian environment is essentially a product of the nature of its crops and the geographical locations and cultural backgrounds of its farmers.

Just as each variant in the pursuit of agriculture produced its own structures, each has brought mobile constructions as well as stationary. This disk harrow from Hillsdale, Wyo., was used to turn fields preparatory to seeding.

Rice culture in the Carolinas, Arkansas, and Texas produced systems of dikes and levees to bring water needed for rice growing. Cotton production in the antebellum South gave rise to great houses and villages of slave cabins and dependencies. Ranching in the West and Southwest called for bunkhouses for cowhands and corrals, blacksmith shops, and tackle sheds for the care of the horses. Grain production in the Midwest, carried on after the mid-nineteenth century with increasingly larger and more sophisticated machinery such as the mower-reaper and the combine, required the construction of large barns or sheltered areas for storage of massive equipment and elevators for storing grain.

The process of growing tulips in Michigan, daffodils in Virginia, roses in Texas, and marigolds in California produced not only showplace fields but also irrigation

systems, warehouses, greenhouses, and retail outlets. Citrus fruit cultivation in Florida, Texas, and California called for broad acres of trees lined with smudgepots in case of severe weather changes and packing sheds adjacent to rail sidings for quick shipping. Apple growing in Virginia, Washington State, New York, and Michigan necessitated different forms of orchards, contoured to hug the hillsides. Truck farming for vegetables produced its own machinery as well as migrant labor camps.

At the Booker T. Washington Birthplace, Rocky Mount, Va., these split logs required no vertical supports and were easily movable, yet provided secure fencing.

Another determinant of the appearance of agrarian structures, as in housing, was geographical location. This established the available materials: stone in hill or mountain areas, logs or timber framing where forests were plentiful, sod in the flat prairie lands, stone or adobe where clays were suitable in the Southwest. Also of crucial concern to farmers were climate changes: the severity of winters and summers, the direction of prevailing winds, the length of growing seasons. These factors dictated the direction structures faced and their relation to each other. In the North and East, buildings faced away from prevailing winds (toward the south and east) and were oriented toward the morning sun. In severe

The shape of a barn often depends on its intended use, cultural origins, or pure experiment. Above: Joseph Battell, founder of the American Morgan Horse Register, did much of his work in developing the breed (named after Justin Morgan) here at the University of Vermont Morgan Horse Farm Barn (1907). Above, right: The unusual half-timber, half-brick Langholff barn (c. 1848), Watertown, Wis., took its form from the farmer's German background. Right: This Arcola, Va., barn (c. 1910) is notable for its two-story wagon way and clipped gambrel roof with eave pents, designed to throw cascading water or snow away from the barn. Below, right: The barns at Woodlawn Plantation, Mount Vernon, Va. (c. 1910), are recurring types since the mid-nineteenth century, banked into a hillside with storage above and animals below, a corncrib on stilts with a central wagon bay, and a tackle and equipment barn. Below: Rev. J. E. Biehler's experimental barn (1914), Easton, Kans., was patterned after one in Missouri. Topped with a cupola, its entire upper floor was turned into a hayloft.

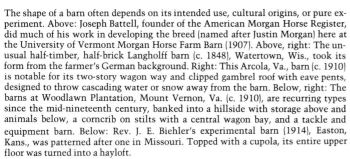

Above, left: With its eighty-foot tower, wooden mill blades, large wooden storage tank, and underground cistern, the Bronson Windmill (1893–94) in Fairfield, Conn., used for the Verna Dairy Farm, is an unusual cross between the American windmill and its European antecedents. Above, right: This Hillsdale, Wyo., windmill is typical of the American windmills that pumped water for nineteenth- and early-twentieth-century homesteads. Its sails revolved with the wind.

Opposite page, above: Farmsteads, like this one in Geneva, Neb., were and often still are self-sustaining clusters, using a minimum of land for the structures necessary to tend the crops or herds. The louvered sails on the windmill and horse weathervane are unusual. Below: The mid-nineteenth-century Fort Laramie Hog Ranch at Fort Laramie, Wyo., provided cards, whiskey, companions, and some agricultural products for the soldiers at nearby Fort Laramie.

New England climates, farm buildings were often interconnected in a continuous row, not just for convenience but to provide protection for humans and animals during bitter winters. In warmer climates, kitchens and bake ovens often were detached from the dwelling.

As protection from harsh New England winters, many mid-nineteenth-century farms, such as this one in Jackson, N.H., joined dwelling and outbuildings in one continuous structure.

No matter where agricultural buildings were located, the major elements of their form were shaped by their use. Smokehouses, for example, whether built as separate structures or located adjacent to chimneys in the attic or basement, had to be dry and tightly enclosed. Icehouses were constructed near sources of supply— lakes or rivers that froze—and had to be well insulated to assure that the ice kept for later use. For this reason icehouses were usually revetted into the ground or placed below ground. Common elements were evident also in barns used to store hay as opposed to those used to house livestock. In the former, the amount of hay stored for winter required strong framing methods and cathedral-like spaces; dairy barns and horse barns had to allow for stalls and equipment rooms.

Tobacco-curing barns show these differences dramatically. Bright-leaf tobacco in the South's Piedmont area was cured by heat, so the curing barn was a fully enclosed square, usually made of logs. Cigar leaf produced in Connecticut, on the other hand, was air-dried, calling for rectangular frame barns with louvers or movable sides to regulate the flow of air. The tobacco of southern Maryland, also air-cured, was hung in rectangular barns as well, but these were generally smaller than their New England counterparts and often had exposed frames with no enclosing walls at all.

The varied cultural background of America's farmers also influenced the diversity of the nation's agricultural environment, leaving more of an imprint than on urban areas; pressure to conform to style did not overpower the farmer, whose main interests were efficiency and self-sufficiency. English farmers, from a verdant country of

Hung on sticks, tobacco plants air-cure in a frame curing barn in Ridge, Md., that is sufficiently closed to protect the drying tobacco from the weather.

gently rolling hills, built simple rectangular barns, windowless, with entrances on the long sides and a passage through them flanked by animal stalls. German farmers tended to bank their barns into the sides of hills, providing entrances at two ground levels. A German barn also was more likely to have windows or louvered vents and an upper level cantilevered over a lower one. These building methods were so prevalent that the two terms, English and German, are now used generically, regardless of the builder's ethnic background.

This early-nineteenth-century barn at Thoroughfare Gap, Va., features a forebay supported on wooden columns and cantilevered out over the stone foundation.

While agrarian buildings are essentially utilitarian, farmers have generally been attentive to detail in their construction; barns and other major outbuildings often rivaled houses not only in the time the farmer spent in them but in their decorative detail—the so-called hex signs that decorate Pennsylvania Dutch barns being only one example. A barn, especially, was an indicator to

As utilitarian as they may be, the outbuildings of a farm were often constructed with an attentiveness to detail usually seen only in houses or public buildings. Left and above: At the Lick Run Plantation, Hedgesville, W.Va., this early-nineteenth-century barn was constructed of native stone carefully arranged in courses, especially at the corners where the large stones simulate quoins. Below: Even farm necessaries, or privies, were designed with special care. This large brick necessary at Huntley (c. 1820), Groveton, Va., features ventilators in a diamond pattern as part of a storage area abutting the main facility, which was cleaned through a metal tray beneath the wooden plate at ground level below the windows.

neighbors of success, but even the smallest and most utilitarian of structures was not overlooked: the necessary was often as well detailed and finished as the dwelling.

Farm complexes show attention to detail and color often reserved for the dwelling, as seen in these barns in La Salle, Mich. (opposite page), and Indiana (above).

Many old farm buildings have remained in use because they still serve the purposes for which they were built, farmers long ago having decided how to solve space problems in the best way. One type of farm that changed little during the first half of the twentieth century is the dairy farm, small, independently owned, and as productive as possible. In places such as southeastern Wisconsin and upstate New York, only the addi-

In experimenting with this round barn in Elkins, W.Va., the builder was able to put a conical roof on the cupola, but had to modify a standard gambrel roof for the main structure.

tion of leased, navy-blue Harvester silos infringes on the architectural integrity of these small complexes. On other farms, visual intrusions into the weathered, natural patina of the agrarian landscape are beginning to make their way in the form of prefabricated aluminum storage structures and concrete block barns. Some cohesive agrarian communities such as plantations are long since gone, destroyed or divided in the aftermath of the Civil War and turned into small farms. Ranches, being larger in acreage and fewer in number, have for the most part been maintained.

Although temporary, haystacks form integral parts of the agrarian landscape. A central frame holds these Dawsonville, Md., stacks securely as the hay cures for winter feeding.

Besides the population explosion that has called for the building of highways across the countryside and the taking of massive amounts of land for large developments, farms and their outbuildings are being threatened by another overwhelming force—the rise of agribusiness, which has perhaps done more to eliminate traditional structures on small farms than any other factor. Freed from tiny yields by the mechanization of labor in the mid-nineteenth century, many farmers, especially in the rich lands of the Midwest, forfeited the self-sufficiency of diversified crops for the profits available in single cash crops such as wheat or corn. Tied to world markets, time and time again farmers have been caught by the vicious circle of overproduction, low prices, and debt. Consistently throughout the 1890s, again in the early twentieth century and in the Depression era, small-scale farmers faced bankruptcy, the division of foreclosed land into smaller parcels, and sharecropping. Today big business operates multiple farms under a single corporate umbrella. This has meant not only less attention to the individual farm and its buildings, but development of newer, larger, more standardized equipment and structures.

Such changes, together with the difficulty of finding new uses for farm structures and the inherent fragility of many of them, make the outlook for saving old agrarian structures seem bleak. Only a small percentage of farms can be converted to farm museums such as the Oxon Hill Children's Museum in Oxon Hill, Md., an operating farm. Only a small number of farm structures can be saved by being moved to museum villages as have the Pliny Freeman Farm buildings at Old Sturbridge Village in Sturbridge, Mass., or the collection of ranching structures at Ranch Headquarters at Texas Tech University in Lubbock, Tex.

A mid-nineteenth-century slave cabin on the Georgetown, Ky., farm of George W. Johnson, Confederate governor of Kentucky, is more substantial than most and reflects the architecture of the era and the owner's attempt to keep in style with the times.

If farm-related structures are to be saved in their original places, Americans will have to develop a greater awareness of the importance of agriculture in American history and its manifestations in the nation's architecture. Several European countries—Holland, Great Britain, and Germany, among others—survey landmarks and maintain registers for barns and other farm buildings. In this country farm museums have found a benefactor in the Association for Living Historical Farms and Agricultural Museums. Rural housing loans, tax incentives, and other devices to lessen the development pressures pushing farmers to sell are also gaining acceptance.

If American farm structures continue to diminish or disappear, we will have lost another irreplaceable reminder of our heritage, or more. For nowhere is architecture tied more organically to the land than in the pursuit of agriculture. Agrarian structures rose because of the

This late-nineteenth- or early-twentieth-century farmers' exchange in The Plains, Va., is of vertical board and batten construction, a handy backdrop for an advertiser's message.

land's riches and depend for their utility on its continued vitality. But not only are structures dependent on the land; in many cases the preservation of the land depends on saving its buildings. If the farm gives way to "progress," so may the land.

Trailerlike curers are beginning to supplant old tobacco barns such as this nineteenth-century log structure at Cypress Hall Plantation, Justice, N. C., once part of a row.

Left: The farmer's French Huguenot background can be seen in the thick stone walls, eaves kick, and divided double doors of the Heinrich Zeller House (c. 1745), Newmanstown, Pa. Above: This early-nineteenth-century outbuilding on the Mendenhall Farm, Mendenhall, Pa., combined springhouse, smokehouse, and storage. Below: Built by settlers from German Silesia, the half-timbered Langholff house (c. 1848) in Watertown, Wis., put dwelling and barn under one roof.

East or West, farm or ranch, the structures built to serve the pursuit of agriculture reflect the dictates of the land, the requirements of the crops or herds, and the cultural backgrounds — and often social status — of the builders or residents. Opposite page, above: This New Mexico hacienda, the Severino Martinez House (c. 1804–24) in Taos, has fortresslike walls with roof parapets that were high enough to protect residents against Indian attack. The house's early adobe portion is incorporated in a thirteen-room structure around an inner courtyard. Opposite page, below: Usually clustered near the plantation house in almost military arrangement, slave cabins were part of the antebellum southern landscape. This cabin (c. 1800) at Prestwould, Clarksville, Va., is part of a cross-shaped complex that also includes a barn, a corncrib, a smokehouse, and various other dependencies. Below: This homestead barn at Plum Bayou, Ark., was built as part of a pioneer farm project that was organized during the 1930s to help tenant farmers and sharecroppers become independent farmers.

The word "farmhouse" usually conjures up an image of a neat little white or naturally weathered frame dwelling, Federal or Gothic in simplicity, with perhaps a faint touch of the Carpenter Gothic around the porch or cornice line. But American farmhouses are in fact as varied as their owners and farm practices allowed. Opposite page: For his house in Abbott, N.M., Senator Stephen W. Dorsey, a rancher and businessman as well as a politician, included busts of himself and his family on the octagonal stone turret that was added in 1884 to the house's original log portion completed in 1879. Also on the landscaped grounds are three fountains and a lake with three islands. Right: The Garland-Buford House (c. 1860) in Osmond, N.C., was built by Dr. John T. Garland on his Hyco Creek tobacco tract. A flamboyant bracketed dwelling with Italianate overtones, even the window sashes with their wave patterns show the liberation of taste accomplished by development of the power-driven jigsaw. Below: At the end of a double row of live oaks, amid a community of slave cabins and outbuildings, Oak Alley Plantation (1836), Vacherie, La., is as individualistic as the owner, the unknown architect, and money from slave-raised sugar could make it.

COMMUNITY

Closely following the human needs for shelter and for food is the need to express ourselves spiritually and intellectually, to look after the well-being of mind and soul as well as body. The first sign of a community, the clue that people intend to stay in a place for at least a short while, is often the building of structures that attend to these needs—schools, churches, meeting places.

Early America, seen by some as the Promised Land, drew people to whom the relationship to their God was central to social habits, to education, to every aspect of life. Just as in medieval times the literal center of a community was the cathedral, so the meetinghouse was often a central structure in most parts of colonial America, at times serving as church, school, and public hall. As in Europe, schools were directly influenced in style as well as in academic direction by the church. Even early entertainment had its roots in religion: the English theater originated in the drama of the liturgy, and other amusements, if they can be called that, were provided by pious pursuits such as reading the Bible. Later frontier towns, cattle towns, and mining towns with names like Weaverville or You Bet frequently numbered churches among their earliest structures; as the Wild West turned more civilized, schools and even theaters were built as well.

At first, churches in each colony tended to be all of a

kind. The Puritans, among many other groups, had sought a place where no other church would compete. Ostensibly, religious tolerance was provided for in the colonial charters, but some colonies favored "established" churches, that is, tax-supported institutions. Protests of Baptists under the leadership of Roger Williams in Rhode Island led to the provision for separation of church and state in that colony's 1663 charter and served partly as the basis for the national constitutional policy of separation. As religious tolerance sanctioned by law spread, it had the effect, coupled with diverse immigration, of proliferating denominations and numbers and styles of churches.

Generally, religious beliefs were broadly divided: Puritans in the North, Catholics in the Deep South and Southwest, Anglicans in the South, with a variety of denominations represented in the area around New York and the Middle Colonies of Pennsylvania, New Jersey, Delaware, and Maryland. By 1790 the colonies included Roman Catholic, Presbyterian, Moravian, Methodist, Mennonite-Amish, Anglican-Episcopal, Baptist, Congregational, Dutch Reformed, German Reformed, French Huguenot, Jewish, and Swedenborgian religious groups.

The main influences on church styles, beyond the

Preceding pages: The University of Pennsylvania Library (1888–91), Philadelphia, whose main reading room rotunda is shown (left), was hailed for its innovative stack plan. Its Art Deco splendor painted over, the Twentieth Century Fox screening room (1930), New York City (right), has been recycled as a school.

Opposite page, left: The American Red Cross was born at St. Mary's Roman Catholic Church (c. 1855), Fairfax Station, Va. Opposite page, right: Infrequently used for churches, the Shingle Style suits the All Saints Episcopal Church (1888) in Bay Head, N.J. Above: The Presbyterian Church (1874) in Fairplay, Colo., a striking late Gothic Revival structure. Its uniform covering of shingles helps to achieve a simple dignity.

Religious structures can be austere and ornate at once. Above: The Shinto KuKui Shrine (1923) in Honolulu commemorates Hawaii's Japanese. Below: The ornate door and lintel relieve the severity of this North Jackson, Ohio, Friends Church (1886).

availability of materials and adaptation of traditional designs to climatic differences, were the beliefs they were intended to embody and the practice of worship to be carried on in them. Puritans, escaping what they considered idolatry in "Popish" worship, decorated little but the altar in order not to distract worshippers from their proper focus. Art was seen by some, such as the Quakers, as an invention of the devil, so many early churches were as functional and as plain as some barns, unadorned by towers or crosses. Moorish overtones on synagogues recall the Middle Eastern Jewish heritage, as Buddhist and Shinto temple designs do their Eastern religions.

In the Anglican territory of the southern colonies and in urban areas, a basic similarity in building style resulted from the use of pattern books. In 1736–37 the newly formed Carpenters' Company of Philadelphia began to assemble a professional library on construction techniques and styles. By 1789 the company had about twenty-two books on civil architecture. Although little is known of this eighteenth-century collection, most of the volumes were English publications, either in origin or translation. A basic pattern for churches was established by James Gibbs, who in his publication *A Book of Architecture* (1728) popularized the steepled and porticoed churches designed by Sir Christopher Wren, architect of St. Paul's Cathedral in London. Gibbs's book not only made the spire and the belfry reaching toward heaven ubiquitous in the eighteenth century, it also had a lasting influence into the twentieth century. American architects such as Asher Benjamin and Minard Lafever in their published pattern books also influenced the forms of meetinghouses and churches, as did the work of Boston architect Charles Bulfinch in the nineteenth century.

Using Indian workers, Roman Catholic priests in the West supervised the building of mission churches that adapted the Spanish Baroque style to local conditions, building skills, and materials, often simple adobe. The mission complexes begun by Father Junipero Serra eventually stretched through 500 miles of California.

During the "Great Awakening" in religion a generation before the Revolution, evangelists such as Jonathan Edwards and George Whitefield preached in the open air, in rural areas as well as in town squares. Listeners stood spellbound through long sermons, even in the snow. The circuit-riding followers of John Wesley in Georgia and other southern colonies furthered the practice of gathering outdoors and foreshadowed the popular camp meetings of nineteenth-century revivals.

Frontier areas, in addition to receiving immigrant utopian groups such as the Moravians, saw the arrival of groups fleeing from persecution in their own communities in America, including the Shakers and the Mormons. These groups built functional houses of worship appropriate to the climate, available materials, and their beliefs. Although many groups tended to put more energy into establishing a living and into worshipping than into the architectural elegance of their early churches, others constructed lavishly designed structures.

Mid-nineteenth-century religious confusion caused by the humanitarian philosophies of Transcendentalists such as Thoreau and Emerson was complicated by challenges to religion from the new scientific thinking, specifically Darwinian theory. These developments, coupled with the social upheaval leading to the Civil War and the influence of John Ruskin, the English critic and great proponent of the Gothic Revival, caused church designers to revert, as designers of other public buildings were doing, to romantic designs of the past, to the Gothic Revival and the neoclassical styles being employed in the secular community. Even the Egyptian Revival style enjoyed a period of popularity. Despite its decorative sun disk and vulture motifs, it was defended as being no less religious than the prevalent Greek Revival style.

Although churches have continued to be influenced by major architectural developments, the tendency has been to cling to conservative styles. Even today, when architects experiment with ecclesiastical structures, they generally design for multipurpose use or return to natural forms and materials like wood and stone, even opening sanctuaries to the sky, as in Philip Johnson's Roofless Church (1959) in historic New Harmony, Ind. Rehabilitated churches are also being adapted to full-time use by the total community, as they were once used in the colonies.

Education, like other aspects of community life, took divergent directions in the North and the South in colonial times. In the New England colonies great emphasis was placed on universal literacy. The first free public school was established in Boston in 1636, and Massachusetts required any town of more than 100 families to hire teachers so that every child could be taught to read. This concern for public education was carried by pioneers into the Northwest Territory, where they built schools as some of their first permanent structures. Public primary and secondary schools in the Middle Colonies were often single-room structures. In the South, plantation owners generally hired tutors to educate their children privately and, if they were enlightened slaveowners, sometimes built classrooms for their slaves.

Although there were few public grade schools in the South until after the Civil War, the area pioneered in state-supported universities. The University of North Carolina, established in 1789, became the first; the University of Virginia (1795) was not far behind, with its classical "academic village" (1819–22) designed by Thomas Jefferson. Private colleges were launched with Harvard in 1636, which had added a medical school by 1783. One notable private southern university, the College of William and Mary, was established in 1693 to train Anglican ministers. Princeton was founded by the Presbyterians in New Jersey in 1746. Yale, Columbia, Brown, Rutgers, and Dartmouth also were well established before the Revolutionary War. The University of Pennsylvania was the first, in 1751, to be free from denominational control. The architecture, as well as the curricula, of the Ivy League was to carry its influence throughout the Midwest.

After the Revolution, the Continental Congress showed its concern for education through a system of land grants, which reserved the sixteenth section of every township to provide funds for schools. As the land opened up for settlement, elementary education moved slowly but surely west. On the plains the three "R's" were taught in one-room "little red schoolhouses," many of which were white. In urban areas humanitarian reformers opened schools to aid the non-English-speaking immigrants who flocked to America before the Civil War. During this era, the primary aim of education changed from the transmission of religious knowledge to the teaching of citizenship.

Galveston's "Old Red" (1888–91), the first medical college building in Texas, is a blend of Romanesque and English Victorian styles that its alumni found worth saving.

In the late nineteenth century, universities were swept up in the Gothic wave that became the new academic architectural idiom, often executed in picturesque and eclectic fashions. The Healy Building (1877–79) at Georgetown University, Washington, D.C., is an aerie of northern European Romanesque towers, spires, and gargoyles outside and an eclectic blend of classic gilt and austere brick inside. Above: This winged alligator or dragon figure is one of a number used on window mullions in the building's Riggs Library (1889). Right, above: Four tiers of cast-iron stacks open onto a central light court. Right: An arched brick hallway is a restrained contrast. Opposite page: The main reading room is the core of Frank Furness's almost ecclesiastical plan for the University of Pennsylvania Library (1888–91) in Philadelphia. Shown is a cusped bracket supporting the skylight.

By 1860 several hundred high schools and more than 250 private and state colleges were in operation. Some sixty-nine agricultural and mechanical arts colleges were subsequently built in the West and Midwest on land grants provided by the Morrill Act of 1862. A prevalent architectural style was the so-called Collegiate Gothic with its romantic spired buildings. Such collegiate Old Mains, as well as smaller schoolhouses, stood out as landmarks of community dedication to education, just as courthouses symbolized the community of laws.

Adult education was provided for by lyceums, established in the 1820s as a series of readings and lectures given on all cultural topics except religion and politics; these were so popular that by 1835 regular lyceums had been set up in more than 3,000 communities. They also inspired the initiation of Bible study and recreation centers called Chautauquas, begun in Chautauqua, N.Y., in 1874. By the end of the century this institution also provided courses in languages, math, science, music, and art. Through the 1890s the public was enriched by philanthropists such as Andrew Carnegie who provided public museums, conservatories, zoos, public libraries, and other educational and entertainment facilities.

Typical one-room schoolhouses, the frame Public School No. 18 (1887) in Marshall, Va. (above), features a woodshed and necessaries, while an 1849 school in Childs, N.Y., clothed its Greek Revival design in cobblestone (right, above).

Before the growth of universal tax-supported education, schooling and learning for many meant temporarily using available public halls or homes. Other than at the major universities, few pre-1850 structures built expressly for educational purposes remain. By 1900 there were more than 6,000 high schools in America serving 15 million children. Rapid growth continued, and by the 1920s half of all children were in school. This necessitated the building of new classroom space, theaters, auditoriums, swimming pools, playgrounds, and other facilities, a task

accomplished in part through the federal construction projects of the Work Projects Administration in the 1930s. More than religious structures, schools since World War II have followed new architectural trends, as have many of the scientific research centers and educational facilities established since the launching of the Soviet Sputnik in 1957 and the beginning of the increased educational demands of the space age.

Few colonial amusements called for separate structures. The basic need to gather and talk was met in homes and in the marketplace. "Court days" drew everyone to the county seat, in the South for horse-racing and picnics. In the Dutch territory on the Hudson River, bowling greens were the center for amusements. Dancing, where not forbidden, required only a spacious room, be it a plantation house or a tavern ballroom or a barn. Outdoor sports and militia training, of which the northern colonists were fond, required only a village green.

Theatrical productions, however, did call for their own buildings. The first was constructed in Williamsburg in 1716, with Charleston's Dock Street Theater following in 1736 and New York City's John Street Theatre in 1767. Simply designed at first, theaters became elaborate by the Revolutionary War era. Charleston's Harmony Hall (1786) had boxes with their own locks, and in 1794 another Charleston theater was ventilated by an air pump. Behind a monumental façade, the Federal Street Theater in Boston, designed by Charles Bulfinch in 1793, had card rooms, tea rooms, and kitchens, and was considered the finest theater in the country.

Opposite page: A community of interests is never hard to find. German residents of Sauk City, Wis., posed in 1902 at their Freie Gemeinde cultural society (above). The Central City, Colo., Opera House (1878) presents operas of the non-equine type (below).

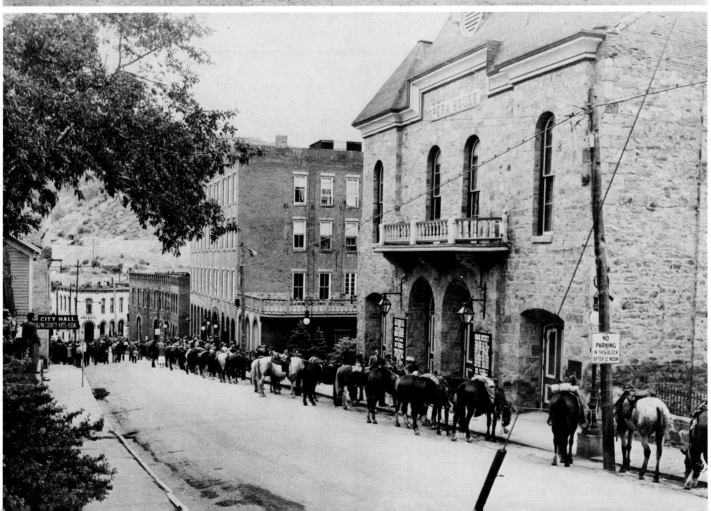

People gather together in a variety of pursuits. Opposite page: Built about 1865 in the golden age of Virginia City, Nev., the Italianate Piper's Opera House (above, left) is said to be where theater manager David Belasco began his career. Germans far from India built the White Elephant Saloon (1888) in Fredericksburg, Tex., using native limestone and cast-iron cresting (above, right). Mission or Dutch with a difference, the Rockham, S.D., community hall (below) served the multiple-use requirements that all communities have. Below: As with many places, much of the history of the Nogales, Ariz., area is left to museums to interpret through glass-encased exhibits. While the region's Spanish architecture is reflected in this museum of Indian and Spanish history at Tumacacori National Monument, the seventeenth-century mission after which it was named is now in ruins.

During the latter half of the eighteenth and the early nineteenth centuries, theaters were built in towns of every size, from the elaborate structures of Philadelphia, New Orleans, and New Bern, N.C., to those in small western towns. By mid-century midland towns were beginning to open what they called "opera houses." A plain pioneer theater was built by the Mormons in Salt Lake City in 1862 under the auspices of Brigham Young himself. Although several theaters were built in New York for the performance of operas, all failed and became playhouses. Only the Academy of Music (1868) was able to produce operas successfully and continuously. With the establishment of the Metropolitan Opera Company and the building of its house (1883), New York acquired prestige as an opera center in addition to its pre-eminence as the theater center of the nation. The architectural team of Dankmar Adler and Louis Sullivan, who had collaborated on ten theaters in the Chicago area, produced a masterpiece for that city in the Auditorium Building (1886–89), which used arches more for acoustics than for structure and employed electric lighting for the first time on such a scale—5,000 houselights, 150 footlights, and scores of lights on stage.

The style for theaters up to the middle of the nineteenth century was generally classical, perhaps because of the Greek heritage of Western drama; today's multi-purpose theaters, theaters-in-the-round, and amphitheaters are returning full circle to the Grecian precedent.

Twentieth-century entertainment learned a lot from P.T. Barnum. Opposite page: Mixing Chinese patterns with stucco, the Paramount Theatre (1926) in Palm Beach, Fla. (above, left and right), was one of the first built just for film. Cinematic eclectic prevails also (below) in the mezzanine of Cleveland's State Theatre (1921). Below: The "Sig" Sautelle Circus Training House (c. 1902) provided the unexpected: pressed tin inside a frame octagonal house in Homer, N.Y.

While drama flourished in urban areas, major pastimes in the rural areas of the South, the Midwest, and the West included the activities at county and state fairs. The more elaborate of these fairs produced large pavilions and other buildings for the judging of livestock and the exhibition of produce and crafts. Circuses toured the nation, taking a mobile built environment with them, while permanent sites for musical entertainment were provided by bandstands in town squares and parks. At box socials and church gatherings the popular game of baseball produced diamonds on the land.

In 1800, less than 10 percent of the American people lived in cities; by 1900, a third did so. Urbanization was beginning, and with it, new amusements for great crowds of people. The beginning of professional sports — baseball first, then football and basketball — produced stadiums for spectators numbering in the thousands. The early twentieth century also saw the rise of amusement parks, sideshow buildings, and fairgrounds flanked by roller coasters, Ferris wheels, and other engineering feats. St. Louis gave birth to the blues, and streets named Bourbon in New Orleans and Beale in Memphis fostered America's own Dixieland jazz; their legends live on even if the clubs and halls where this music got its start exist mainly in reputation.

From peep-show beginnings the movies had become respectable enough by the 1920s to warrant their own

Decorated with corn, native grass, and murals by an American Indian artist, the onion-domed Corn Palace (1921) in Mitchell, S.D., has served as a community exhibit and special events hall since the original was built in 1892.

buildings. Many were noted for their Art Deco style, featuring geometrical forms and earthy colors lavishly decorating interiors as well as exteriors. Other movie houses were literally transformed into Spanish and Moorish palaces, with Baroque-like plasterwork, winking stars, and moving clouds. The movies also took over burlesque halls left empty when vaudeville died. The perfection and mass production of radio and television during the 1920–50 period, however, and the phenomenal interest in these home entertainments dealt a blow to many

community activities. With communications media that could transport viewers anywhere in the world, fewer families saw the need to leave their living rooms.

The desire remains strong, however, to congregate for worship, for learning, for amusement. While some churches in downtown areas have been abandoned by congregations moving to the suburbs and some schools have been closed because of dwindling enrollments, many communities are increasingly putting these pivotal structures to new uses. Theaters too are becoming multimedia centers, refusing to usher in the act that brings down the house.

This Queen Anne–style cottage (1881) at the Los Angeles Arboretum in Arcadia, Calif., is a tribute to the jigsaw's capacity to create wooden extravaganzas.

For leisure or learning, a community gravitates to its focal areas and structures. Left: In Kennebunkport, Maine, the Kennebunk River Club (1889–90) served boaters in fashionable Shingle Style. Below: From a roller-coaster past, Glen Echo Park on the Maryland bank of the Potomac River near Washington, D.C., is making a comeback as a crafts center operated by the National Park Service. Launched in 1891 as a summer Chautauqua Society camp for lectures and entertainment, Glen Echo later became the area's chief amusement park. Its Dentzel Carrousel (1921) is now the center's new landmark and a link with its recent past. Opposite page: Although designed to be only a temporary celebration of the opening of the Panama Canal, San Diego's 1915 Panama-California Exposition has left the community with a complex of buildings, many saved at residents' insistence, forming its world-famous Balboa Park. The Moorish entrance to the main botanical garden building contrasts sharply with the soaring elliptical arches of the dark conservatory frame.

PUBLIC WELFARE

Promoting the general welfare—a primary reason for the creation of the federal government—requires the provision of a variety of services and buildings to house those services: buildings in which laws are made, interpreted, and enforced (legislatures, municipal office buildings, courthouses, police stations, jails); buildings that house facilities and people who see to the public safety and health (hospitals and firehouses); structures that provide public utilities (water reservoirs, sewage systems, electricity and gas plants for light and power); and buildings for the defense of the people (forts, army and navy posts, air force bases, missile sites, and other military installations).

Categorizing these building needs as federal, state, county, municipal, or private responsibilities is complicated by the fact that throughout the nation's history a fundamental tension has existed on the question of who should supply what. The source of the dispute over responsibility lies in the fact that some specific powers to provide for the public welfare were granted to Congress, among them levying taxes, supervising the national defense system, coining money, regulating interstate and international trade, and running the postal service. Others are implied powers, also given to Congress in Article I, Section VIII, of the Constitution. Steadily, as the federal government has grown in size in response to population growth, shifting political and social goals, and emergencies such as wars and depressions, the scope of its powers has also reached into areas formerly thought to be within the domain of states or of the private sector: hospitals, facilities for the aged and the unemployed, housing, public education, and recreation.

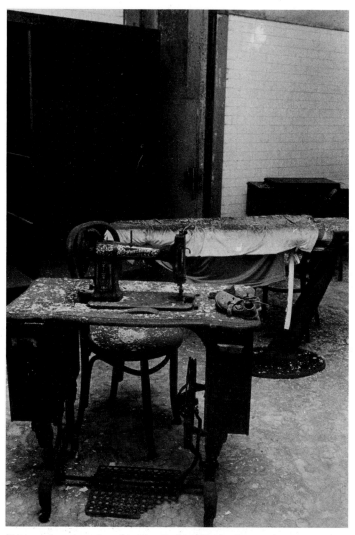

Preceding pages: As stated boldly in Art Nouveau letters, the Wissahickon Valley Public Library (1895), Skippack, Pa. (left), was built as a school. Behind a shingled false front in Crested Butte, Colo. (right), is a combined city hall and firehouse (1883). Below: Going to the poorhouse once meant structures such as the Lombard Farm (c. 1821), West Barnstable, Mass., used until World War II.

Using workrooms such as this, New York's Ellis Island received America's immigrating tired and poor from 1892 to 1954. The island is being restored for visitors.

One example of this shift is the most influential and controversial of the New Deal programs, the Tennessee Valley Authority, established in 1933. Seeking to break the utility corporation monopoly on public power supplies and to provide electrical power to the area, the federal government authorized the construction of more than twenty dams. Its supporters maintain that this program not only protected and provided economical power to an area about the size of England, but also restored the soil and brought low-cost housing to a needy region.

This change in political responsibility has influenced the built environment in two ways: directly, by the fact that many of the buildings housing these services were financed or designed by the federal government, and indirectly, by example. Just as state and municipal governments are patterned somewhat after the federal system, so in buildings that deal with like services, especially those constructed prior to the twentieth century, reflections of a central "Washington" style can be seen. At the same time, pivotal buildings such as courthouses, hospitals, and public schools have also made unique individual statements about the community itself. Even if a pattern was used again and again, such buildings, in the use of native materials, special touches in design, or regional craftsmanship, nonetheless announced aspirations and civic pride unique to a particular community.

Before the establishment of the federal government, northern colonial town-meeting halls grew up from a communal system of government. New Englanders used

the town hall for other purposes, including education and religion, but its main function was as a public forum. Jefferson called meetinghouses "the best school of political liberty the world ever saw."

In the early days of Virginia and Maryland, New Town Acts were passed to establish centers where land acquisition, property assessments, the disposal of property for tax and customs, and other legal matters could be attended to. Williamsburg, Fredericksburg, and Annapolis were set up for this purpose. There, in buildings reflecting Georgian and Adam styles, lawyers' and clerks' offices, jails, taverns, and inns were available to landowners when they had to register deeds, settle disputes, and otherwise keep the domestic scene tranquil. Although it was hoped that towns would grow up around such centers, the geography of a plantation economy often dictated otherwise, and initially they were filled mainly on days when court was in session.

Bills for materials and services plus the builder's own description survive to document Maine's oldest court building still in use, the Lincoln County Courthouse (1824) in Wiscasset, whose galleried main courtroom is shown.

State capitols, up to the time of the establishment of the federal capital in Washington, were also in the Georgian style. Jefferson's 1785 Roman-temple design for the state capitol of Virginia at Richmond set a new tone and was copied widely, for it was accepted in the new republic that buildings reminiscent of ancient Republican Rome (and later Greece) expressed the ideals of democracy and would inspire virtues such as loyalty to the state. The many-tiered tower and cupola of Philadelphia's Independence Hall (1732–1828) was also a major influence throughout the country. After the Renaissance-inspired classical U.S. Capitol (1793, William Thornton) was given its cast-iron dome (1863, Thomas U. Walter), many states looked on it also as an appropriate prototype for their highest seats of government.

State capitols seldom neglect their symbolic role. Left: Although classic revival, Minnesota's capitol (1896–1905) in St. Paul used ornate Victorian detail inside. Above: With its massive dome, the Beaux-Arts Mississippi State Capitol (1901–3), Jackson, shows its debt to the Washington model. Opposite page: Later wrought-iron features contrast with the Greek Revival simplicity of Tennessee's capitol (1845, 1854) in Nashville.

In the mid-nineteenth century such outstanding architects as Ammi B. Young, Isaiah Rogers, and Alfred B. Mullett served as supervising architects of the U.S. Treasury Department. Buildings designed from Washington by these men and others under their direction included customhouses, courthouses, post offices, and other federal office buildings that introduced the latest styles and technology to cities across the nation.

In early and frontier towns court was convened variously in a house or in the saddle, as Judge Roy Bean ("the Law west of the Pecos") often handled matters. But as towns strove to proclaim their permanence in the latter half of the nineteenth century, courthouses were proudly erected in the centers of county seats. By that time, the nation's best-known architects were no longer as active in designing the federal government's buildings, but the work of private architects such as the prolific Henry Hobson Richardson nevertheless had a great influence on the styles of public buildings. During the latter quarter of the century a large portion of America's courthouses departed from earlier classical motifs in favor of the newly popular Richardsonian Romanesque, mansarded French Second Empire, and Victorian Gothic styles, and their derivations.

Military buildings provide a wealth of examples of government architecture. Forts, although primarily thought of as wartime defense posts, were built also to protect boundaries from other encroachments. Fort Laramie, Wyo., was expanded by the government in 1849 from a trading post to headquarters for campaigns against Indians, and Fort Bliss in El Paso, Tex., to protect wagon trains bound for the California gold fields. Others were built for special government purposes, such as the Fort Knox complex (1917) near Louisville, Ky., which houses the federal gold deposit in vast steel and concrete vaults. Fort Leavenworth, Kans. (1827), once a defense outpost in Indian territory, now encompasses the U.S. Army Command and General Staff College as well as the military prison. While some forts remain active military installations, others, including Fort Worth, Tex. (1849), and Fort Smith, Ark. (1817), have become thriving civilian cities.

The *Maine* sailed to Havana from this isolated "Gibraltar of the Gulf," Fort Jefferson (1846), once a strategic defense outpost in Florida's Dry Tortugas Islands.

Hospitals—the first was Pennsylvania Hospital in Philadelphia (1755–56)—began as private ventures, financed by subscription, and thus developed relatively slowly. By 1825 there were hospitals in New York City, Boston, Baltimore, Cincinnati, and Savannah, but most doctoring in small towns was done in the home. During the Civil War, however, many hospitals were developed for the care of the wounded. In the postwar era Dorothea Dix and other reformers pioneered new treatments for mental illness, and the first of a system of federal hospitals for the insane, St. Elizabeth's in Washington, D.C., was built in 1855. Increasingly, hospitals, medical schools, and special treatment centers have been aided by federal financing and construction.

That jails and prisons are designed in part as work places is based on the Quakers' treatment of offenders. Because workers were badly needed in their communities, offenders were punished by being put to work chopping wood in the hope that hard labor would have a reforming influence. In contrast to the foul prisons of

Left: Three walls of the Old Colfax County Jail (1872), Cimarron, N.M., survived a lynching party's dynamite. Above: Seemingly as secure as a pharaoh's tomb, Philadelphia's Egyptian Revival Moyamensing Prison (1832) was razed in 1968. Below: The officers' quarters at Fort Davis, Tex. (1854), built to protect westward-bound travelers, overlook buildings now being restored.

Europe, penal complexes like Pennsylvania's Eastern State Penitentiary (1823–29) began reforms such as individual cells. Nineteenth-century prison architecture was predominantly a gloomy Gothic style with battlements and turrets for guard stations, but in more recent times the architecture has reflected the varying needs of maximum and minimum security.

Nineteenth-century attempts at penal reform evidenced themselves in prison architecture. Below: Although the entrance and administrative offices of Philadelphia's Eastern State Penitentiary (1823–29) retained the popular medieval-like Gothic Revival style, its innovative design provided for a central rotunda with seven cell blocks radiating out like spokes. With improved light, heat, ventilation, and cell space, including solitary confinement facilities, the prison was ahead of its time. Opposite page: Also Gothic in style, the Old Baltimore City Jail (1855–59), Baltimore, Md., seemed so progressive that it was criticized as a "palace for felons." Now only the gatehouse remains. The barred open arches provided light for the prisoners while giving guards an overview of the tiered cell blocks.

During the last decade of the nineteenth century, groups of local citizens, led by municipal art societies, also took up the reform banner on behalf of the appearances of cities. Under the name "The City Beautiful," the movement focused its efforts on making streets and other public places more attractive. From the great influence of landscape architect Frederick Law Olmsted's plan for the 1893 World's Columbian Exposition in Chicago came the development of comprehensive city plans in such cities as New York, Philadelphia, Chicago, Cleveland, Hartford, and San Diego. Although the designs of planners such as Daniel Burnham, the Olmsted Brothers, Albert Kelsey, Charles Mumford Robinson, and John Nolen were never fully implemented by local government officials during this period (1893–1909), the movement stimulated further city planning, sociological and scientific analysis of urban growth, and government concern for the well-being of citizens. Parks, playgrounds, and boulevards, all with their associated structures, were to become part of America's planned and built environment.

The era of most prominent direct government influence on public buildings was the Depression. Between 1935 and 1943, the Work Projects Administration (originally Works Progress Administration) granted more than $11 billion to states, municipalities, and other public bodies for local construction, seeking to match local needs with those of architects, engineers, and construction workers for employment. Among the structures built were hospitals, reform schools, airfields, naval and submarine bases, parkways, tunnels, dams for flood control, low-income housing, municipal swimming pools, sewage treatment plants, water supply systems, schools, grain elevators, electric power plants, radio stations, garages, warehouses, university dormitories, labs, greenhouses, administration buildings, courthouses, city halls, quarantine stations, and Coast Guard inspection stations. The government also began slum clearance and provided low-income housing in the Virgin Islands, Brooklyn, Birmingham, Ala., and Omaha, among other places.

Because the buildings were designed by local architects, the quality and styles varied from region to region. Some of the best structures were built in Missouri: new prison facilities throughout the state, the Forest Park Zoo and Conservatory in St. Louis, and the St. Louis and Kansas City municipal auditoriums. Technological strides were also made in lighting and plumbing systems and safety measures in schools. Air conditioning was developed further and used first to relieve conditions in southern hospitals. Improved seismic protection devices were employed on buildings in the West, and materials such as concrete were used innovatively for major engineering projects including tunnels and dams. One showpiece of technology is Hoover Dam (once also known as Boulder Dam), built in 1930 on the Colorado River at the Arizona-Nevada border.

Constructed by the Bureau of Reclamation for flood control and reclamation, Guernsey Dam (1927), Guernsey, Wyo., is now part of a series of recreational sites.

As combustible gas was pumped into or withdrawn from gasholders such as this 1872 example in Petersburg, Va., the holder, which floated on water, would be raised or lowered between the Doric-style iron supports, maintaining compression.

Many structures built by the federal and state governments and local municipalities are being threatened by the same sectors. The proliferation of the bureaucracy during World War II caused government personnel in all regions of the country to outgrow their facilities. During the 1950s and 1960s many communities, seeking to modernize, simply tore down courthouses, post offices, municipal office buildings, and city halls, along with trees and other parts of the environment, regardless of their historical or architectural value. Especially sad was the loss of many nineteenth-century buildings not yet old enough to have come back into fashion.

Above: This log hut built by Ukranian settlers served as the Grassy Butte, N.D., post office from 1914 to 1963. Right: Two late-nineteenth-century variations on the false-front style of firehouse architecture are found in Georgetown, Colo.: the Alpine Hose Firehouse No. 2 (above) and the Old Missouri Fire Station (below).

Many communities are just now beginning to realize the value of these irreplaceable structures, recognizing that as symbolic focal points for community identity and pride, older public buildings cannot be duplicated. Some are constructing inconspicuous appendages to old buildings to alleviate space problems and are renovating instead of demolishing. Typical of the groups that have promoted this are the New York State Bar Association's Committee for the Preservation of Historic Courthouses and similar groups in Kansas, Arizona, Oregon, Ohio, and Virginia.

The federal government is now authorized to transfer its retired buildings to states and communities for a variety of purposes; thus, forts are being turned into amphitheaters, mints into museums, and customhouses into community centers. Since the issuance of Executive Order 11593 in 1971, all federal agencies have been directed to locate, record, and assure the maintenance of their own historic buildings, for the federal government, too, has come to recognize that many of its own buildings are indeed worth saving.

Below: The cast-iron Marcus Garvey Park Fire Watchtower (1856) in New York's Harlem has not been used since 1870. Right, above: This New York Edison Company Powerhouse (c. 1910) in New York City belies its utilitarian function. Right, below: Shingled and Chateauesque, the Lawson Water Tower (1902), Scituate, Mass., was built to hide a steel frame. Opposite page: Conversion of this city coal bunker on Boston's waterfront to a fire and police station is under consideration.

TRANSPORTATION

"You can't get there from here" may well be one of the oldest tag lines in American humor, but in that statement is the challenge that has shaped the history of American transportation and communication—the story of how people found ways to get "there."

The needs that produced the first American transportation systems have remained basically the same to this day. In the early colonies, for example, the prime need was for routes by which farmers could get their produce to market. In the northern colonies, with buildings encircling common land, this often meant a

walk across the village green or a short trip on horseback to trade at the next village. In the southern colonies, however, it usually required a major trip down inland waterways from the forest or the plantation to get lumber or tobacco to market for shipment to England. Throughout the colonies, especially before the Revolution when the fate of the country depended so heavily on the exchange of ideas, the need for roads on which to carry the post was crucial.

In addition to transporting goods and ideas, early Americans transported themselves as well. They traveled to visit friends and to see new places, but the hazards and discomforts of early travel over dusty, uneven roads—at times quagmires—made standard visits last several weeks or months. Colonists also moved their households in search of better lives, a motivation not too different from that of Indian tribes who traveled to find food and to escape the seasonal harshness of climates.

Today our transportation systems are still based on trade, on the need to communicate, on travel for pleasure, on the need to keep "going west"—to find better jobs and better climates. In a lifetime the average American moves fourteen times. Methods of travel have

changed drastically, and each change has produced a variety of new structures and new sites, even new cities. Perhaps no other aspect of American life, dependent as it is on technology, has had a greater impact on the built environment than transportation and communications.

In the earliest days, when there was little technology and nature alone controlled the environment, explorers edged the coastlines, coming inland only so far as navigable waters would permit. This natural movement established coastal towns that become centers of fishing or trading: New London, Conn., Salem, Mass., New Bern, N.C., Charleston, S.C., New York City, Boston, Baltimore, Philadelphia, New Orleans, San Diego. Once on land, colonists also followed the lines of least resistance: trails and paths made by the native Americans, natural passes through the mountains, or animal paths, "buffalo streets," through the least dense areas of forests.

Built before steel replaced wrought iron, the Laughery Creek Bridge (1878) in Aurora, Ind., is a triple intersection through-truss span probably prefabricated on-site by one of the early companies specializing in bridge building.

Preceding pages: Gothic Revival stations like Wallace, N.Y.'s (left), are sprinkled across the land. H.H. Richardson's Union Station (1885–87), New London, Conn. (right), has finally survived the threat of demolition. Below: Last of a breed, the sternwheeler *Delta Queen* (1924) anchors near Natchez, Miss.

Right: The towns of Walpole, N.H., and Rockingham, Vt., combined funds to build this bowstring truss bridge at Bellows Falls, Vt., opening it to the public in 1905. Below: At the time of its construction in 1848–49, the Wheeling, W.Va., Suspension Bridge was the longest suspension bridge in the world and is believed to be the oldest cable suspension highway bridge still in use. When not sufficiently stiffened, suspension bridges tend to oscillate in high winds, and Wheeling's consequently has been rebuilt and strengthened several times.

Above: The Sand Key Lighthouse (1853) in Key West, Fla., combines light and keeper's house in one cast- and wrought-iron structure. Opposite page: Built about 1885 to carry horse-and-buggy traffic across Massachusetts' Duxbury Bay, the wooden Powder Point Bridge (above) is being restored so it can continue to carry automobile traffic. By this "rude bridge" at Concord, Mass. (below), the Revolution's "embattled farmers stood,/And fired the shot heard round the world."

Within these early towns, support facilities began to develop: taverns and inns (complete with bowling alleys, pool tables, and gambling equipment) where weary riders, walkers, or sailors could find rest and entertainment. Tired animals were well cared for in livery stables and boats went into drydock in comparatively sophisticated ports. Other tangential structures became necessary. Horse-and-buggy travel created the need for carriage manufactories, warehouses, blacksmith shops, tanning mills, harness manufactories, and carriage houses. By the mid-1700s post roads accommodated (barely) travel between the major cities; by the late 1790s turnpikes were initiated and the first tollhouses were built. Canals along waterways created the need for such things as locks and lock-keepers' houses. Fords and ferries were developed where the rivers were easiest to cross, and by 1820 bridges of many types were making it possible for travelers to get over rivers and chasms. On the coast, those depending on the sea for their livelihood had developed such safety measures as lightships and lighthouses.

Opposite page: This plaque on the Walpole-Rockingham Bridge at Bellows Falls, Vt. (above), acknowledges Lewis F. Shoemaker & Co., Philadelphia, as the builders. A span being built over the Ohio River between Louisville, Ky., and New Albany, Ind., in the 1960s echoes earlier prototypes. Right: Built when horses were still a major mode of transportation, the early-nineteenth-century Grange Carriagehouse in Havertown, Pa., was Victorianized with an Italianate tower, tin roof, and stamped Renaissance Revival door hinges. Below: Instant communications and Coast Guard patrols have made obsolete the hundreds of life-saving stations constructed by the U.S. Life Saving Service beginning in 1871. The Chicamacomico Life Saving Station (1874), North Rodanthe, N.C., was one of seven constructed on the treacherous Outer Banks. Decommissioned in 1954, the main building is in the weather-resistant Shingle Style favored by the Life Saving Service.

Now automated or replaced by automatic light towers, lighthouse complexes were built to be instantly recognizable. Opposite page: Built 1787–90, the 90-foot-high Portland Head Light (left, above) at Cape Elizabeth, Maine, was authorized by President Washington. This cast-iron stairway is later. The Old Rock Harbor Lighthouse and Keeper's House (1855) in Isle Royale, Mich. (left, below), guided Lake Michigan traffic. The octagonal lighthouse (1818) and later generator shed of Baldhead Island Lighthouse (right, above), Southport, N.C., are abandoned. The 1901 Portland Head Light keeper's house (right, below) is a shingled Queen Anne. Below: The octagonal New London, Conn., Harbor Light (1801) is thought to have been the fourth U.S. lighthouse.

The drive to the west in search of new lands and new starts set America against the problem of vast distances. One solution to the hardship of travel by Conestoga wagon was the Cumberland Road or Great National Road from Cumberland, Md., to Vandalia, Ill., begun in 1811 and completed in 1852, an event that opened up new territory to rapid settlement. The beginnings of modern technology were further evidenced in the first few years of the nineteenth century with the invention of the steam engine. The launching of a steamboat in 1807 was to revolutionize river trade, then carried on by keelboats propelled by a pole. By the 1860s more than 1,000 steamboats were literally racing up and down the major waterways, making such river towns as St. Paul, New Orleans, Pittsburgh, Wheeling, and St. Louis into prosperous cities. In the East the construction of the 363-mile Erie Canal from Buffalo to the Hudson River at Albany created cities such as Rochester and Syracuse and served as a national model after it opened in 1825.

The technological advances brought by the inventions of dynamite and black powder and the Bessemer process opened the westward movement; railroad tunnels were blasted, roads leveled, canal locks constructed, and bridges built. In 1828 the inauguration of the Baltimore and Ohio Railroad began what became the most influential transportation system yet seen in America. The routes of a railroad could make or break a town; the histories of a thousand communities read in two parts; the last part is either prosperity or decline depending on whether or not they "got the railroad" (a situation repeated in the era of the interstate). By 1869 the transcontinental railroad was completed. With it came modest stations at small junctions as well as elaborate station-hotel complexes, roundhouses, warehouses, and massive terminals in larger cities—and entire towns where before there were none. Besides the miles of track, bridges, dams, tunnels, and other structures that made the journey itself possible, the system necessitated hundreds of steel mills and factories to produce rails and ties. The need for long-distance message relays on the rail lines gave rise to semaphoric and electric telegraph systems, which in turn developed their own contributions to the built environment. Also dotting the continent from St. Joseph, Mo., to Sacramento, Calif. (1,966 miles), were Pony Express stations, a communications network that had a brief but blazing career in the 1860s.

The open spaces of Baltimore's Mount Clare roundhouse (1884) are natural display areas for historic locomotives in the Baltimore & Ohio Transportation Museum.

Once a major passenger station on the route to Rochester, the late-nineteenth-century Lehigh Valley Railroad Station, Rochester Junction, N.Y., is no longer used, although its stature indicates its former importance.

Above: Wells, Fargo & Company's red sandstone office (1877) in Silver Reef, Utah, looks as if it were designed to be more than one floor—but then stopped in mid-second-story when the town's brief but bright boom ended about 1888. Below: The cabs that wait at New York's Pennsylvania Station now do so outside the structure that replaced the original monumental station (1906–10).

In the cities mechanized streetcars were the forerunner of such mass transit systems as elevated trains and subways, which necessitated the construction of power and cable houses and car barns. By the turn of the century the invention of the internal combustion engine made the dream of the automobile a reality and ushered in the era of the commuter. By the 1920s automobiles were being mass-produced, and the nation's road system—built for horses and buggies—demanded serious overhauling. The need was answered by a cooperative effort of federal, state, and municipal governments that ultimately provided some one million miles of interstate highways. Cars, buses, and trucks now rivaled the railroad in terms of wider range and lower expense. Little towns that had died as a result of being bypassed by the trains came back to life, and oases of truck stops, garages, and gasoline stations sprang up alongside the highways. Motor hotels, bus terminals, and parking lots were brought into being, as were factories for the production of rubber, fabric, glass, and other auto-related products. Mass travel opened the way for mass culture.

Indicative of the important place of the railroad in turn-of-the-century society, the nation's best architects often were commissioned to design train stations. From the hands of McKim, Mead and White, New York City received in its Pennsylvania Station (1906–10) a classical monument based on the Baths of Caracalla in Rome, but whose most notable feature was its totally modern steel and glass concourse. After barely half a century, the station was demolished in 1963–66.

Above: This Hamlet, N.C., passenger depot (1900) may be recycled as a rail museum. Right: Now a drive-in bank, the Chateauesque Lincoln, Neb., station (1893) proudly bears the Chicago, Rock Island and Pacific logo. Below: The Mt. Airy Station (1883), Germantown, Pa., picturesquely blends brick, frame, and shingle.

Left: The important point where the B&O Railroad branched on its east-west route, one line leading to Washington, D.C., the other to Baltimore, is marked at Point of Rocks, Md., by this Gothic Revival station (c. 1875). Above: The brick walls, slate roof, and High Victorian Gothic tower of this Whitman, Mass., station seem out of place surrounded by an asphalt parking lot. Below: The Hammondsport and Bath Railroad Station, Hammondsport, N.Y., adapted itself well to a location between the tracks, using a tower on the approach end.

Simultaneously, the quick development of air travel following the first flights of the Wright brothers in North Carolina in 1903 virtually opened the entire world for trade. Through two world wars and the jet age of the 1950s the air as a more rapid route for travel and transportation of goods and mail rendered the old systems relatively obsolete. Since the 1960s the space age, with its missile sites and launch facilities, has created or inflated such towns as Huntsville, Ala., Cape Canaveral, Fla., and Houston, Tex., just as the first travel systems did in the colonies. In 1969, with the first lunar landing, a bit of built environment was transplanted even to the moon.

Gas stations were not always sterile landmarks along the road, as these imaginative service centers in Dallas (above) and Detroit (below) show.

Opposite page: The interior of one of H.H. Richardson's masterworks, the New London, Conn., Union Station (1885–87), has been converted to a two-level restaurant-office-and-rail complex. Above: To compactly transport pedestrians as well as cars and trucks, the Brooklyn-Queens Connecting Highway at Columbia Heights, N.Y., cantilevered the pedestrian promenade over the highway lanes, requiring no extra land. The new freeway itself is balanced over the old street.

Ironically, the great range of transportation systems America today enjoys is jeopardizing the quality of life that makes traveling possible and desirable. Because of air and noise pollution and a massive expenditure of limited resources, especially petroleum, we are looking carefully at our modes of travel for their efficiency and economy. Methods only recently considered obsolete are now beginning to make sense as alternatives to congested highways and knots of cloverleaves. It may be that new, adaptive uses of transportation structures from bygone eras will no longer be the only way to save these buildings; we may soon be using some of them again for their original purposes.

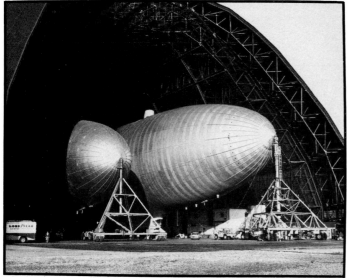

Some technological wonders of America's modern age of transportation have an uncanny resemblance even though their modes of transport are as different as air and water. Left: A domicile for dirigibles, the Goodyear Airdock (1929) in Akron, Ohio, was built for construction of the zeppelins U.S.S. *Akron* and U.S.S. *Macon.* Made of sheet metal attached to parabolic arches, the airdock is 1,175 feet long, 325 feet wide, and 211 feet high. Goodyear is seeking new uses for the structure, now used partly for storage, and they have not been hard to find—even a golf course has been suggested. Below: The world's first atomic-powered submarine, the *Benjamin Franklin,* was launched in 1954 from Groton, Conn.

Waterside portals are often the first—and sometimes the last—landmarks travelers see. These structures at the tip of New York City's Battery are near the site where ships embarked even in the days of the Dutch colonists. Right: The fire-boat station Pier A (1886) sports a tower and clock donated as a memorial to World War I servicemen. Ships' bells ring the time. Below: Like three tunnels opening into the canyons of the city, the water façade of the Battery Maritime Building (1907–09) is a monumental Beaux-Arts reminder of the time, before the East River was bridged, when seventeen ferry lines scurried between Manhattan and Brooklyn. Now serving as the Governors Island Ferry Terminal, the structure is in need of restoration, its blend of cast iron, pressed copper, and steel decaying in the salt air. The city has suggested turning it into a multi-use cultural, entertainment, and museum facility.

COMMERCE & INDUSTRY

Competition in America's free enterprise system has not always produced a better mousetrap, but it has produced a variety of structures in pursuit of that goal: buildings for assembling and processing raw materials; mines, power plants, coke ovens; factories for manufacturing goods from raw materials; mills for grinding grain, spinning and weaving fabric, and producing steel; and outlets for making these goods and attendant services available to the public: warehouses for wholesale transactions and markets, department stores and shops for retailing products to individual customers. Commercial and industrial activities also have given rise to office buildings to house the administration of such things as manufacturing, labor, and sales, and banks to provide the capital to keep it all going.

Every American industry has produced its own forms, and thus its own monuments. Preceding pages: Two 1882–83 blast furnaces (left) are among the survivors of the Sloss Furnace Company, Birmingham, Ala., one of the first iron-producing companies in the area. The twentieth-century buildings of the American Aggregate Company, Oxford, Mich. (right), follow earlier patterns. Opposite page: The pipes, tanks, and valves of this Michigan Consolidated Gas Company pumping station in northwestern Michigan are so well cared for that they seem more sculptural than industrial.

Above, left: An ore loading station (1901) is among the mining era relics remaining at the Silver King Mine, Park City, Utah. Above, right: In Moscow, Idaho, is a group of structures that reveal the evolution of grain elevator design from 1885 to 1942. This Idaho Seed Company Elevator was built in 1927. Below: By this century, grain elevators such as this Rock Island Railroad complex at Goodland, Kans., reflected the new industrial technology and massing.

Although agriculture was the main source of livelihood in the early days of the colonies, trade flourished as well, and by 1770 the colonies were also carrying on substantial fishing and lumber industries. These activities dotted the coast with shipyards, docks, and warehouses, and the forests with sawmills. Ships regularly carried dried cod, turpentine, pitch, tar, and tobacco from port to port along the East Coast as well as across the sea. The infamous triangular trade also flourished. Traded for rum, native Africans were taken as slaves to the West Indies, where they were again traded for molasses; this in turn was shipped to the colonies, where it was turned back into rum at American distilleries.

Cottage industries were practiced to perfection by the Shakers. Shown is the loom room in an 1851 shop at the Mount Lebanon Shaker Society, New Lebanon, N.Y.

Besides distilling, cottage industries included the manufacture of beaver hats, iron forging, and spinning and weaving in most colonial homes. By the 1790s some large-scale manufacturing was also under way. Especially active was the Brandywine River Valley of Pennsylvania, where paper, corn, and wheat were milled. Gunpowder was produced in Delaware and New Jersey. But even though England was already producing textiles through an established factory system, this industry did not take an early hold in America for a number of reasons. In addition to manufacturing and trade restrictions imposed by England, there was little money for capital investment; raw materials were virtually undeveloped; there were not enough people living in proximity to each other to provide either the necessary labor or a domestic market; nor was there a dependable inland transportation system for the exchange of goods. In any case, as immigrants who had been starved for land, the colonists were eager to expand their agricultural operations over the plentiful acreage they found in the New World.

America's entrance into manufacturing in the early 1790s was based on the cooperation of enterprises in both the northern and southern states. Imperfect spinning machines were available for the manufacture of cotton thread, but a shortage of fiber kept America out of the market. A slave, working by hand, took a full day to produce an average of one pound of cotton fiber. Not until after 1793, when Eli Whitney invented the cotton gin, was it possible to provide large quantities of raw material for textile manufacture. In that same year Samuel Slater established a mill at Pawtucket, R.I., for cotton spinning. Grown in the South, the cotton was processed primarily in New England and the Mid-Atlantic States, where the area's rapid rivers supplied the power to drive the mills, shipping provided the necessary capital, population centers supplied the labor, and natural harbors gave easy access to the raw materials being shipped in and finished products being shipped out.

Mills harnessed water power to provide America's first large-scale manufacturing. Below: Shepherd's Mill (1734, 1880), Shepherdstown, W.Va., has the largest overshot waterwheel in the world. Opposite page, above: In Malvern, Pa., a miller and his wife built their spring mill and house (c. 1793) of strong native stone. Below: The Yates Mill (c. 1760), Raleigh, N.C., ground corn and wheat, milled lumber, and carded wool.

New England mill towns became centers for the manufacture of cotton goods in the 1790s, and their mills were the towns' architectural focus. Opposite page: The Everett Mill (1909–10) in Lawrence, Mass., was said to have been the largest cotton mill under one roof at the time of its completion. Below: The crenelated Gothic tower of the Lower Pacific Mills (c. 1875), also in Lawrence, stands alongside the canal that supplied its water power, an unmistakable industrial landmark.

By cutting the colonies loose from the domination of England, the Revolutionary War spurred new industry and trade. The War of 1812 provided a further incentive for making America even more self-sufficient and contributed to the rise of native industries. Thereafter, a series of inventions again changed the face of manufacturing. The concept of producing firearms with interchangeable parts, pioneered by Whitney, Colt, and others before 1850, opened up assembly-line methods of production. The sewing machine, invented in 1846, made possible the manufacture of clothing and shoes, and this, too, called for the building of factories and worker housing.

Although the machines of industry led America into its own industrial revolution, their physical legacy is being diminished even more quickly than that of buildings because they do not adapt so easily to the wheels of progress. Some do remain as casebook examples of lost industries. Used originally as a saw and grist mill, the Easton Roller Mills (c. 1870), Easton, W.Va., was converted to rollers in 1894 with the advent of steam power, an innovation that produced a finer-ground and more nutritious flour.

Areas now included in American territory also were active centers of trade and industry during the first two centuries of the country's development. A thriving sugar industry existed in the Danish Virgin Islands during the eighteenth century. In the Southwest, Spanish colonists traded with the Old World in silver and agricultural products. In the Mississippi River Valley the French managed busy centers in furs, as did the Russians in Alaska.

The discovery of metal and minerals during the 1850s and the railroad boom in the 1870s were times of great change in the built environment. The rush to mine major deposits of gold in California in 1849 created new towns there, and the subsequent discovery of gold and silver in Nevada in 1859 caused towns to spring up in the surrounding states of Utah, Montana, and Colorado, as prospectors stampeded west to try their luck.

The deposits of iron ore first found and exploited in the Great Lakes region in the 1850s provided raw material for the production of steel. The resources of the large Mesabi Range in Minnesota, discovered in the 1890s, provided a stronger base for the rise of steel manufacturing, which was to become a keystone of the national economy. The high-heating Bessemer process of making steel from iron required an abundant supply of coal as well, and in places such as Pittsburgh these two resources were ideally found together. The town became a

The built environment boomed but also went bust during the mineral rushes. Above: Lead mining in Mineral Point, Wis., attracted an influx of Cornish tin miners after 1830. Many left their imprint on the town's buildings. Below: Silver City, Idaho, seen here in its boom days after the 1863 silver discovery, had become a ghost of itself by 1942.

prototypical factory environment. Following its model, other commercial and industrial structures in America changed from predominantly wood and brick to steel and iron construction, beginning with the railroad tracks and support facilities and the ore-breaking machinery brought into boom towns by big mining companies when the busted prospectors went back home.

In the first half of the nineteenth century cast iron was used occasionally for interior columns, beams, and joists. By the 1850s and especially after the Civil War, the taste developed for its use as exterior decoration, producing the so-called cast-iron architecture. By pouring molten iron into a mold, elaborate and seemingly carved "prefab" façades could be produced, with ornament that would have been prohibitively expensive if carved in stone. The New York City factory of James Bogardus mass-produced some of the most interesting iron fronts, which were used on commercial and public buildings and even some residences. The tendency of the façades to collapse in fires, as happened in conflagrations in Chicago and Boston, limited the use of cast iron in the 1870s.

Steel and cast iron opened up new dimensions inside and out. Above: Cast iron helped to create a palazzolike façade for New York's McCreery Department Store (1868), now apartments. Above, right: Technological advances led to skyscrapers such as the Reliance Building (1895) in Chicago, notable for terra-cotta sheathing over a 200-foot-high steel frame. Right: Cast-iron detail in the Rockefeller Building (1903–5), Cleveland, would have been prohibitively costly in stone. Opposite page: Another High Victorian Italianate fantasy, the Stearns Block (c. 1865–69), Richmond, Va., was made possible through cast iron.

The coming of the railroads also made feasible the shipping of cattle long distances. Up from Texas came the herds on so-called Long Trails to terminal points such as Dodge City and Abilene, Kans., and Cheyenne, Wyo. From there cattle were transported via railroad to stockyards in Chicago and Kansas City and other cities, where there were meat-packing plants as well as factories to turn hides into a variety of products. Beef and pork were shipped east in the newly invented refrigerated boxcars.

At the outbreak of the Civil War, more than 85 percent of America's manufacturing was carried on in New England, the Midwest, and the West. This brought prosperity to the North, as evidenced by its great houses and factories of that era, but it brought vulnerability to the South. Although the South had pioneered in both fields, it had to build up its ironworks and railroad system quickly in preparation for conflict. After the war, the South, once so dependent on cotton and large plantations and now bereft of slave labor, had to develop a new economic system. Railroads spurred industrialization of the South, for they made interdependent trade possible on a nationwide basis. The mass manufacture of cigarettes, which began in the immediate postwar period, gave rise to new factories in the Deep South; northern cotton mills moved there to be nearer materials and cheap labor, and some northern iron manufacturers transferred their factories to the South, too, to places such as Birmingham, Ala.

After 1840 urban centers in the East and Midwest mushroomed with the influx of Irish and German immigrants (some three million by 1860), who worked as day laborers on canals and railroads and in factories. After the Civil War, freed slaves joined a new wave of immigration to the cities, inheriting the inner-city areas of their predecessors, some of whom had managed to acquire skills and move up the economic ladder and away

This twentieth-century Baltimore & Ohio Railroad coal dump near Rochester, N.Y., is almost a railway roller coaster. Cars approach the dumping area by gravity, are emptied, and roll to the end and up a small incline, where they are switched to the exit ramp.

from run-down neighborhoods. Other laborers found themselves in the almost feudal system of "company towns" owned by impersonal corporations. Company stores often granted credit to ensnare consumers in permanent debt. Although regarded by some as a dictator, George M. Pullman, president of the sleeping-car company, tried to provide better living conditions for his employees in the model industrial community he built (and named for himself) in 1880 near Chicago.

The spreading network of railroads and the breakthrough in communications enabled captains of industry to assemble the administrative facilities of their operations in central areas of trade, often far from the sites where their goods and services were produced and sold.

Supermarkets cannot duplicate the intimacy and pleasing clutter of stores such as the early-twentieth-century Philomont, Va., general store and post office (right) and the Thomas Meskell Store (1796–1803), Greenwich, N.J. (below), seen here as it appeared in 1941.

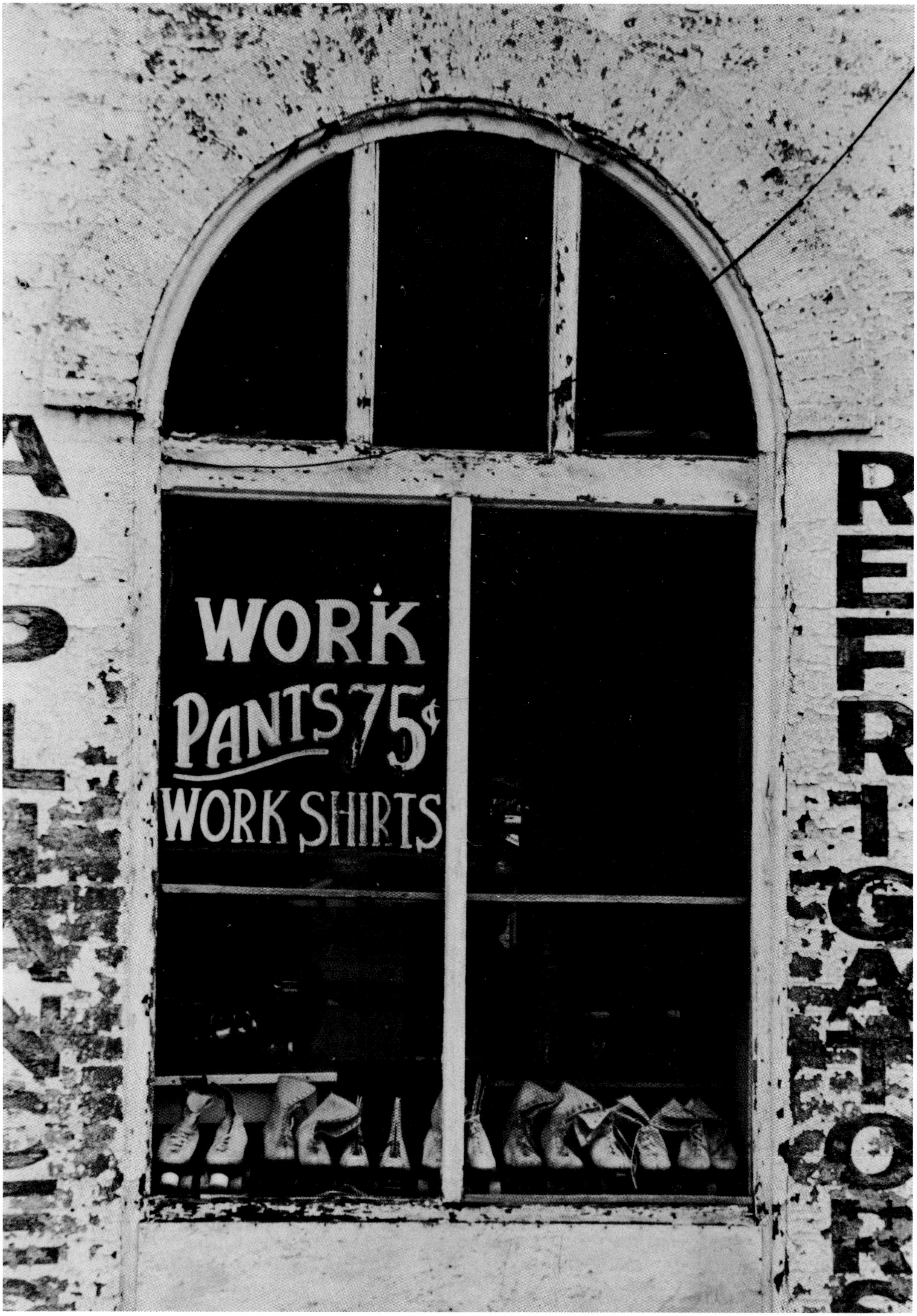
WORK
PANTS 75¢
WORK SHIRTS

Leaders of such monopolies as the sugar, tobacco, leather, and petroleum trusts that developed in the 1870s and 1880s located their headquarters in key cities and controlled hundreds of outlets and factories across the country. John D. Rockefeller, Sr., for one, controlled from his Standard Oil Company offices and main plant in Cleveland the operation of 95 percent of the nation's refineries before that monopoly was dissolved.

The ability to centralize sales and planning also brought about the development of mail-order houses such as Montgomery Ward, established in 1872 in Chicago to serve consumers in all parts of the country through published catalogues. Chain stores and other outlets for goods were located wherever there were accessible railroad terminals.

Accommodating the personnel for these industrial networks required spacious office buildings, and the rising costs of city land indicated that there was nowhere to build but up. The development of steel frame construction methods and the invention of the elevator made possible the erection of skyscrapers to meet the need. In the last quarter of the nineteenth century, efforts in such cities as Philadelphia, Chicago, and New York City signaled the beginning of a drastic change in the nation's skyline. The work of Chicago architects Dankmar Adler and Louis Sullivan in such structures as the Wainwright Building in St. Louis (1890–91) was among the most notable. By 1931 the world saw the Empire State Building reach a phenomenal 102 stories.

The wars and economic vagaries that marked the first half of the twentieth century also increased the number of industrial and commercial structures. World War I provided a great stimulus to most industries, under the supervision of the War Industries Board and its director, Bernard Baruch. By the end of the war, 350,000 workers were employed in 341 bustling shipyards, giving this industry twice the construction capacity of the rest of the world. The prosperity of the 1920s was reflected in

Opposite page: Like this Indianapolis, Ind., store window's, turn-of-the-century commercial messages fitted their buildings sympathetically. This is in one of a three-story trapezoidal building's ten ground-floor arches.

Built early this century as a brewery, this crenelated Gothic complex in Dobbs Ferry, N.Y., has adapted to a number of commercial uses over the years, including the Methodist Book Concern. It is now divided into several offices.

the rise of the automobile industry. In 1929 there were 26 million automobiles on the roads, and the country bristled with factories related to their production and with gas stations and garages to service them. During the Depression the WPA supervised the construction of more than 116,000 public buildings, 77,000 bridges, 285 airports, 800 airport improvements, and 650,000 miles of roads, providing jobs for 8.5 million people. World War II saw another proliferation of shipbuilding and munitions plants an l brought the construction of aircraft factories, airfields, and submarine bases.

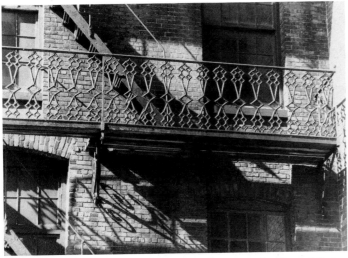

The revitalization of industrial structures not only preserves buildings of distinction but also is an increasingly viable economic alternative. Opposite page: The American Brewery (1884–87) in Baltimore, Md., closed in 1973, is being considered for reuse by a local community group. Above: A wrought-iron fire escape graces the Davol Mills (1867–68) in Fall River, Mass., a manufacturer of galvanized ware. Such fine craft work is comparable to that found in houses of the period.

Today, the manufacture of a range of space-age materials such as synthetic fibers and plastics, the ever-increasing demand for fossil fuels, and the need for the development of new energy sources have made the environment more industrial than ever. Based in part on the German Bauhaus influences, industrial design has become in itself a twentieth-century building form, leaving many of its predecessors behind in terms of currently accepted standards of efficiency and beauty. Even though threatened by alleged obsolescence, older commercial and industrial structures are not popularly regarded as being as architecturally valuable as houses or public buildings. The failure of these older industrial structures to excite wide public interest and respect may be due to the fact that they connote exploitation of labor and the dirt, sweat, grime, and pollution associated with it; neither are their typical locations in decaying inner-city and waterfront areas readily thought particularly attractive or conducive to reuse.

Yet the adaptation of utilitarian structures has led to the development of lucrative multi-use complexes such as San Francisco's Ghirardelli Square, which grew out of an old chocolate factory, and Salt Lake City's Trolley Square, a group of theaters, shops, and restaurants brought to life in old trolley barns. Commercial projects such as these in Seattle, Kansas City, Tacoma, Wash., Denver, Georgetown, and other cities have turned deteriorating areas into showplaces. In the restoration and revitalization of the buildings, many are discovering that the craftsmanship and even the decorative details of these structures often rival those of houses and more "respectable" buildings of the same eras.

Decorative details in nineteenth-century industrial structures indicate their social importance. This elegant window with cast-iron lintel and sill was part of the Detroit and Cleveland Navigation Company Warehouse (1854), Detroit, Mich.

In addition, the very space that is now abandoned is often ideally suited to the needs of modern production, allowing a building's former industrial life to be continued. With rising demolition and construction costs, mounting evidence indicates that the reuse of yesterday's industrial and commercial buildings may be the only rational and economical business choice.

COMMERCE & INDUSTRY

By the late nineteenth century, commercial buildings in small towns increasingly used manufactured pressed metal for façades, cornices, and detailing. In New Harmony, Ind., pressed metal was used in the cornices of the two buildings on the left and for the entire façades of the buildings on the right.

This closer view of the entranceway to the New Harmony, Ind., Medical Building shows more of the rich detailing incorporated into the building design. The pressed-metal paneling duplicates that of the gable end. The doors are ornamented with machine-made sawn work.

A wealth of architectural detail projects an image of stability and prosperity suitable to financial institutions. Opposite page: The façade of the Ladd & Bush Branch of the U. S. National Bank (1869), Salem, Ore., is prefabricated cast iron. Above, left: The seal on the banking room floor of the Virginia Trust Company, Richmond, Va., employs a safe, key, and watchdog to symbolize "The Safe Executor." Above: The eagle above the entrance of the Merchants National Bank (1912), Winona, Minn., signifies national pride. This small-town bank is one of many throughout the Midwest designed by Purcell, Elmslie & Feick. Below: Banks built during the Victorian era display exuberant detailing from a variety of architectural traditions. The High Victorian Gothic-style Syracuse Savings Bank (1876), Syracuse, N.Y., is believed to be the first commercial building in Syracuse with a passenger elevator, a technical improvement that made its height commercially marketable. Left: The Princeton Bank and Trust Company (1896), Princeton, N.J., flamboyantly uses Dutch design elements.

Cast iron and glass provide distinctive decoration in many commercial buildings. Above: The palm and floral motifs on the first floor of the W. & J. Sloane Carpet Store (1881), New York, N.Y., are cast iron. Opposite page, above: The great glass dome of the City of Paris Department Store (1896), San Francisco, Calif., is open several stories to the ground floor. A decision by the owner, Neiman-Marcus, to raze the nearly vacant building has been hotly contested by preservationists. Below: The former Second Ward Savings Bank (1911–13), Milwaukee, Wis., is now used as the Milwaukee County Historical Center. The windows of the Beaux-Arts building show Art Nouveau influence.

Grillwork, skylights, and open stairwells create an interplay of light and space in commercial building interiors. Above: The skylight of the Pioneer Building (1890), Seattle, Wash., brings sunlight and moonlight into the building center. Opposite page: Commercial buildings in Cleveland, Ohio, effectively use grillwork that creates patterns varying with light and viewpoint. Above, left and right: The arched window inset with the city seal in the Cleveland Federal Reserve Bank (1922) and the detail of decorative grillwork in the Cleveland Public Library (1925), were designed by Frank R. Walker and Harry E. Weeks. Center above, and below: The Cleveland Arcade (1888–90), designed by John Eisenmann and George H. Smith, with an open stairwell and five tiers of galleries around a central skylighted court, was the largest and tallest of its type in the United States when constructed. Offices and shops ring the court.

Art Deco or Art Moderne, popularized during the 1920s and 1930s, was more than just a mode of ornamentation. Its aerodynamic, streamlined style soon became an architectural symbol for the progressiveness of commerce and industry, and was interpreted in stepped-back skyscrapers, white stucco walls, curved façades, glass bricks, and stainless steel in such quantity that current generations still have difficulty distinguishing these structures as landmarks. Below: The Syracuse Lighting Company Office Building (1932), Syracuse, N.Y., features the winged "Spirit of Power" on the façade and geometrical stainless steel detailing, both testimonials to technological advance. Opposite page: New York City's Chrysler Building (1929–30), a 1,048-foot-high skyscraper tapering into a stainless steel point, employed decorative metal motifs throughout, many symbolizing the automobile. This detail is above the entrance's revolving doors.

SITES & MEMORIALS

A site is a place where something happened, a mark—visible or just in memory—left on the land by an event or an era. A site may be a battlefield, an airfield, a launching pad, a river crossing, or a mountain pass. It may be a natural formation on or in the land, or the ruins of earlier structures: the foundation stones, the machinery, the debris of a past way of life. A memorial, on the other hand, is intrinsically more a part of the built environment although it may serve the same function to viewers as a site. A memorial is something deliberately erected to mark a spot or a time or an event. It commemorates a place or thing. A memorial can be a plaque, a statue, a park, a headstone, a row of tombs, even a full-scale building—anything purposefully set up to mark the land in memory.

Preceding pages: Deceptively serene, Death Valley (left) is now the site of a battle to halt open-pit mining. "Once scarred, the desert is slow to heal itself," says California Senator Alan Cranston. In the middle of farmland, this country grave-yard (right) in Wayne County, N.Y., is still in the mainstream of tradition with its obelisk and imposing fence. Opposite page: Long after the winged angel face had replaced the skull and crossbones, this pagan symbol was used (above) on the Christian Graham tomb (1742), Aquia Church, Aquia, Va. Scratched onto a sandstone block, a prehistoric petroglyph (below) in the Petrified Forest National Park, Holbrook, Ariz., is appropriately called Newspaper Rock. Above: The sand-stone cliffs at El Morro National Monument, N.M., encompass prehistoric Zuni ruins and inscriptions dating to 1605.

No matter what the nature of the event or place that they mark, sites and memorials have the same effect: they say "remember." Like the "memento mori" of the ancient world, the talisman that reminds all humans of their mortality and thus keeps their pride in check, sites and memorials call us to remember the life and death experiences that we share, regardless of origin or status. They fill few basic physical needs (such as the need for shelter), yet they are a part of every culture.

The statue of "Energy" (1922) guards Cleveland's Federal Reserve Bank both literally and figuratively: it is said to have once housed a machine gun in its base.

Memorials generally follow the styles and perpetuate the values, traditions, and some even the forms of classical times. Predominantly, what they commemorate are ways of dying and views of death; a major subject for honor is "those who fell in battle." Whether they take the form of statuary or parks or bandstands, they echo memorials once erected to conquerors such as Pompey or Hadrian or the Caesars. There are markers in America to the soldiers of all wars in which the country has been engaged. The Princeton Battlefield statuary of Washington and his troops is a typical memorial: its message is that all soldiers are loyal to their commander, brave and true through hardship and in conflict, even to death. Like the national Tomb of the Unknown Soldier, the lone figures often found on Civil War memorials symbolize the sacrifice of one life for many.

Above: The object of vandalism by some and fascination by others, the burned-out ruins of Windsor Plantation (1861) in Port Gibson, Miss., have been proposed as the setting for an amphitheater and trails, even an enlarged lake to picturesquely reflect its haunting Corinthian remnants. Opposite page: Marking a private moment of grief in an early 1900s memorial, an angel classically pauses before a roughly worked cross at the grave of Henry Towar in Elmwood Cemetery, Lyons, N.Y.

The other major type of memorial, the structure built to the memory of the civilian population, is based on similar factors. Statues in noble poses honor philanthropists or founding citizens with their likenesses; unknown pioneers have to be content with prototypes in stone. Memorials to other citizens of the community that are erected in family cemeteries, in church burial grounds, or in impersonal secular plots of land set aside by the community often feature a gate of some sort, a symbol of transition, either the departure of the individual from this life to a reward or a new dimension, or the change from one form of energy to another.

The architectural design and landscaping of cemeteries reflect some of the styles seen in houses and other buildings of their eras. But they span a narrower design range, because what is always called for is a sense of continuity and dignity—not always hope, but forever dignity. The Romanesque, the Gothic, the Italianate, the Egyptian Revival styles are natural and standard choices.

On the individual memorial, ideas of reconciliation, peace, and occasionally victory are echoed through classical motifs and shapes. Plain arched headstones carry words to mark the passing of sixteen-year-old girls in "a triumph of faith." Hebrew gravestones carry messages of consolation in ancient script, some in the shadow of smokestacks that convey basically the same message: life goes on. Scenes sculpted on markers make universal statements: stone flowers defy the transience of beauty; varying combinations of skulls and angels' wings express changing views of death; clasped hands signify the continuation of friendship or of marital fidelity; and the

cruciform, here outlined in overturned bottles, there underscored by a pagoda, shows the hopes or assurances of those left behind. Whether a lone grave in the wilderness or a large cemetery in a densely populated city, memorials everywhere mark the continuity of generations.

Even in the peace of a Jewish cemetery in the Bronx, N.Y., the tombstones are crowded together, like a miniature city, echoing the smokestacks of the worldly cities that are left but never far behind.

As much as it tries, the tropical growth never totally erases the machines of war from sight or memory. This tank on the Micronesian island of Ponape was left by the Japanese, a reminder of the struggle for territory now in America's trust.

Memorials are deliberate in what they signify. Sites, on the other hand, are signs that can be and are found anywhere and in any form. Usually they tell something of a way of life now past—the good and the bad, the constructive and the destructive aspects. Archaeological sites mirror the way in which land reclaims itself and give evidence of the destructive forces that menace the built environment. But because sites are not purposely designed to convey an idea or information, they call on our careful research and our imagination to reconstruct the past and supply an interpretation.

War leaves its traces in incongruous combinations of machines and landscape from the jungles of the Pacific to the deserts of the Southwest. A Japanese plane and tank, riddled with bullets and covered with vines, speak to everyone who comes upon them. Streets in an Arizona desert whisper of internment camps once located there. Other sites—the peaceful edge of a river, a stretch of empty prairie in the Dakotas—leave the sights and sounds of clash and massacre to the onlooker to guess at.

Other messages of bygone but less belligerent days are left to be read: building techniques in Hawaii and the patterned brickwork of a West Virginia barn; the ruins of a southern mansion destroyed by fire; a boundary stone marking the limits of a geographical entity; the weathered remnants of a ghost town, leaning drunkenly; the elaborate stone piles that were once a fort or factory or the abutments of a railroad crossing over a stream. The gloomy pleasure that ruins afford is attested to by the fact that during the late eighteenth to mid-nineteenth century, while the Gothic Revival style was at a height of popularity, European architects even went so far as to purposely design buildings to look as if they were crumbling. Landscape architects created elaborate combinations of "ruins" and vegetation.

Messages are also left in the land itself, through the petroglyphs of an ancient civilization, by the ceremonial mounds of Indian tribes, in the cliffs used by Plains Indians to kill buffalo, in the threateningly beautiful dunes of the Death Valley area that challenged travelers to reach the promised land of California, and in the Teapot Dome, still challenging nationalistic pride with the memory of scandal in high places.

Right: Untamed even in the twentieth century, Death Valley, Calif., lives up to its name. Below: Today only melted adobe walls testify to what Fort Union (1851) near Watrous, N.M., once was: the largest fort and supply depot on the southwestern frontier, a base for battles against both Indians and Confederates.

By our definition, sites and memorials are sometimes one and the same thing. The Watts Towers of Los Angeles, built with cast-off material of a wasteful society and set in the midst of a decaying area of the city, are a tribute to creativity and life and a self-made memorial to their creator.

It may be thought that sites and memorials are sacrosanct, that their preservation is a foregone conclusion. But the pressure for land to use, to live on, and to grow crops on has already begun to attack the expansive memorials of yesterday; weather also works away at vulnerable monuments and statues. Those areas and sites not protected by law are no longer guaranteed protection by past values and traditions—and taboos. Just as some irreplaceable natural areas are now protected as wilderness, perhaps one way to guarantee a future for sites and memorials is to treat them the same way: to stabilize them and then simply leave them alone to their memories.

Opposite page: Between 1921 and 1954 Simon Rodia, an Italian immigrant, built the Watts Towers (left) of steel rods, mesh, mortar, and broken bits of refuse to fill a fantasy desire for immortality. "I had in mind to do something big, and I did. You have to be good-good, or bad-bad, to be remembered." On the grounds of Gallaudet College in Washington, D.C., sculptor Daniel Chester French captured the image of Thomas Gallaudet (right, above) teaching his first deaf pupil to make the letter "A" (1889). Before 1850, the great Oregon Trail migrations crossed Robidoux Pass near Gering, Neb., as this historical marker commemorates (right, below). Right and below: The resting place of slaves as well as free blacks, Mt. Zion Cemetery in Georgetown, Washington, D.C., slipped into decay and became the developers' prey before court action assured that restoration could proceed.

Death, either man-made or natural, is a prevalent theme of the historic sites that are set aside and the memorials that are erected as reminders. Opposite page: The battle of Antietam at Sharpsburg, Md., September 16–17, 1862, was a turning point in the Civil War. Here on this country roadway (above) now known as Bloody Lane, Confederate forces fought two Union divisions. Combatants crossed and recrossed the lane, literally over their fallen comrades—some 4,000 of whom fell during the three-hour battle. In a Wayne County, N.Y., graveyard (below), memorials mark a more peaceful passage. Below: All but the dead have left the nearly inaccessible ghost town of Kelton, Utah, once a water station on the now abandoned Central Pacific Railroad line west of Promontory Point.

PRESERVING IT ALL TOGETHER

A foreign visitor who sees only the New York City skyline or San Francisco's Golden Gate Bridge can hardly return home and claim to know what America is all about; American tourists who snap the Eiffel Tower with a Kodak cannot be considered experts on things French. Yet many make these mistakes, thinking that a community is only as interesting as its tallest building or its plushest residential area. Just as an appreciation of America depends on the understanding that the sum is infinitely greater than any one of its parts, so one's enjoyment of a community or a neighborhood depends on viewing it in its proper setting and in its totality.

The built environment worth saving is made up of special groups and ensembles: large units—islands such as Nantucket, Mass., and towns such as Marshall, Mich.; and small—a pair of houses in Kentucky, leaning on each other for support; and simple street scenes—a row of adobes, with their entrance ladders set out in welcome, an alleyway in Puerto Rico, deserted in the blinding heat of afternoon. Single structures or sites do indeed speak to sensitive listeners, but groups of buildings may be said to carry on conversation among themselves. By listening in the right way, a place's history, its beginnings, its changes through the years, its past and current values, even its opinion of itself, can be heard clarion clear.

A treeless square surrounded by once ornate Victorian stores, banks, and offices, their façades hidden behind metal siding and neon, can tell of a time of prosperity, followed by a time of decline, a scramble to keep up with the Joneses in the next community—and a failure to appreciate the past. An industrial city viewed from a train speaks of its beginnings through its smokestacks, its current economy through abandoned or bustling warehouses, its values through acres of row houses turned into slums. Well-tended lawns, bright new coats of paint, and flowering borders between houses indicate, on the other hand, cordial relationships and a sense of pride in that neighborhood, just as broken or barred shop windows, peeling billboards, and unswept litter in an inner-city neighborhood speak volumes about the nature of its inhabitants' lives.

Beyond these broad impressions, knowing a place better depends on knowing something about its collective architecture, on being able to look with some knowledge at the quality of its design and construction. The relative ages of key community buildings such as churches, banks, schools, and courthouses, the relationship of commercial to residential districts, even the juxtaposition of similar neighborhoods, the styles and condition of street furniture, the scale of the buildings on a single street, gaps or major changes in the streetscape: knowledge about these factors can give the viewer an understanding of a place that a history book seldom does, because history is written intimately, three-dimensionally, upon the environment.

For building watchers and listeners, ghost towns are an obvious place to start looking, simply because, like collected butterflies, they stand still long enough to be examined. Once-lively places like Madrid, N.M., and Bodie, Calif., seem to have been abandoned in the twinkling of an eye. Stores full of prospecting supplies lean on their neighbors, old bottles stand empty in saloons, while next door (in studied proximity) the bank is completely open, vulnerable to nonexistent outlaws in search of its nonexistent money. The remains of a get-rich-quick town built overnight tell of a sudden and profound change before the place had a chance to come of age.

Plantations, built on slave labor and one family's economic fortunes, give evidence of a life-style that now exists for most people only in novels. The arrangement of the outbuildings, the size of the kitchens, the gardens for vegetables and flowers, the smokehouse and other

The built environment is composed not of single structures but of many elements working all together. Preceding pages: Two essentially similar rows of late-nineteenth-century commercial buildings, one in Madison, Ind. (left), one in the Shockoe Slip Historic District, Richmond, Va. (right), show the difference between caring for the cityscape and not. Below: Italianate, Chateauesque, and other styles exist in harmony on this Wilmington, N.C., street.

structures speak of guests and lavish hospitality. Livery stables, blacksmith shops, and harnessmakers' tools tell how animals were cared for. The slave quarters speak, too, so that the plantation in its entirety helps tell what life must have been like—not necessarily what we have been told or what we would like to believe.

Other towns that depended on one resource like the Cotton Kingdom plantations and the boom towns that went broke have escaped their unhappy fate. Some either hit more paydirt or developed enough peripheral trade to keep alive. In towns like Ouray, Colo., and Deadwood, S.D., where the first temporary buildings were put up mainly to relieve miners of their money, false fronts that once proudly displayed the latest Victorian exteriors

Most difficult to preserve are those areas that outlive the life-styles for which they were built. Left: The sturdy stone structures of Mogollon, N.M. (1889), indicate that it was never intended to become a ghost town. Below: The Greek Revival mansion at Milford Plantation (c. 1839), Pinewood, S.C., known as "Manning's Folly," survives as the figurehead of a way of life since gone.

from "back East" have turned into permanent commercial structures. Banks and clusters of competing saloons, now respectable inns, guard a tradition of prosperity. Straight-edge main streets and grid town plans recall Congress's early system that produced land-grant townships of 640 acres laid out in sections, a system picked up and carried by private speculators over the mountains all the way west. Neighborhoods surrounding the rougher business districts are filled with great houses trimmed in gingerbread that seems to curl just to show off in front of viewers or to challenge the competition next door.

In other living towns and in industrial areas, commercial structures reveal the past. The waterfront area of Annapolis, Md., tells of its earliest colonial days as a

The Central Block (1887) of Sutton, Neb., retains its pressed metal windows and cornice, and, even rarer, original street-level storefronts.

On asphalt or water, Main Streets have a purpose that never goes out of style. Below: Through continued commercial use, the Bow Street waterfront of Portsmouth, N.H., has transited two centuries.

busy port, political center, and home of the U.S. Naval Academy. Through its name, Portsmouth, N.H., reveals its ability to adapt to new life; in its docks, warehouses, and shops can be seen the evolution of an eighteenth-century town into a twentieth-century city, still employing its built resources, just as it uses the natural resource on which its life depends. In the mountainous West Virginia countryside, strange old wooden contraptions strung across acres of woodland testify to a still profitable enterprise, using gravity and cables and luck, a Rube Goldberg system of derricks and pumps to draw oil.

A little rural neighborhood in Michigan with brilliant white late-nineteenth- and early-twentieth-century houses, set down cleanly on close-cropped lawns, is anchored to the landscape by ancient trees and the fact that home-owners have "always" been there, quiet, industrious, thrifty. Its serene atmosphere is echoed in a tiny village in Virginia, full of unaltered Federal houses, left behind by a railroad and a trade route, managing somehow to live without traffic lights or paved roads; it tells of modest but determined Quaker founders who built to last.

Essentially a one-person operation, this Volcano, W.Va., pumping field (1885–89) relied on wooden wheels as a power source for several oil wells.

PRESERVING IT ALL TOGETHER

The main street of Sutton, Neb., on the other hand, intends to keep up with the twentieth century by proudly proclaiming its longevity. Its row of elaborate nineteenth-century office buildings speaks of agricultural prosperity translated into community pride and a definite sense of place. Wilmington, N.C., assumes the viewer needs no reminder of its history and importance, and quietly allows its main street to juxtapose four of its outstanding architectural achievements with modern necessities like parking lots and radio towers.

When the mills of Harrisville, N.H., closed, the town faced almost certain change. But through innovative preservation programs, its buildings were recycled, intact, for new uses. Below: Across the Milldam Canal to an 1847 church. Opposite page, below: "Peanut Row" (c. 1864), housing for the Cheshire Mills.

Towns can even be brought back to life. Two-hundred-year-old Harrisville, N.H., its textile production falling off, faced a major crisis when the 1849 Cheshire Mills declared bankruptcy in October 1970. A private school a mile away also closed, and its 500 acres were ripe for development. A traumatic change in the town's historic character hovered in the wings. A group of its residents, acting on the advice and support of the National Trust, the Society for the Preservation of New England Antiquities, and the Nature Conservancy, organized to save it. With a $10,000 loan from the National Historic Preservation Fund of the National Trust, they formed Historic Harrisville, Inc., and sought to attract new industry.

They were successful. The Filtrine Manufacturing Company of New Jersey moved its entire operation into the millworks of Harrisville. The land around the school was purchased by local investors, and the school buildings were made into a graduate-school extension facility by Antioch College. To keep the textile tradition active in Harrisville, a small company was formed to manufacture looms and yarns for hand weavers. Private interests have purchased mill housing for rehabilitation. Historic Harrisville also has moved to assure long-range protection by holding preservation easements on twenty-six buildings, avoiding incompatible development while providing new owners with professional architectural and preservation counsel. The fight to save Harrisville may continue, as preservation efforts do, but this town at least has found sophisticated weapons to keep itself alive.

Madison, Ind., has found a wide variety of buildings worth saving, including the old Indiana Gas Company (c. 1840s), now used as a warehouse.

PRESERVING IT
ALL TOGETHER

Whether structures and sites are saved or lost depends on how they are seen. If viewed one by one, chances are that they will certainly be lost; as each demolition takes its toll, the fabric of a community is gradually diminished. Buildings cannot exist in a vacuum. Only if protection is provided to structures as part of the total environment—whether this means neighboring buildings or a natural setting—can they and that environment be saved and saved properly. The way to start is to learn to see the environment, not bit by bit, but with larger vision, so that it will be preserved all together.

Small-town America takes many forms, but because of their size small towns have in common a more workable opportunity to preserve their special character as a unified whole. Below: Its frame houses, yards, and street trees made Frankenmuth, Mich., typical of a well-preserved community until these same qualities made it a historic "boom town" and it had to cope with success. Opposite page: Madison, Ind., is often called a living museum of styles, building types, and eras, but the emphasis is on the living. Preserved all together in Madison are structures as varied as a sparkling example of "Steamboat Gothic" woodwork (above, left), a pressed-metal-front house that served as the business card of its ironmaker-owner (above, right) and a cast- and wrought-iron fence and brick walk in front of the Regency-style Shrewsbury House (below).

SOME PRESERVATION DEFINITIONS

Preserved. This is the word a lot of people use to describe what they have done to a building or area of a certain age. They "preserved" the colonial village, although only half of it was around before the Revolution (and the second half not until yesterday). They "preserved" the home of the town founder, even though they first had to go out and buy the bricks and the mortar and the framing and the windows and the roof. They "preserved" the old factory by gutting the interior and making three floors where only one had existed, the better to put in more boutiques. They "preserved" the bank by sandblasting its façade. They "preserved" the old house, after moving it, by stripping the Victorian additions and ordering out for colonial-style replacements. And they "preserved" the neighborhood by demanding that the new building down the street be Federal-style and not that avant-garde thing, even if it would have been the right size and its materials would have fit right in with all the others on the block.

Demolition comes as often from neglect as from a wrecking ball. This ruin of a colonial house in Brookfield, Mass., has been stripped so that its pieces could be sold. Opposite page: Bared and patched, the Jillson House (1825–27) in Willimantic, Conn., awaits restoration under an urban renewal program.

Demolition is not just a wrecking ball swinging against brick and mortar. Any building or structure or site that is not being cared for properly is being demolished. Demolition can be inaction; in fact, it often is, destroying buildings and their environments by neglect. Demolition can also take place when people think they are preserving. Out of slavish devotion to what they believe or have been told the past is, they strip real structures and put on deceptive masks, or tear down the really old and construct new "old" buildings, actions that stem from misconceptions of what preservation is and can be.

At one time, everyone who thought about it had a fairly sure idea of what constituted historic preservation: it was an effort to save buildings that were considered important for one reason or another in the development of the country. But because preservation now covers a broad spectrum of activities, what "preserving" means is not as simple any more. In its dictionary sense, preservation means saving something pretty much the way it is. This often takes much work to accomplish. On the most basic level, it means keeping things in good condition by maintaining them. According to general priorities supported by the National Trust for Historic Preservation and other preservationists: "It is better to preserve than repair, better to repair than restore, better to restore than reconstruct." In other words, the less done to good structures the better, and if it is done in time, more extensive work will not be necessary.

"BETTER TO PRESERVE . . ."

By the time most preservationists enter the picture, a structure has usually passed the point of needing only the status quo—preservation in its literal meaning. Because the world is not static, buildings too must adapt to change, especially if they are to continue their prime function of use. Thus, preservation means not stasis but an effort to ward off detrimental changes—to maintain the qualities and contributions that made a structure or area a candidate for protection in the first place.

Maintenance of existing buildings is a vital means of preservation. Old farms can be maintained by being farmed, old business structures by being rented, and old houses by being lived in. Preservation by maintenance is taking place in areas like East Baltimore, where householders scrub the marble steps of their row houses, proud of a trademark that is both useful and beautiful and that gives residents a sense of identity. Preservation is taking place in towns where county courthouses and city halls are maintained in use either as courthouses or for other services because they are recognized as unique symbols of civic success and continuity. Some department store and business owners are proud of their landmarks and take steps to assure their preservation because

Maintenance of the Honolulu House (1860), Marshall, Mich., has not been stinting. Reputedly modeled on Hawaiian prototypes, this unique house has a pagoda-roofed central tower and a full-length veranda, whose Tudor arches and voluptuous brackets are shown here.

the condition they are in serves as a visible statement of the continuing success of the owners' enterprises. Preservation is also happening where civic organizations keep the park bandstand painted and in use or where they persuade their government to exercise control over the kinds of commercial signs used in a downtown area.

Although some may not even know the term, all of the people involved in these activities may properly be called preservationists. They value their property, the structures and sites they have collectively inherited, and appreciate them as factors that create the quality of life in their environment. The stabilization and the maintenance of older buildings without undue change is a holding action against the tooth of time.

"...TO REPAIR..."

Buildings, like people, need care. If care is constant, if maintenance is carried out, the capacity for a long and productive life remains. Just like people, however, buildings and structures, sometimes even with the best of care, develop problems. Shingles begin to weather,

plumbing wears out, wood warps, or paint cracks and chips off. Replacements are needed.

In the world of modern building technology there are such things as "genuine reproductions"—aluminum siding that comes in Weathered Colonial, fake stone that purports to re-create Gothic fortresses, and asbestos shingles that recall the days of wattle-and-daub (but not quite). If repair is not done with care, the result can destroy the essence of an old building. Repair work on the exteriors of old structures is therefore regulated in some communities. The Boston Redevelopment Authority and the Commission on Chicago Historical and Architectural Landmarks are among the public agencies that issue guidelines to owners of older structures who want and

Aluminum and asbestos siding, fake stone: technological improvements and a means of preservation, or are they? More often, good details disappear behind a false front, as here with this fake-stone covered brick house in the historic Logan Circle area, Washington, D.C.

nah, Ga., for example, a team of architects and urban planners analyzed the existing structures in one of the city's core historic areas. The study developed sixteen common denominators shared by the buildings, criteria usable in planning for future compatible design. These criteria included height, proportion of the buildings' front façades, rhythms of solids to voids, spacing on the street, relationships of materials such as brick, trim, and color, relationships of architectural details such as balustrades, cornices, arches, direction of the buildings' front elevations (horizontal or vertical), and roof shapes. On these predominant elements the community based compliance standards to regulate future construction.

Designing new structures for older areas is one of the most difficult activities in preservation because even when criteria are quantified, design decisions are ultimately subjective. Some communities, faced with the difficulty of agreeing on flexible standards of compatibility, have drawn rigid design controls. In Santa Fe, N.M., a 1957 city ordinance spelled out such restrictions for its historic area that today new buildings in the district look as if they are constructed of adobe; ironically, modern technology has made them of stucco acting like

Constructed of materials organic to its location, I.M. Pei's National Center for Atmospheric Research (1961–67), Boulder, Colo., epitomizes how a new structure can retain its contemporaneity while reflecting the area's pueblo heritage.

Respectful of the past as well as the present, the Frank Andrews III House (1974) in Santa Fe, N.M., incorporates materials and design elements from the region's earlier Spanish and pueblo styles without slavishly copying either.

adobe. Some local architects complain that besides having their creativity stifled, they are also forced to build buildings that leak (the pueblo-style flat roofs let in water). The architects suggest that design criteria should include three-dimensional factors such as how a building relates to other structures, and not just two-dimensional façade symbols of style, like vigas (protruding wooden beams) or battered walls.

Other historic districts have similar tight controls. The Santa Barbara, Calif., historic district, "El Pueblo Viejo," is controlled by a strict ordinance that requires all construction to conform to a few specific buildings of the Spanish Colonial style. In Nantucket, Mass., property owners follow the strictest controls (even to the point of having an approved color chart), for the town believes that architectural integrity is the keystone of Nantucket's tourism, one basis of its economic well-being.

Architect Philip Johnson, who speaks from his own experience in designing new buildings in such historic areas as Georgetown and New Harmony, Ind., maintains that what spells catastrophe is not a change in style but a change in scale. The matching of scale accounts for the successful juxtaposition of two major buildings at Georgetown University in Washington: Healy Hall (1877–79), a Romanesque-style structure complete with a 200-foot tower, dormers, chimneys, cast-iron finials and gargoyles, and Lauinger Library (1970–72), designed by John Carl Warnecke and Associates in a Brutalistic style. In color, in rhythm of solids and voids, in open slab towers, and in roof slopes, the new structure echoes the lines of the old and provides a balance to it, making an exciting combination of forms seen from any angle.

Loose guidelines, however, cause problems for some.

A series of plans for the Jehovah's Witnesses headquarters in the Brooklyn Heights Historic District of New York City showed increasingly unsympathetic designs before a solution acceptable to the New York City Landmarks Preservation Commission was executed in 1970. The first proposal placed a twelve-story building in a neighborhood of predominantly five-story Greek Revival and Italianate buildings; four other designs, although toned down in scale to six stories, superficially aped Georgian, Federal, and Richardsonian styles; a fifth was characterized by the commission's chairman as "Times Square variations on the New Brutalism." Finally, another architectural firm was commissioned and designed a building that used the materials and scale of the surrounding buildings and yet did not violate the best of present-day design standards.

A new style did not meet the commission's approval

Through its massing, height, windows, and use of brick, the new Jehovah's Witnesses headquarters became a contemporary statement in harmony with its historic neighbors.

in another historic New York neighborhood, however, pointing up the delicate balancing act needed in keeping the new in line with the old. One building in a row of Greek Revival houses in Greenwich Village dating from the 1840s was destroyed in 1970 when a bomb being built in the basement accidentally blew up. In the gap that was left on West 11th Street, architect Hugh Hardy decided to build a home. In designing the infill structure, Hardy considered the context of the whole street and added what he thought was a minor distinction to indicate its modernity: a window set diagonally into the façade so that it jutted out slightly. Because the street is part of the Greenwich Village Historic District, Hardy had to submit his plans to the landmarks commission for approval. To his surprise the members were divided in their opinion and the protests of his prospective neighbors, who wanted him to replace the lost building with one that matched the row's traditional design, were heated. This preference was seconded by those who contend that row houses should be considered as one structure, and that if one unit is destroyed, it should be replaced as would a portion of a single building. The diagonal window has not yet appeared on 11th Street, but neither has the hole disappeared—a gap as much a consequence of the nature of bank financing as of what constitutes acceptable new designs in old areas.

The problem of integrating new with old is common to nearly all communities, for very few are homogeneous. Most have buildings that reflect their eras of growth. In the past, replacements called for relatively simple decisions because the limits of technology and styles dictated most designs. Although some eyebrows may have been raised when a High Victorian Gothic building went up next door to a Federal row house, it was not until technology gave us the ability to put up structures so entirely out of scale with their historic neighbors that streets and whole cities started losing the quality of being pleasing ensembles. Today, successfully choosing the elements of new design calls for the education not only of architects but of communities—for it is their appreciation that is the key.

That preservation requires an appreciation of existing environmental resources, new and old, is illustrated by the following tale. Some years ago the Washington *Evening Star* carried a photograph of a fire training exercise in Annandale, Va. In the picture firetrucks surrounded an empty, deteriorating house that had been repeatedly set afire and extinguished by fire fighters. Close up, readers could see on each truck the seal of the city, beautifully painted, and on it a picture of Ossian Hall, a plantation house built in Annandale about 1783—a structure historic enough to give the community a sense of its heritage and its identity.

The house being burned in the training exercise was Ossian Hall.

Recently Annandale took a look at itself and decided that a new start should be made. Away with the ugly signs that proliferated on the streets. Away with the shopping strips, the treeless landscape, and the faceless buildings. In with planning, design, amenities, and beauty. Conspicuous by its absence is Ossian Hall.

A community's belated appreciation of what it once had is not rare. There is no lack of Maple Streets, named for the groves they replaced. Every Barnyard Lane, Sawmill Road, or Church Street suggests similar substitutions. There are more than a few housing developments

This new row house in the Georgetown Historic District of Washington, D.C., blends into the streetscape because of its height, materials, small windows, and entrance treatment.

with ironic names like Poplar Forest—where there is no longer a tree; New Gardens—where any gardens have to be new because the buyers have to plant them; and Heritage Preserve—where there is nothing left worth saving.

In new developments like the planned communities of Reston, Va., Columbia, Md., Irvine Ranch, Calif., Heritage Village, Conn., and Sea Pines Plantation, S.C., land has been treated with respect and so have people. Homes are clustered to make more space available for common recreational use, but each dwelling has amenities of its own. Likewise, Merritt Parkway in Connecticut is designed not just for cars but for cars with people in them; it is a scenic as well as a functional highway.

What must be learned is the wisdom to discern what is useful and worth keeping and what is not, what is a linchpin to the rest and what is superfluous. To a certain degree we have learned to be sensitive to the interdependence of parts of the natural environment so that we know, for example, when to protect the watershed that supports a marsh to make certain that the marsh survives. It is just as necessary for preservationists to identify the watersheds of areas important to them and to use these to maintain standards. To do this, we must learn to appreciate what our environment has to offer.

DOCUMENTING THE BUILT ENVIRONMENT

DOCUMENTING THE BUILT ENVIRONMENT

The horror of that moment," the King exclaimed to Alice and the Queen after a breathless journey through the Looking Glass, "I shall never, *never* forget!"

"You will, though," said the Queen, "if you don't make a memorandum of it.

Lest they also forget where they have been and where they may not want to go again, many communities have taken the Queen's advice and are beginning the preservation task logically by literally making a memorandum of their built environments—by documenting their physical assets as a prelude to planning for their preservation.

In *Building the Future from Our Past*, the published survey of St. Paul's Historic Hill District, Old Town Restorations, Inc., recorded the area's architectural development. The house on the left is Queen Anne style (c. 1890), the one on the right is Stick Style (1888).

Planning for preservation begins with a survey to identify and evaluate a community or area's resources. Not just major landmarks but every physical resource

and every characteristic in the designated survey area needs to be identified—from the best to the worst of the old and the new, from buildings to street furniture, landscaping, open spaces, views and vistas. A clear picture of a community's character and physical growth emerges from a comprehensive survey, a picture that can help guide future development in protecting the good and avoiding the horrors of the past or present. Preservation surveys have numerous goals and results: they identify structures and sites that meet criteria for listing in national, state, or local landmarks registers, and thus become eligible for whatever protection is available; they define areas to be designated as historic districts; they provide the impetus for creation of preservation agencies and private groups; they sensitize residents to their community's value. Above all, preservation surveys are a tool for comprehensive planning, identifying elements that not only are as integral to a community's development as the provisions for education, health, safety, housing, transportation, business, and recreation more routinely studied by urban and regional planners, but that, in fact, have the potential to serve all these needs. If inventoried properties and areas are seen only as isolated objects, the survey becomes little more than a guidebook to what is there (and what may be gone tomorrow). But if they are regarded as useful components that give a place its unique character, they can be the cornerstones of all future development—comprehensive blueprints for living environments of quality.

As more and more preservation documents are doing, a recent survey and plan for the Historic Hill District of St. Paul, Minn., asserted that its purpose was not to create an urban museum but to develop workable procedures for integrating preservation into the process of growth and change. Its intent, says the report, was "to find ways of guiding new development in such a way as to be compatible with, and actually enhance, the historic and architectural qualities." In addition to a historic preservation component, its proposed planning policies for the area covered "human services," land use, design standards, open space, lighting and utilities, traffic and circulation, and commercial and economic development. "When the staff assembled and began to discuss general items to be included in the plan, it became apparent that it would indeed be 'comprehensive'—more than just land use, or just zoning, or just structure preservation was involved. What was involved was an attempt to affect nearly every aspect of daily life in the Historic Hill District—to keep high quality where it existed and to improve the quality of life where it was low."

The St. Paul report also used documentary photographs, such as this from the Minnesota Historical Society, to trace the rise and fall of residential areas that once rivaled Historic Hill. Shown is the J. F. Stevens residence (c. 1896).

THE SURVEY

Who conducts preservation surveys? Today, the answer is: just about anyone and everyone. Federal agencies are responsible for inventorying their own historic properties and assuring that their actions do no harm to protected sites; other federal offices exist for the sole purpose of conducting preservation surveys in one form or another, while still others aid survey work by providing funding. State governments produce statewide surveys and preservation plans to participate in federal preservation programs as well as to fulfill their own long-range planning objectives; some state arts councils fund or guide architectural inventories as part of their cultural responsibilities. Regional and community planning agencies are increasingly undertaking preservation surveys or including preservation components in their comprehensive plans, spurred on recently by community development block grant programs in particular. And desirable as it is for public agencies to undertake preservation surveys as part of their total planning responsibilities, experience often has shown that not until publicity from private inventorying increases public awareness do many planners turn their attention to preservation.

Although the words "survey" and "inventory" are often used interchangeably, a survey usually refers to the actual gathering of historical and physical data and illustrations through research and field work, while the inventory is a selective list of sites or amenities from the survey professionally evaluated for their retention value or need for protection. Planners striving to be objective recognize that these resources represent a continuum and a value greater than their individual worth, and consequently try not to distort their assessments by setting up a good-better-best system or unduly emphasizing first or last, biggest, oldest or only, or most curious. A group of workers' houses is as representative of economic and social patterns as the factory owner's mansion or the factory itself. Assigning points for significance is one method of evaluating preservation potential, but if not used with caution, it turns into little more than a system of hunting licenses, declaring open season on the structures and areas at the bottom of the point list.

There are as many kinds of surveys as there are specific reasons for carrying them out. A survey can be limited to a carefully defined geographic area such as a neighborhood or enclave of buildings, or it can encompass the nation or an entire state or community. It can be limited to places of obvious cultural significance or certain individual building types such as industrial or commercial structures, or it can cover all built and natural resources. The amount of information about individual structures that a survey provides also varies. On the

A survey of Oak Park, Ill., a town identified with Frank Lloyd Wright, set out to evaluate all its built resources — and found more than 300 worth preserving, from Victorian structures through examples of the Prairie School, as well as some intrusions due to changes in land use.

one hand it may only suggest the rudiments such as construction dates and architectural style, or it may provide an in-depth analysis of an individual structure, including measured drawings, photographs, chain-of-title information, and other historical data and technical architectural descriptions. The most far-reaching surveys also include the area's social and economic factors, development patterns, visual relationships, and design elements. A problem inherent in preselecting survey contents is that not until after comprehensive documentation has been gathered can significance be adequately assessed; a limited survey often excludes properties or areas that research shows to be of importance. Until one knows what is there, one may not know what to look for.

The Doylestown, Pa., survey, done in 1969 and published in 1972 as *Design Resources of Doylestown*, includes such conventional approaches as a description of the historical development of the area and an architectural inventory that found samples from all periods of Ameri-

Historic Savannah rated the Savannah Cotton Exchange (1886), now the chamber of commerce building, an "exceptional" survivor of the Romantic Revival movement. "It is a rich mélange of materials and forms, a period piece of distinction," said the surveyors.

"The tree imitates the voices of the rain," reads this Moravian tile produced in Doylestown, Pa., following a revival of an old tile works in 1899—one of the artistic objects that surveys often "completely overlook," says the Doylestown survey.

can architecture. The survey also included several other elements that too often are not assessed for their worth to the community, utilitarian objects such as benches and street lights, vistas and viewpoints, surface qualities displaying textures, colors, and patterns of brick, and artistic objects such as stained-glass windows and general topography. In all, *Design Resources of Dolyestown* is a full assessment of the qualities that make up the town and provides a thorough basis for planning for their future preservation and use.

The scope of some surveys is determined by their intended use or the organizer's preservation goals—whether to locate properties for nomination to national or local landmarks registers, to gather data to aid local planners, to stimulate public awareness, to create the basis for community-action programs to improve neighborhoods, or to guide property owners in their rehabilitation. In 1962 the Historic Savannah Foundation undertook a comprehensive survey of the 2½-square-mile downtown area of Savannah, Ga. "It was thought," said the survey sponsors, "that an authoritative survey of all the structures in the historic area was an absolute necessity to buttress and substantiate the theory that the historic buildings of Savannah were valuable economic assets as well as irreplaceable cultural amenities." Approximately 1,100 buildings were surveyed and rated. The results of the Savannah survey enabled the group to target structures and areas on which to concentrate their rehabilitation and restoration work. The results of the survey were published in 1968 as *Historic Savannah*, a book that

Savannah's Forsyth Park (1851) typifies the humanly scaled quality of the town's imaginative 1733 plan. Providing open spaces and broad vistas, Savannah's squares complement its architecture to produce a collective statement that buildings alone cannot provide.

became valuable in publicizing the architectural and historical legacy of Savannah. According to Leopold Adler II, one of the leaders of the organization, it also served as the basis for the historic zoning ordinance enacted by the City of Savannah in 1972.

From the standpoint of preservation content, geographic scope, and planning impact, some of the most comprehensive surveys are being done in the states. Because it established a broad and clear-cut system for registering important places, expansion of the National Register by the National Historic Preservation Act of 1966 gave rise to the need for a consistent, professional system of surveying historic sites in the states and territories. Statewide surveys of historical, architectural, and other cultural resources are being undertaken to guide nomination of properties to the National Register as

Landscaped esplanades, fountains, statuary, and planter urns help to create the special urban amenity of Woodruff Place in Indianapolis, Ind., a 77-acre residential park platted in 1872 and recorded here by the Historic American Buildings Survey.

well as to take advantage of funding and protective programs open to inventoried and registered properties. The survey also forms the basis for a preservation plan in each state and territory analyzing the resources and developing an annual program for their protection. In some states, separate agencies were created to administer the program and carry out the survey, while in others existing agencies such as historical, environmental, or parks and recreation offices were designated (see list of State Historic Preservation Offices on pages 291–293).

Professional staffs do most of the survey work in some areas. In almost all cases the state agencies, anxious to survey their states as painlessly and economically as possible, accept assistance from individuals and groups who have experience in conducting surveys. A survey locally funded and conducted in West Virginia's Jefferson and Berkeley counties, for example, is being used by the West Virginia Antiquities Commission as part of the statewide survey. Most state agencies recognize that the survey is not complete until all structures in a state have been examined, and that as changes occur—demolition, new construction, discovery of new material relating to sites—the importance of individual sites in the survey changes.

To assure that surveyed sites are taken into account in state projects, the Eastern Massachusetts Regional Planning Authority has computerized the location of area sites included in the Massachusetts survey. The information is available on data print-outs to locate sites within given distances of the center strip of proposed highways or highway-widening projects, for example. Because of this, highway planners are aware from the beginning what effect any highway program may have on surveyed sites.

Many states also are considering state land-use planning as a means of assuring that important land resources are used intelligently for the greatest benefit. A number of pieces of legislation long proposed at the federal level would aid such planning by providing grants for state inventories of key resources such as coastal areas, agricultural land, and places rich in raw materials, as well as those supporting sites of cultural and historical significance.

While the federal-state partnership of the National Register inventorying program is one of the most visible and active, other federal programs are also surveying cultural sites. "Preservation Through Documentation" has long been the motto of the Historic American Buildings Survey, initiated in 1933 to record important examples of American architecture through a nationwide program of intensive, detailed studies including measured drawings, photographs, and architectural and historical data. Often with the aid of local groups and funds, HABS to date has recorded more than 16,500 structures and area studies in fifty states and three territories through some 34,750 measured drawings, 44,800 photographs, and 15,450 pages of data. Nineteen catalogues to HABS collections have been produced or are about to be; a half dozen privately published books have highlighted selections from the HABS records, and several preservation calendars and books and other publications draw heavily on its written and illustrated material.

Its tools and dies intact, the Gruber Wagon Works (1882) in Pleasant Valley, Pa., is one type of structure surveyed by the National Park Service's Historic American Engineering Record in its effort to document the growth of American engineering.

Since 1969 the Historic American Engineering Record has conducted similar surveys concentrating on particular regions or industrial structural types. During the summer of 1969, HAER surveyed the Troy, N.Y., area to identify and record industrial and manufacturing structures. The survey results were published by the Smithsonian Institution in 1972 as *A Report of the Mohawk-Hudson Area Survey*. The profusely illustrated report provides a picture of the extant physical resources of late-nineteenth-century industry in a specific area.

The National Historic Landmarks Program, established by the Historic Sites Act of 1935, surveys sites of national significance based on a series of historic theme studies, from prehistoric archaeology, agriculture, and architecture through literature, the military, politics, religion, and science. Numerous other federal agencies are undertaking inventory programs under Executive Order 11593 directing them to locate and protect their own important properties; others conduct brief surveys or studies as part of environmental impact compliance requirements.

The net effect of all these programs is to produce a set of general concepts of what is worth saving. Having such concepts as guidance has become even more important with the growth of local survey efforts by both government and private sectors, and especially with passage of the Housing and Community Development Act of 1974. That act encourages urban and rural community planning through block grants from the U.S. Department of Housing and Urban Development and puts on local communities the burden of satisfying federal protective laws and procedures as a condition of receiving project funds. In many cases, this means that a community will have to undertake a survey to assure that projects do not adversely affect historic and other protected sites. This is putting surveys back at the local level, where many of them began.

Like so many other preservation techniques initiated and carried out by a community with its own resources, the first architectural survey made its debut in Charleston, S.C. In 1931, the city adopted a historic-district zoning ordinance—also the first in the country—to preserve the historical and architectural variety of certain downtown areas. A decade later it became apparent that not enough was known about the sites within the districts and that the areas designated for protection were themselves not large enough. So, horse after cart, a building-by-building architectural survey was conducted in 1940–41 under the aegis of the Carolina Art Association with funding from the Carnegie Corporation and the Rockefeller Foundation. The original survey covered 1,168 buildings, including warehouses, train depots, gates, stables, firehouses, various outbuildings, factories, gasworks, a powder magazine, carriage houses, a jail, schools, a bathhouse, and fences. Buildings and spaces were photographed, located on city maps, and given architectural descriptions and available historical information (name of structure, name of architect, and date of construction).

But by the early 1970s it had become apparent that unless the Charleston historic district were expanded to include more of the architectural resources of the city, all that would be left would be a well-preserved enclave of eighteenth- and early-nineteenth-century structures surrounded by a sea of asphalt parking lots, gas stations, and highways. To forestall this, a large area of the Charleston peninsula was surveyed to identify and analyze its architectural resources. The survey, carried out by

The one-room-deep "single house" with its side piazza reminiscent of the West Indies is a Charleston trademark. Two designated "valuable to the city" in *This Is Charleston* are St. Philip's Rectory (c. 1807), center, and the Thomas Legaré House (1760), foreground.

an expert team of architectural historians and preservationists, concluded that the historic district should indeed be expanded and that many more of the peninsula's structures ought to be protected and preserved.

The first of four editions of Charleston's survey, *This Is Charleston*, was published in 1944. Photographs and descriptions of 572 of the city's buildings were presented on a street-by-street and area-by-area basis. As architect Albert Simons commented in the foreword to *This Is Charleston*, the survey stemmed from an already well-developed pride of place.

No Charlestonian can be expected to speak or write about his city objectively for it is so much a part of the background of his mind and emotions that detachment is never possible. The lovely and the shabby are all woven into the same warp and woof of the familiar scene. The stucco façade of some old house, its chalky colors weather-faded, its surface mapped with earthquake patches and crumbling at the windows, through a sort of empathy assumes a character akin to an aged face looming out of one of Rembrandt's later portraits, infinitely world-weary yet infinitely enduring and wise in human experience.

Because Charlestonians knew their city, they did not compare their city with another but instead looked at it for what it was, determined for themselves what it had to offer, what gave their place its special character, and recorded it.

Ornamental ironwork is another distinguishing characteristic of Charleston's built environment. The lantern standards on the South Carolina Society Hall (1804), recorded by the noted photographer Frances Benjamin Johnston in 1937, are pre-Revolutionary.

Over the years the published Charleston survey has become a popular tour guide and an invaluable aid in promoting real estate sales in the historic areas highlighted. It has also served as an impetus and a model for efforts in other towns that suspected that they, too, had something to be proud about and wished to document that fact in order to help protect it.

Few places can match Charleston's long involvement in historic preservation. Some communities are just beginning to take stock of their surroundings. In 1975 the Department of Environmental Affairs in Fairfield, Calif., argued for preservation in its published survey, *The Way It Was,* and suggested several courses of action for what

the town might be. The document was viewed as "a program for the preservation of local things," but "not a plan." The report suggests that "in the final analysis, it is up to the various governments and to the people to decide the importance of historic preservation to this community." Some forty-nine "local things" were enumerated in the book through photographs and descriptions, such things as Algonquin petroglyphs, 1940–41 sidewalks where "the WPA imprint may be seen as one walks the streets," early-twentieth-century company workers' bungalows, and Thompson's Corner, a 1902 building housing "the oldest bar in Solano County." Also included are churches, mills, schools, houses, government buildings, all of styles and times that make them important to a northern California town—pieces of its own individuality.

Before the entry of government into preservation surveying, surveys too often were regarded as little more than quaint guidebooks put together by nice little old historical groups; without official recognition, they and their subjects were overlooked in community development planning. Now local surveys, regardless of who conducts them, are gaining maximum impact as a planning instrument by obtaining official endorsement or sponsorship of local governments. Just as the barn-raising was the big event of early American communities, barn-saving and recording today bring together people of diverse interests. Local preservation groups, historical societies, junior leagues, garden clubs, students, individual property owners, and others are turning into seasoned field workers, learning the art of research and photography by recording their neighborhoods. They also help document the built environment by using other people's memoranda: library and court records, private collections, contemporary newspaper accounts, letters, diaries, old photographs, deeds, wills, store ledgers, epitaphs, tax records, plats, elevations, past surveys, and maps.

Many state preservation agencies such as those in Colorado, Massachusetts, New York, Georgia, South Dakota, and California have published manuals that establish guidelines for local groups and individuals who want to assist in the surveys. Almost all of the state agencies have staff available to provide advice as well as survey forms and guidelines and to help assure that the completed survey is in a form useful in the statewide program. Coordination with federal agencies and private organizations carrying out survey work opens up new sources of information and possible cooperative projects.

Realizing that the architectural heritage of Marshall, Mich., a town founded in 1831, was unusually rich, the Marshall Historical Society undertook a survey as part of the Michigan statewide survey, with funding from the state's National Register planning apportionment and a consultant service grant from the National Trust for Historic Preservation. A team of preservation consultants was retained to evaluate the structures and sites on four bases: historical value, architectural value, physical value, and environmental value. To judge historical significance the team drew on data provided by the historical society. Architectural importance was judged against the prototypes of particular styles and in comparison with others built during the same period. Buildings were also examined for structural soundness. Most important, the team evaluated each structure for its visual impact on the environment—its place on a street, its relation to the landscape, its location in the community's traffic patterns. Because the evaluation was done in such a comprehensive manner, Marshall gave full credit to each structure and to the collective impact of all parts of the built environment, avoiding the danger of underrating some buildings, which then often become targets for demolition. "Each community can be its own visual history book, recording for all to see where it has come

Because of a series of economic setbacks, little new construction rose in Marshall, Mich., in the late nineteenth century to alter the town's appearance. Today it looks much as it did during this turn-of-the-century parade.

from and where it is going," says the preface to the published survey, *Marshall: A Plan for Preservation* (1973). "But even more important, when the values of preservation are fully understood and knowledgeably injected into the community, they can become vital forces in the local economy and a guide for future progress."

A survey produces a wealth of material—historical data, development statistics, photographs, drawings, maps. As many preservation agencies and organizations have discovered, unless these are translated into a program of action, the survey remains little more than an academic exercise, a picture of a neighborhood or community at a point in time, static as a photograph. Charleston, Savannah, Marshall, Fairfield, as well as places from Maine to Utah, Cambridge, Mass., to San Francisco, have turned to publications to communicate their surveys to professional planners and the general public. Among the types of publications derived from inventory material are the detailed surveys themselves, often circulated only in-house; illustrated selections from the survey, guidebooks, monographs, rehabilitation guidelines for property owners, manuals on how to carry out surveys, even brochures, posters, and notecards. A survey of the architecture of Duluth, Minn., conducted by the city's Department of Research and Planning with the aid of a HUD comprehensive planning grant, was published in 1974 as *Duluth's Legacy. Volume I: Architecture*. The first edition of 5,000 copies sold out within two weeks, and more than half the second printing of 10,000 was presold—a more than comfortable sales record in a city of 100,000.

THE PLAN

In too many cases, however, the preservation survey has not moved out from the hearts and minds of preservationists and into a comprehensive plan where it can have a positive effect. Preservation plans range from general documents that are essentially site surveys or inventories with identified goals to urban design plans for historic areas and comprehensive master plans of which preservation or conservation of existing resources is only one element, although a vital one, among a range of social and environmental goals. Despite their variations in form, common factors characterize plans for preservation: a history of the surveyed area's growth and a general description of the population, land use, and building types and conditions; the surveyed physical resources, often ranked or grouped by priorities, usually form the nucleus. What sets a plan apart from a survey is a state-

Duluth's survey uncovered structures and elements as varied as cherubic capitals on the Richardsonian-style Old Duluth Central High School (1891–92); the Bayha Furniture Company Barn (1909); and the Northwestern Oil Company Filling Station (1921), now a store.

ment of goals and techniques to implement them. Goals can be as limited as maintaining the architectural or physical integrity of significant individual structures or as broad as protecting whole enclaves or even maintaining and enhancing the overall environmental amenities and social character of the area. Courses of action can include the common preservation techniques — historic district zoning, creation of landmarks commissions, protective easements, favorable tax advantages and valuation assessments, revolving funds for property purchases — as well as general planning procedures for accommodating new development to the old, safeguarding natural areas, and meeting growth needs through enlightened development policies.

San Francisco is one of the places where the preservation element has been successfully integrated into the general planning process. The *Urban Design Plan for the Comprehensive Plan of San Francisco*, prepared by the Department of City Planning with an urban planning grant from the U.S. Department of Housing and Urban Development, not only identifies and describes the important elements of the city's unique environment, but also

The plan for New Mexico's Acoma Pueblo views built elements such as its adobes as only "furniture" in the larger "land house" of the pueblo itself. Acoma is one of the oldest continuously occupied settlements in the United States.

assesses how the desires of people to conserve and improve the livability of their neighborhoods can be accomplished. The plan stresses human variety and scale and recommends such things as protecting vantage points, restoring some historic areas, keeping open space open, and putting parking underground or behind berms as a means of keeping or making the city people-oriented. Says the report:

> *Urban design planning is a response to human needs. It is part of the process of defining quality*

in the environment, and quality is based upon human needs. Quality means degree of excellence, and when applied to cities it depends upon pleasing physical relationships, a fitting together with scale and interest and without jarring contrasts. Over time, quality means cultural heritage, and things and values that last.

Other places, from cities to small towns, have comprehensive plans in effect that take full account of preservation. Towns such as Roswell, Ga. (5,430), Long Grove, Ill. (1,196), Willard, Utah (1,000), and Ephraim, Wis. (236), use preservation in their comprehensive plans. Plans also cover areas that are primarily open space. The historic preservation and design study for Acoma Pueblo in New Mexico addresses the problem of preserving traditional Indian uses of a 245,000-acre reservation by preservation and traditional zoning, which would allow different types of development in accordance with established planning criteria. Similar to the Savannah plan, which sees the city's squares as its "living rooms," the Acoma plan views the pueblo as a "land house," with highways and paved roads for corridors, the San Jose River as its "plumbing," arroyos as its private rooms, grazing land as carpet; houses, corrals, and other built elements are its furniture. This type of evaluation is not so much whimsical as practical if all elements of our environmental homes are to be taken into account.

All too often a preservation plan is the result of the loss of one or more important buildings. These losses often make people look beyond the immediate crisis to a means of assuring that there are mechanisms to protect buildings and places in the future.

In Grand Rapids, Mich., the impetus in 1969 was the fight for and eventual loss of the Grand Rapids City Hall to urban renewal. As the dust from the demolition settled in Grand Rapids, those who had come together to try to save the eighty-one-year-old landmark learned that they had more in common than the preservation of a single monumental edifice. They learned, for instance, that they cared about the expansion plans of a local college, about the deterioration of in-town neighborhoods, and about the effects of the continuation of the urban renewal project on their city. They became excited about the rest of their community. In doing so, they began to look systematically at the assets of one of the city's neighborhoods, a place they named Heritage Hill because of the past it reflected and because it overlooked the main section of downtown.

Proceeding from the expanded goal of preserving the Heritage Hill area, the new Heritage Hill Foundation began to refine goals and aims to achieve its overall objective. With the assistance of a grant from the National Trust, the citizens hired a consultant to inventory

Rehabilitated and readied for sale, this house in the Heritage Hill area of Grand Rapids, Mich., is one of a half-dozen acquired for restoration and resale by the Heritage Hill Foundation to implement its master preservation plan.

For this Oyster Bay, N. Y., commercial row, Vision, Inc., advised removing imitation brick siding, painting architectural details, and unifying signs and street furniture.

the structures within the neighborhood. This was the basis for a master plan for preservation of the area and also served as the basis for listing the Heritage Hill Historic District in the National Register of Historic Places. The course of action elaborated in the plan included a program for upgrading the residential housing stock of the neighborhood through a revolving fund for property purchases. The inventory was thus the beginning of making Heritage Hill once more a convenient and pleasant place in which to live.

Working on the premise that the centers of many communities are basically nineteenth-century in character and as such are more properly attuned to the pedestrian than to the automobile, a nonprofit Cambridge, Mass., corporation, Vision, Inc., uses visual surveys to provide design expertise as another means of preservation. It first draws up a catalogue of an area's physical and visual characteristics and then develops an urban design and preservation plan. In a number of cities such as Portsmouth, N.H., and Bellows Falls, Vt., the plans call for enhancement of the old center-city areas by coordinating signs and graphics for commercial establishments and developing areas that cater to the pedestrian. Design counseling is provided to local merchants. Maintaining the uniqueness of place and developing the vitality of Main Street and other central areas often mean that alternatives to use of the automobile have to be developed, with new areas found for cars so that they do not terrify and overwhelm the pedestrian.

Logan Circle, an area of large Victorian town houses in Washington, D.C., not far from the Capitol, was a prime residential section of the city in the late nineteenth century. But by the early 1970s it had deteriorated badly and become part of an urban renewal area. A preservation plan developed to revitalize the area recog-

nized the neighborhood's important features and made recommendations to stabilize and improve Logan Circle. The plan proposed flexible guidelines and standards for the exterior rehabilitation of the structures around the circle to recapture their architectural integrity. The standards included specifications for exterior elements such as brickwork, windows, doors, and fencing. It also proposed street improvements and modification of heavy traffic patterns. Finally, the plan proposed changes in the zoning of the area and adaptation of the urban renewal plan and presented cost estimates and means of financing some of the proposed improvements. In all, the Logan Circle report is a good example of what a preservation plan can be—even though its full implementation still has to be counted among the plan's goals.

Usually a plan is only that: a suggested means of achieving a specific goal. As such it is constantly subject to change and updating as attitudes and conditions change and new techniques are developed. A survey considered definitive a decade ago may not include many of the elements of the built environment that today are thought worthy of attention. The boundaries established for the Heritage Hill District in Grand Rapids, for example, were based on factors such as architectural coherence and geography. But when Gerald Ford became Vice-President in 1974, it was discovered that his boyhood home lay just a block outside the boundaries of the historic district and thus outside its protection—showing how rapidly what is considered important can change. Surveys that include only eighteenth- or nineteenth-century structures, or only buildings and not their settings, are now outdated. Yet there is no substitute for the documentation produced by surveys. The more thorough they are, the better the assessment of which buildings, streetscapes, and open spaces are necessary to maintain and improve the fabric of an area. Not everything can or deserves to be preserved as is. The survey is the tool for determining what additions or subtractions or retentions will enhance the built environment.

But as the organizers of St. Paul's Historic Hill District survey found out, a planning program "is only as good as the concrete results it achieves in the improvement of the physical and social subjects it studies. . . . without implementation, the planning program is time, money, energy, and ideas wasted."

METHODS OF PRESERVATION

METHODS OF PRESERVATION

A look at the history of the preservation movement in both the private and public sectors makes one pattern clear: What began as a rather narrow—first patriotic, then architectural—activity became, because of the nature of its goals, a movement of broad environmental proportions. In many instances preservation began with a concern for saving a single building of documented historical, cultural, or architectural importance. It quickly branched out to take a broad approach to what should be saved and used—from single sites to streets and neighborhoods and cities; from only structures to their settings, their landscaping, their street furniture; from sites associated with the rich and well placed to sites associated with all of us. When preservationists saved one structure, they found that they also had to save the one next to it and the trees around it and the air above it. To keep the quality of one place they had to protect others.

One important change occurred when it became evident that purchasing sites out from under the bulldozer would not solve all preservation problems or fit all situations. Preservationists have become increasingly sophisticated, adapting ideas and techniques from related endeavors and developing many of their own—using financing methods of the marketplace (discussed in the next chapter) and expanding and launching new protective techniques. Preservationists communicate, and because of this, what is found to be a successful approach in one area is often adopted and used in other places. Preservation in the last decade has been characterized by the pebble-in-the-pond effect: every time a new idea or technique has been found to work in one area, it has made its way into all parts of the country, everywhere that the value of preservation is recognized.

As the nation's oldest registered distillery, in Lynchburg, Tenn., knows, plaques and listing in the National Register provide invaluable public recognition.

RECOGNITION PROGRAMS

Programs that recognize buildings, places, and areas of importance are among the long-standing preservation techniques. The largest recognition program is the National Register of Historic Places, with more than 15,000 entries to date. But recognizing and cataloguing important places was taking place years before the National Register took on its present role in 1966. There are many programs in both the public and the private sectors that identify landmarks and signify their value.

Erecting plaques and markers is one of these. Through a desire to call attention and to single out a place, plaques and markers have been put up by national and state governments, patriotic associations, local preservation organizations, city and town governments, and now such Bicentennial agencies as Boston 200. Indeed, some individuals proud of the buildings they own have erected their own plaques.

Plaques and markers are, however, merely the tip of the iceberg of recognition programs. Many if not most recognition programs do not award plaques but are instead aimed at identifying the important elements of the built environment so that they will be preserved in some way. Recognition programs lead to public education and to mechanisms such as historic districts, which are designed to protect and enhance the important elements of the built environment.

Reaction to plaquing buildings has also arisen in recent years; it has been attacked as an exercise of little import as well as for the fact that plaques can detract from the exterior appearance of a building. In one East Coast city a building of some importance is virtually covered with bronze plaques, attesting to and noting everything from the historical importance of the building and the founding of the town to the townspeople who sacrificed their lives in the world wars. Apparently, whenever an occasion or event demanded some sort of commemoration or memorial, the townspeople could think of nothing better than to put a plaque on this building. The result is that today the building's main exterior wall seems to be made more of bronze plaques than of the original stone.

Beyond merely educating the public, however, recognition programs with defined criteria do serve as the basis for the protection of important buildings. For example, buildings that have been officially recognized by government bodies can be protected from demolition, insensitive alteration, inharmonious or incompatible new construction, and other adverse effects, depending on local regulations. As has been noted, buildings officially recognized by listing in the National Register, including National Historic Landmarks, are afforded some protection from federal and federally licensed or funded projects such as highways through the review mechanism of the Advisory Council on Historic Preservation.

Many preservation-minded people support the idea of broadening the criteria for listing in national and state and local registers, expanding the idea of what is worth protecting. General criteria that now guide the state and federal governments in evaluating potential entries for the National Register are similar to those used by other recognition agencies. Chief among them, in the words of the National Register, is a certain "quality of significance"—significance in American history, architecture, archaeology, or culture. This quality is present in districts, sites, buildings, structures, and objects that possess integrity of location, design, setting, materials, workmanship, feeling, and association. Although properties that have attained significance within the past fifty years are not generally considered, along with cemeteries, birthplaces, graves, structures that have been moved or reconstructed, and those that are predominantly com-

The Frank Lloyd Wright–designed Pope-Leighey House in Mount Vernon, Va., a National Trust property, is only 35 years old yet has already been added to the National Register—as well as moved from the path of a highway.

memorative in nature, such properties do qualify if they meet additional criteria of significance. It is urged that places that have a less tangible quality of being workable and livable environments, places with "vital street life," be recognized also, and many in fact are.

Moving beyond past definitions of what constitutes landmark quality, planning and preservation agencies are beginning to view the "vital street life" of places such as New York's Mott Street as worthy of official recognition and protection.

PRESERVATION ORDINANCES

It might appear that recognition programs do little except create a lamentation list that becomes operable each time a valuable building is torn down. The important facet of recognition programs, however, is the protection that can be afforded listed properties. For federally funded projects affecting National Register proper-

ties, the recourse is to the Advisory Council, which has mainly the power of persuasion behind it. In other jurisdictions listed properties are protected through preservation ordinances.

Although each place is unique in what it legally protects, all use basically one of two kinds of statutes: landmarks commission ordinances or historic district ordinances. Sometimes the two are combined. Today between one half and two thirds of the states have legislation specifically authorizing municipalities to create historic districts or landmarks commissions. In others, such as New Jersey, historic districts have been created under the general zoning power of a community.

Generally, these ordinances define the architectural and historical standards of value in the area (usually based on an architectural survey). Each sets up an agency with authority to review proposals to alter or demolish designated structures and to restrict such actions. Each provides a procedure by which decisions can be appealed by applicants—either to a higher administrative authority such as a zoning board, city council, or mayor, or directly to court. The basic difference between the two kinds of ordinances is the scope and nature of the jurisdiction they give the governing agency.

Landmarks commission ordinances grant a landmarks commission jurisdiction over an entire area such as a city, but its power generally applies only to single buildings or objects within that area; some commissions, however, also have authority over historic districts. Generally speaking, a commission is authorized to recommend landmark designations to the city council, which makes the designation official. Powers of a landmarks commission may include the ability to review and control exterior alterations and to order a stay of demolition of a landmark. The structures and sites covered in landmarks commission ordinances tend to be widely scattered throughout the area, and the commissions seldom have power to prevent construction, alteration, or demolition of structures adjacent to designated landmarks.

The New York City Landmarks Preservation Commission, established in 1965, has broad powers. It can restrict not only exterior alterations but in some cases interior changes as well. Subject to the approval of the mayor and seven other members of the Board of Estimate, the City Planning Department designates historic districts. Today the commission has review authority over twenty-five districts containing some 9,000 buildings and more than 450 individual landmarks. It is empowered to prevent demolition of a landmark with proof that the building or site is capable of earning a "reasonable

Designated a municipal landmark by Chicago's landmarks commission, the Rookery Building (1886) of Burnham and Root presaged modern steel-frame office construction and is representative of the type of landmark more usually recognized.

return'' (defined as a net return of 6 percent of the assessed value of the building and its site). In conjunction with this, the commission can also have a say in granting partial or complete tax exemptions or remissions of tax to bring the net return up to that figure.

Historic district ordinances encompass a defined area of buildings, structures, sites, or objects. Their administrative commissions or boards are authorized to supervise the *tout ensemble,* what the community has deemed worth saving "all together," including not only significant landmarks but also street furniture, street façades, open spaces such as squares and courtyards, and natural features such as trees and hills and vistas.

Historic district ordinances sometimes grant the supervising agency power to restrict demolition or alteration within the area. The commission overseeing Santa Barbara's El Pueblo Viejo, already cited for the strictness of its architectural design controls, has absolute power over demolition. The commission supervising the College Hill Historic District in Providence, R.I., may engage in financial arrangements and allow zoning variances to preserve historic structures.

"The lovely and the shabby are all woven into the same warp and woof of the familiar scene," wrote Albert Simons in *This Is Charleston.* The cobblestoned Chalmers Street and the pre-Revolutionary "Pink House" at left help to create the special character of Charleston, S.C., site of the nation's first historic district.

Historic district legislation is never an end in itself, as Nantucket Islanders have found out since the once isolated community became a successful tourist attraction. While its historic district act protects typical grey-shingled cottages, mansions, and other amenities of the town, outlying areas are being overdeveloped, threatening the town's essential character and necessitating new conservation and land planning efforts.

Chicago's Rookery Building encloses a large interior light court and a lobby remodeled by Frank Lloyd Wright in 1905. Even in designated municipal landmarks such as this, interior features like the Rookery's spiral cast-iron staircase generally are not protected by the ordinance's review provisions.

The purpose of historic district ordinances parallels the goal of zoning laws used by communities since early in the twentieth century to regulate growth and to control the distribution of people and traffic. While land-use zoning sought to keep commercial or industrial enterprises out of residential neighborhoods, historic area zoning grew from attempts to protect environmental amenities and keep them for public enjoyment. The first historic district, created in Charleston in 1931, was followed in 1937 by the establishment, through a special amendment to the Louisiana State Constitution, of the Vieux Carré Historic District in New Orleans.

Commissions are in effect in such different areas as Albuquerque, N.M., Bethlehem, Pa., Columbus, Ohio, Lexington, Ky., Mackinac Island, Mich., North Kensington, R.I., Schenectady, N.Y., Tombstone, Ariz., and Windsor, Conn. In Miami and Dallas, historic districts encompass twentieth-century upper-middle-income residences; in Walker's Point, Milwaukee, a district covers nineteenth-century worker housing. First used in cities, such ordinances are now part of the laws in counties, townships, and small towns; in fact, the preponderance are used in towns under 10,000 and, in several states, in towns of fewer than 5,000 people.

With buildings dating from 1840 to 1910, Walker's Point is one of the last relatively intact neighborhoods in Milwaukee, Wis. The preservation goal here is "to preserve not just one building, but a community."

Whatever type of ordinance is operative, its success depends on the interest and the experience of the administrators. Most ordinances, whether administered by landmarks commissions, historic district commissions, or architectural review boards, demand professional qualifications for members. Yreka, Calif., has specific requirements for each member of its commission: one must be a member of the county historical society; another must have special knowledge of nineteenth-century architecture in order to deal with Yreka's heritage.

Most commissions include local historians, lawyers, architects, and real estate people, for the decisions of a commission are based on a multitude of factors germane to these professions; in addition to answering to the preservationists of a community, the boards have to interpret decisions to applicants and to the general public.

Because ownership of land and the freedom to do with it what a person wills have been sacrosanct aspects of the American way of life, the constitutionality of some development controls has been questioned in litigation. It has been charged, for example, that designating landmarks or placing any restrictions on a property's use without compensation constitutes a "taking" of private property without due process of law, action forbidden by both the Fifth and the Fourteenth Amendments to the United States Constitution. The right of the government to regulate private property to promote the general welfare, however, is equally well established in the law. The test is whether or not development controls promote legitimate public purposes.

Because Walker's Point was a typical nineteenth-century working-class neighborhood, efforts are being made to preserve its unique workers' and ethnic characteristics through preservation means that do not displace residents.

Preservation is now essentially deemed a desirable public goal that promotes the general welfare, and many court decisions have supported preservation controls. One of the most important recent cases is *Maher* v. *City of New Orleans*, decided in 1974. After a decade of litigation, the United States District Court upheld the denial by the Vieux Carré Commission of an owner's application to demolish a one-story historic residence to build a seven-unit apartment building. The owner claimed that the ordinance reduced his potential income from a building that "wasn't historic" anyway. The court ruled that any zoning ordinance, being an exercise of police power, would naturally reduce the rights of some, but that it was not by that fact unconstitutional, for other options were still open to the owner. To his argument that the building was not historic, the court ruled that just as important as the saving of buildings of great worth was the preservation of "the setting or scene in which those comparatively few gems are situated."

Preservationists and protective agencies themselves have gone to court over the years to uphold the constitutional rights of old buildings and people who like them—including what Justice William O. Douglas in 1954 declared to be the right of a city to be beautiful. Actions also have been brought under protective statutes and directives such as the 1966 Preservation Act, the National Environmental Policy Act, Executive Order 11593, and local and state ordinances. From Alaska and Grand Rapids, Mich., to Green Springs, Va., Louisville, Ky., and New York City, cases have been won and lost as the law of preservation continues to grow. In one of the most celebrated cases, a New York State appellate court in December 1975 ruled that designation of Grand Central Terminal was in the public good and that the time for "full implementation" of the New York City landmarks preservation law had arrived.

Other zoning devices are used to protect older structures and sites. Residents of Old West Side in Ann Arbor, Mich., wanted to stop decline and preserve the envi-

The Old West Side area of Ann Arbor, Mich., observes a recent survey, "exhibits a remarkable continuity of development. . . . Its architecture is a major asset that helps to establish much of the neighborhood character."

By restoring this typical frame house, as the sign says, Historic Walker's Point is demonstrating how the entire neighborhood can be improved.

ronmental quality of their neighborhood. They began simply by taking political action to change the city's policy of granting multifamily zoning variances in single-family areas. By rehabilitating salvageable homes they stopped uncontrolled change, and today the neighborhood is listed in the National Register. In Galveston, Tex., a referendum to create a 100-block historic district under state law was defeated in the late 1960s because residents thought the police power of the governing board was too broad. Instead, in 1970 the city council approved the addition of special historic preservation regulations to the city's regular zoning ordinances and now any area can become a historic district once a development plan is approved by the city planning commission.

Ann Arbor's Murray Avenue forms a distinctive enclave of small, closely spaced classic revival homes. It was protected as an ensemble because it represents a typical, well-preserved worker's house neighborhood of the 1890s.

PRESERVATION BY DEED

Preservationists are now frequently looking to less-than-fee legal techniques (that is, less than full ownership) as added tools for preservation. Approaches such as deed restrictions have been used with some success in a number of areas. Deed restrictions, although based on ownership of property, actually pertain to only a few of the "bundle of rights" that come with a property. Thus, one or two of the rights can be sold or given away without affecting the others. A preservation organization, for instance, may acquire and then sell a property subject to a covenant and reverter clause in the deed. The reverter clause might specify that the purchaser must comply with certain restoration guidelines. Should this not be done, the property would revert to the preservation organization. In this way, the preservation group can assure the future of a property without actually owning it.

An ironic twist to the use of such preservation-oriented clauses recently occurred in New York when the state purchased a 1,500-acre camp in the Adirondack Mountains to add to its "forever wild" Adirondack Forest Preserve. A state constitutional provision was interpreted to mandate that the state was indeed to keep the area "forever wild," meaning that any not-so-wild buildings it purchased in the area had to be demolished. In the case of its new acquisition, structures on the property happened to include the Vanderbilts' 1897 rustic camp lodge, Sagamore. Another clause, however, this in the sales contract, gave the state time to resell the property to a preservation group and thus relieve itself of the mandate to demolish the buildings while preserving the forest.

The most flexible and widely used less-than-fee controls are easements. An easement is one interest in property sold or given by the owner to another either for profit or for public benefit; the owner retains the remaining interests. In preservation usage two kinds of easements are most common: exterior or façade easements and open space or scenic easements. (A third possibility is the protective interior easement.) The holder of a façade easement may control the exterior of a structure, including barring inappropriate alteration or requesting specific improvements. If a preservation group purchases an exterior or façade easement, it can, for example, stipulate that certain actions must be performed on the exterior of the structure. Such things as painting or cleaning the façade of a building could be required as part of the easement purchase agreement.

Open space or scenic easements are used to save a structure from contiguous development that would change or interfere with its visual surroundings. Generally, an easement runs with the land, meaning that it is a permanent interest. Holders of easements, which can be preservation groups, governmental bodies, or organizations legally entitled to do so, are also qualified to enforce the protective restrictions.

Easements give the preservationist the power to protect the historical, architectural, or aesthetic value of a site or structure, and because they are generally less costly than owning and maintaining a structure, easements on numerous properties can be held by a group. The public benefits two ways: the property retains its architectural or historical quality, thus contributing to the visual richness of the total environment, and it remains in active use on the community tax rolls, continuing to bring in revenue. Easements are palatable to property owners, too, for usually owners choose to remain free to use the portion of their property not covered by an easement. An exterior easement, for example, would not usually preclude alteration of the interior.

The owner may benefit from a purchase price, or if the owner donates the rights, the donation may qualify as a charitable contribution for federal income tax purposes. Relief from state or local real estate taxes may be possible as well. In Virginia's Loudoun and Fauquier counties, property owners who agree to maintain their land for a specific length of time as open space or in agricultural use (rather than allowing it to be developed) are taxed at a lower rate—for actual rather than for potential use of the land.

Suffolk County on Long Island is a 65,000-acre area of rich farmland within easy reach of Manhattan's development pressure. The land yields $30 million a year from potatoes, cauliflower, and other products, but private owners are under intense pressure to develop. Residents, realizing the benefits of the open space, have sought to safeguard the land. A $60 million preservation program has been proposed to allow the county to pay farmers for scenic easements on their property. The land would remain in agricultural or at least undeveloped use, so that it will be saved for everyone to enjoy. New Jersey is also beginning a program of farm preservation in an attempt to assure that valuable agricultural land remains just that and does not give way to subdivision.

A potentially difficult problem with easements is enforcement of the provisions. While the original donor or seller of an easement may fully and carefully abide by all the easement provisions, subsequent occupants of the structure may not be so cooperative or they may not be fully informed of the easement provisions. Although easement holders have recourse to legal proceedings to enforce their interests, legal proceedings are costly and may not well serve the ultimate purpose of preservation. Periodic inspections are necessary to assure that the easement provisions are being complied with. This can prove burdensome for a preservation organization that holds many easements, because it does require that someone physically inspect each easement.

The federal government has accepted easements since 1935 under the authorization of the Historic Sites Act. In 1974, to block highway and ferry landing construction, the owner of 130 acres of land on the south bank of the James River gave the property outright to the National Park Service for incorporation into the Colonial National Historical Park and also donated a scenic easement on the rest of his land in Surry County, Va. The easement stipulates that no structures may be built there by current or future owners and that the property cannot be used for any industrial or commercial purpose except farming.

Roughly a third of the states and American Samoa and Guam have specific enabling legislation that allows them to accept and hold historic preservation easements.

Each has its own particular system, however—some combining open space and façade easements in a single set of statutes, others authorizing the acquisition of easements by eminent domain, some authorizing existing agencies to accept easements and some creating new ones. Arkansas has special provisions for the acceptance of easements on archaeological sites. In Montana the Department of Fish and Game is the agency authorized to accept easements. The State of Maine's Bureau of Parks and Recreation accepts outright donations of historic property and holds easements, as the Maine Historic Preservation Commission also is authorized to do.

Private nonprofit preservation groups also hold easements. In a program begun in 1968, the National Trust for Historic Preservation has acquired more than a dozen easements on historic properties from Maryland, Virginia, Washington, D.C., and Pennsylvania to California. Open space easements protect the surroundings of Oatlands, a National Trust property near Leesburg, Va.; easements on the house and portions of the estate were given to the Trust for protection in 1973. The Virginia Landmarks Foundation has an aggressive program to acquire easements for properties listed in its register. Between 1969 and 1975 it acquired thirty-one such easements.

Although the Queen Anne–style Haas-Lilienthal House (1886) in San Francisco is owned by a local preservation group, a façade easement and reverter clause held by the National Trust will protect the house if the group can no longer maintain it.

Use of easements for preservation purposes is still relatively new and much experience is still to be gained. Despite the potential problems, they do appear to be a useful tool for assuring preservation of property.

BUILDING CODES

Building and fire codes have long presented one of the greatest challenges to preservationists. Such codes are intended to assure public safety through requirements designed to apply principally to modern buildings. Restoration architects and code enforcers have worked in an admitted atmosphere of conflict: the one charged with saving and adapting old buildings in a condition as close to the original as possible; the other, with assuring high standards of safety. "Should we preserve from the ravages of time," one architect asked at a recent national conference on preservation and building codes, "but lose to the ravages of fire that reduces the preservation effort to zero?" His answer was, of course, "No."

Within the framework of the codes, it has been difficult not only to achieve historical authenticity—to restore without visible "intrusions" such as fire exits and steel supports—but also to adapt old buildings to new uses for which they were not built. Where restorers were tenacious and code officials sympathetic, ways have been found to comply with the codes. But even where they were, it has been difficult to apply the same methods to other places, because codes vary greatly from area to area.

Compromise and flexibility are increasingly becoming the keystones of relations between preservers and code enforcers, as both work to uphold the intent of the codes. In the past several years, a significant number of moves have been made to alter prevailing building codes to more easily accommodate preservation of older structures. Three of the four national code organizations had by 1975 approved amendments acknowledging the special problems of historic buildings; these provide review procedures to certify that even while work on such structures does not have to meet all standard code requirements, it nonetheless meets all standards of public safety. More than a dozen states, from Oregon to Virginia, have introduced similar review procedures, and even more cities have other provisions taking into account restoration problems.

COMBATTING DISORIENTATION

No matter how comprehensive and farsighted the preservation methods, often there are problems to deal with. Sometimes it is success itself: a historic residential area like Old Town in Alexandria, Va., becomes a prestigious address, and when housing is no longer available inside the district, the area becomes ringed with new high-rise construction that casts shadows—figuratively as well as architecturally—over the historic area. Or historic tourist meccas like Gettysburg, Pa., the Vieux Carré in New Orleans, and other sites begin to suffer the so-called terminal cutes—a surfeit of gaslights and specialty shoppes. Or small towns and scenic areas draw visitors in flocks to the open spaces, causing vacation condominiums to mushroom.

Far more troublesome are the social effects of preservation when it has been planned only in terms of buildings and not in terms of the human beings who live in them. All too often when restoration begins (especially in urban areas with acute housing shortages), old neighborhoods suddenly become fashionable places to live and newcomers squeeze out old residents who have made their own unique community out of the area's only recently unloved housing stock. Blacks and whites, Chicanos and Puerto Ricans, Indians and others have been forced out by affluent new residents—by the very economics of the situation, even if no intensive development pressure is involved—and their need for decent housing remains unsolved and usually becomes worse. They often leave neighborhoods that work to go to less cohesive ones where disorientation compounds economic woes. Sociologist Marc Fried, studying persons displaced by urban renewal, found that even when people were relocated in better housing, they reacted to leaving their homes with feelings akin to grief over losing loved ones.

Revitalizing neighborhoods without displacing the residents is more than ever an integral goal of preservation.

After years of having their neighborhood neglected by

Opposite page: Conversion of New York's old Astor Library to the New York Shakespeare Festival Public Theater necessitated accommodation to the building safety and fire codes. Below: Residents of Cincinnati's Mt. Auburn area have undertaken a grass-roots effort to make streets such as this livable again.

absentee slumlords, residents of Mt. Auburn, a primarily black section of Cincinnati, set up their own development corporation in 1967 with two objectives: to own and renovate the area's houses, and to integrate the neighborhood by bringing in middle-income whites and blacks. Dynamic leadership and a carefully prepared plan for revitalizing the area helped secure an initial $169,000 loan, with which the corporation gutted and renovated the "largest and ugliest" buildings it could find. To these were added amenities such as basketball courts and barbecue pits to make the buildings attractive to as many people as possible. So successful was this method that twenty-nine of the largest local savings and loan associations now contribute to a revolving loan fund to assist homeowners in the crosstown neighborhood of Madisonville in renovating their property.

The easement program of Historic Annapolis, Inc., although designed primarily to preserve historic structures by keeping speculators from assembling property parcels, at the same time makes it possible for owners to restore

To stop the rooming-house-and-decay syndrome in the Mexican War Streets area of Pittsburgh (below and opposite page), a program was begun in 1966 to revive the mid-1800s buildings. Historic district designation provided encouragement.

Another Cincinnati neighborhood, the Over-the-Rhine district, is getting needed community facilities through a process of infilling new buildings among the old. The 1840 church attached to the spire (above) was lost to the cause.

their homes with the easement income. This provides a tool for maintaining the existing social and economic status of the neighborhood at the same time that the buildings are saved and the environment enhanced.

The Pittsburgh History & Landmarks Foundation, in cooperation with the Pittsburgh Urban Renewal Authority, has set a similar goal for the Manchester Renewal Area, a scene of riots in 1967. The foundation certified historic buildings, and the housing authority, using federal urban renewal funds when the program was still in operation, paid owners for the right to restore exteriors. Owners took on the responsibility of making needed repairs and restoring interiors through regular renewal grants and loans. Residents of the neighborhood initiated the idea of setting up a limited partnership with the foundation for future preservation programs.

The preservation objective in Butchertown in Louisville, Ky., is to preserve the existing early-nineteenth-century housing stock (now threatened by industrial encroachment). Butchertown, Inc., a nonprofit corporation established in 1967, raises money for rehabilitating units by selling stock and also by holding an annual neighborhood festival, which stimulates cultural and community awareness.

Although the pigs are no longer driven through the streets to the slaughterhouse, Butchertown in Louisville, Ky., maintains its link with the past through buildings such as these vernacular brick and frame structures.

Varied styles and rich decoration contribute to the visual interest of Pittsburgh's Mexican War Streets district. Its neighborhood preservation effort was inaugurated with private support and the federal leased housing program.

FEDERAL PROGRAMS

The Housing and Community Development Act of 1974, which consolidates previous HUD preservation and urban renewal programs, authorized the three-year expenditure of $8.4 billion to states, counties, and units of local government in need of housing and employment opportunities. Its declared goal is to produce communities with decent housing, suitable living environments, and expanding economic opportunities principally for persons of low and moderate income. It calls for more rational use of land and other natural resources, better arrangement of residential, commercial, industrial, recreational, and other "activity centers," reduction of the geographical isolation of income groups in ghettos, promotion of greater income mixes, and restoration and preservation of properties of special historical, architectural, and environmental value. At least in its language the act is a stimulus to farsighted community planning.

Of course, whether or not all these things will be accomplished depends on the public input in each community, for the allocation of funds is decided by local officials. Preservation organizations have already made starts in that direction, using experience gleaned in past preservation programs to bring about other improvements in the community.

Relatives of the mansard-roofed Mt. Auburn House, focal point of Cincinnati's Mt. Auburn neighborhood revitalization program, can be found in almost any city.

In South Bend, Ind., and Los Gatos, Calif., monies will be used to establish revolving funds for loans and grants to rehabilitate housing in low-income areas. In Boston, homeowners with incomes of less than $16,000 a year will receive a 20 percent rebate on home repairs up to $3,000 under a new plan financed by the block grants. In Albany, N.Y., the Historic Albany Foundation and three other area organizations have formed the South Mall Community Development Coalition to coordinate planning and implementation of nearly a half million dollars in HCDA funds. The group has contributed substantial data to city officials and has surveyed residents, asking them about their interest in home ownership and their need for subsidized low-interest loans, and has also targeted buildings that need rehabilitating. The coalition additionally investigated other approaches to neighborhood rehabilitation—urban homesteading, nonprofit housing corporations—and has met with key lending institutions to assess the availability of mortgages.

Nearly $400,000 has been committed to new preservation programs in Louisville, Ky., including $35,000 for historic preservation planning and design services for older neighborhoods, $100,000 for a revolving fund, and $27,600 for the first phase of a three-year comprehensive inventory of historic resources—a program that will tally the number of potentially usable housing units.

In the face of dwindling energy sources and the consequent fade-out of across-the-board technological solutions, it is obvious that the approach we take to the things we have inherited will have to be governed by something besides the throw-away mentality of recent years. If the preservation philosophy—the appreciation and full use of all important resources—can become an integral part of the national outlook, and if these resources can be put to use for the good of all the people, then the things worth saving will be saved—not by special programs but as a natural part of our way of life.

The Soulard area of St. Louis, Mo., once an amalgam of ethnic "sub-ghettos," is making a come-back through private and city efforts and historic district designation.

FINANCIAL ASPECTS OF PRESERVATION

FINANCIAL ASPECTS OF PRESERVATION

A Preservation Daydream: The demolition crew assembles and machines line up for the initial swat. All of a sudden, who should appear but Preservation Person! By the sheer power of rhetoric, the bulldozer is stopped in mid-doze. A deft turn of phrase stirs in the workers a latent appreciation for vermiculated stone. And as the visitor points dramatically to the quoins and joists they were hired to destroy, strong workers weep and the crew walks off the job rather than tamper with such artistry.

Probably every active preservationist has had a similar daydream, or one in which someone knocks on the door with the check that will miraculously solve all the financial problems of saving a building. The thought of John D. Rockefeller, Jr., repeating his performance as the angel who restored Williamsburg dies hard.

If there ever was a time when such daydreams could become reality, that time has passed. Today there is lit-tle wisdom in waiting to bump into angels or calculating the cost of preservation in bake-sale receipts. Even the most eloquent of eleventh-hour laments is drowned out by the noise of the marketplace.

Economic pressures are a constant fact of life in preservation. Little has been achieved through rhetoric alone, no matter how brilliant. What saves old buildings and rejuvenates them is money. Historic preservation was once viewed as a charity that must be subsidized. As it has moved out of the realm of the historic house mu-

San Francisco's Hallidie Building (1918), a forerunner of the glass-curtain-walled office building, has been economically restored for office use.

seum and into the reuse of existing built resources, preservationists have found that reliance on private charity and, recently, government grants is not enough. The surest means to save a structure is to buy it. This is not always possible. Therefore, preservationists have been developing a variety of financial and economic tools and methods that can be used to save buildings.

Even with admirable purposes and realistic goals, saving and rejuvenating historic structures is not easy. Built into the current economic system are a number of disin-

Economic pressures in prime areas often destroy delicate urban balances created over decades or centuries, bringing about "Beauty and the Beast" situations such as on this stretch of Chicago's LaSalle Street.

centives to preservation. New construction and development are encouraged in many ways over preservation. The tax structure tends to favor new and bigger buildings. Building codes have for too long been geared to new construction. And lenders often do not consider old buildings good risks.

Not much hard data on the economics and financing of preservation can yet be readily found, but organizations such as the National Trust for Historic Preservation are beginning to systematically gather financial figures from preservationists and even developers, who have in the past been somewhat reluctant to divulge the secrets of their trade. With the City of Seattle's Historic Seattle Preservation and Development Authority, the National Trust in 1975 sponsored the first conference on

Below: The photographer who recorded the dismantling of Chicago's "economically unviable" Old Stock Exchange (1893) died accidentally in the wreckage. Opposite page: Not all rehab projects meet with immediate success. Although it opened up unique views of Portsmouth, N.H., conversion of the Rockingham Hotel (1885) to condominiums met with initial sales resistance.

the economic benefits of preserving old buildings, bringing together bankers, investors, developers, and preservationists from around the country. Proceedings of the conference, which investigated case studies of adaptive-use projects and the investment potential of old buildings, have been published by the National Trust's Preservation Press. The Urban Land Institute, a national organization of developers, also has begun collecting statistical material on the economics of preserving versus starting from scratch. Several analyses of adaptive-use projects have been presented in ULI's Project Reference File, a periodical providing detailed financial information on land development projects.

There are still a host of unknown factors in the economics of preservation, and not until further experience is gained and made available will some of the roadblocks to conserving the resources of the built environment be removed.

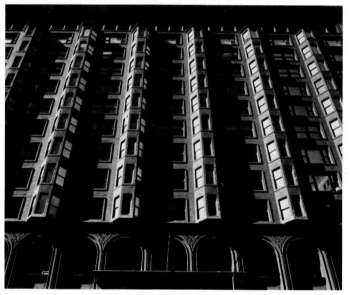

Some of its incomparable Sullivanesque details, removed and saved during demolition, are all that remain of the Old Stock Exchange in Chicago. Now the landmark's replacement also has been called "economically unviable."

COMMERCIAL AND PUBLIC BUILDINGS

Even the most outstanding landmarks are not safe from economic pressures. The Old Stock Exchange in Chicago, built in 1893 and designed by Chicago School architects Dankmar Adler and Louis H. Sullivan, is a classic case. Although the masterpiece generally enjoyed 100 percent occupancy through the years, its owners called it "economically unviable" in 1970. When the Chicago City Council refused to award the historic structure protective designation as a city landmark, preservationists, from private individuals to the Advisory Council on His-

toric Preservation, tried to save it through court battles, economic development proposals, legislation, and fundraising drives, all to no avail. The building was demolished in 1972. With an irony that often accompanies preservation tragedies, the owners of the forty-three-story building that replaced the Stock Exchange had to seek court approval in early 1975 for financial reorganization: the new structure had proved itself "economically unviable" within two years, when no more than one third of the space had been leased.

Yet citizens will rally round landmark structures and sometimes save them. What concerns us most in this book is the preservation of background buildings, those structures which en masse make up a vital part of the community—the groups of buildings and sites, the ensembles that provide integrity and character.

Warning preservationists of the nature of the commercial marketplace, Peter Blake, architect and critic, writes:

> I hate to be so cold-blooded about it, but it is just plain silly to believe that our cities are, as all those planning booklets say, "for people." They are not. They are for some people—i.e., investors. They exist for the sole purpose of making money.

Advice from investment counselor Edgar D. Schraub suggests that Blake's observation is true:

> A client of my office owned a large apartment house in New York City on a prime avenue. The building—18 stories high and occupying half a block—had been built by his family in the 1920s and had always been well rented. It was a very profitable operation. Several years ago, this client had asked me to advise him regarding a complete modernization program to update the building. He had in mind retaining the exterior "period" façade, but installing all new kitchens and baths, new elevators, new heating system and air-conditioning, etc. After a careful and intensive survey, my advice to this client was to tear down this 18-story fully-rented apartment house because the underlying ground had become worth more than the building. The price he would have gotten for the property as an income-producing deal would have been even less than the value of the vacant ground. Obviously, putting over a million dollars into a renovation program would have been throwing money away.
>
> After much anguished thought, my client went along with my recommendation, tore down the building, and erected a 47-story office building. He now has a real top-notch money maker.
>
> So, appreciation of the ground far outstripped the appreciation of the property as a whole. And who knows? Fifty or seventy-five years from now, it

may be economical to take down that 47-story office building to erect something else.

One of the important economic arguments for preservation, especially of commercial buildings, can be that it may be less expensive to use what is already there rather than start over—better to recycle than to reinvent the wheel. Developers and architects who work with older buildings indicate that costs of rehabilitating a basically sound structure can be competitive with new construction. What also counts is the rate of return on investment results. In many commercial rehabilitation projects, lower construction costs plus the acquisition costs, which are geared primarily to the value of the land rather than the building, have combined to produce a favorable rate of return.

When urban renewal plans called for tearing down a major portion of Denver's older buildings in 1965, a

The Larimer Square complex was one of the few survivors of Denver's Skyline Urban Renewal Project, which razed blocks of late-nineteenth-century buildings like the Cheesman (right) and Groff & Collins buildings (below).

partnership, Larimer Square Associates, was formed to develop one block of Victorian structures to twentieth-century use as a shopping complex. Even in 1973, the rehabilitation costs were running only about two thirds the average new construction cost in Denver. Trolley Square, a 13-acre shopping and entertainment center in Salt Lake City, Utah, was created in 1969 from old trolleys and turn-of-the-century car barns, costing about $20 a square foot to renovate.

A stained-glass dome from a demolished building adds to the exuberant nostalgic atmosphere of Salt Lake City's Trolley Square, a shopping and entertainment complex that proved to its developers that profitable commercial rehabilitation could succeed in a medium-sized city.

In the Pioneer Square Historic District in Seattle, Wash., during the last four years the cost of exterior restoration and interior renovation of twenty-one buildings from the 1890s has run from $18 to $22 per square foot, about two thirds the average new construction costs, even with the inclusion of air conditioning, seismic (earthquake) safety measures, and complete sprinkler systems. A 1974 feasibility study on restoring Baltimore's Old City Hall found that, taking into account a 12 per-

cent inflation rate, restoration costs in 1975–76 would be $29.50 per square foot as opposed to new construction costs ranging from $40 per square foot for city office buildings and from $60 to $100 per square foot for new city hall construction. A group of four 1860s cast-iron-front office buildings in Richmond, Va., is being restored for approximately $23 per square foot (compared with $40 per square foot for new construction) and in ten months rather than the eighteen months projected for a new building.

The U.S. General Services Administration, which is responsible for finding work space for federal agencies, agreed in 1969 to restore the Pioneer Courthouse in Portland, Ore. Its decision was based on the cost difference: $35 per square foot for rehabilitation versus an estimated $50 to $75 for new construction; a strong preservation boost from the court's judges did not hurt, however.

Commercial renovation and rehabilitation, besides being less costly to investors, also is profitable to the community. One of the oldest examples of how property values grow in a historic district is the Vieux Carré, the French Quarter of New Orleans. Protected by the Vieux Carré Commission, set up by the City Council in 1937, the area's commercial and residential property values have steadily increased, with the sharpest gains after 1960; today they are among the highest in the city. In

Faintly Mission Style, Trolley Square's buildings were erected in 1908 to house streetcars. The spacious and sound industrial complex adapted easily to its new use, providing an intangible quality plus competitive costs.

Even though the power of the purse is often controlling, the power of persuasion is still a necessary preservation ingredient. Rehabilitation of the Pioneer Courthouse (1869–73), Portland, Ore., was found to be cheaper than building new offices, but not until the judges personally intervened did the federal government decide to keep the old. The open-cage elevators, emblazoned with the initials "U.S.," were enclosed in new cabs and shafts.

Seattle's Pioneer Square Historic District, property values quadrupled between 1970 and 1973, from $1 million to $4.6 million; the value of building permits in the area rose 800 percent between 1970 and 1972, compared with permits in the rest of the city, which decreased 6 percent. The Capitol Hill area of Denver, which has only 0.7 percent of Denver's total land area and 6 percent of the city's dwellings, represents 18 percent of the city's property values, $250 million. As Annapolis, Md., restored its historic buildings from 1964 to 1971, the assessable tax base rose 112 percent, and at the rate of $8 to $10 million per year thereafter. Since 1968, tax revenues in both city and county have risen 85 percent, and tourism tenfold.

Preservation gives a community useful tools for stabilizing its economy. For example, it can make a town's business district competitive with regional shopping centers. It works best, however, if a community or neighborhood cooperates fully in the effort. When owners improve their property and the neighbors do not, the instigators are penalized and the recalcitrants benefit from their locations. Only when everyone cooperates can everyone benefit.

One of the names of the game is trust. In 1971 merchants in the Birmingham area of Pittsburgh, a declining

Businesses sometimes restore for noneconomic reasons. Inland Steel Development Corporation moved the canal-front Duvall Foundry (1856) in Washington, D.C., moved it back, and restored it "for good public relations."

neighborhood, were encouraged by the Pittsburgh History & Landmarks Foundation to embark on a speculative venture, renovating the interiors and restoring the exteriors of their nineteenth-century stores to attract shoppers and revitalize the area. None was willing to be the first, however, and the project was held up for several years. Recently, the local chamber of commerce pledged funds to provide rehabilitation loans, and new investors are venturing into the neighborhood.

Medina, Ohio, a town of 12,000 near Cleveland, went through a typical phase in the early 1960s of trying to bring its downtown "up to date" with aluminum siding and modern signs, despite the wealth of Victorian public and commercial buildings that made the town unique. In 1967 a citizens group provided merchants with free designs showing restoration possibilities, even suggesting paint colors. Voluntarily, without using a penny of government funds, the property owners restored the area— banks, department stores, the courthouse, and the public square. In 1975 the Medina Community Design Committee was cited for significant achievement in historic preservation by the National Trust.

Because cities cannot often afford to give up the tax revenue of "highest and best use" of structures in central business districts and few owners of historic structures can be expected to cheerfully ignore the unused development potential of their landmarks, attempts to relieve this pressure by transferring air or development rights

have been made in recent years. Pioneered in New York City, the concept was developed for a broader application by law professor John J. Costonis. Transfer of development rights as used in New York City allows the owner of a historic structure to sell unused development rights of the landmark site to the owner of an adjacent or contiguous site. That owner may then use the development rights to build a structure taller than is normally allowed for the site. The cost of preservation is thus absorbed by the development process itself, rather than by the city or the property owner. In Washington, D.C., sale of the development rights of the 1892–94 Christian Heurich Mansion to an adjacent property owner has been attempted to allow the developer to increase the density of his building. The money from the sale would be used to finance much-needed work on the mansion, which is located near Dupont Circle, a principal shopping and office area.

Although primarily aimed at the preservation of structures in downtown areas, where development pressures are most intense, the plan has also been adapted for use on property in suburban areas. In Montgomery County, Md., an ordinance to allow such transfers was adopted

Peer pressure helped to produce a revitalization of the business district of Medina, Ohio, along with increased patronage. Its bandstand and Victorianized courthouse (1841, 1873) also were restored and a historic district created.

and used to save a late-eighteenth-century farmhouse and its outbuildings. The group of historic structures is to become a community center; the development rights are to be used on high- and low-rise apartment buildings on adjoining land.

Some have criticized development rights transfers as being a form of "bribery": saving landmarks by allowing developers to violate ceiling limitations or to expand outward in larger structures than normally allowed. The city zoning exemption granted the Christian Heurich Mansion is a case in point—taken to court by a citizens' association opposed to the transfer. In general, though, the principle represents one approach to the complex problem of saving urban landmarks and it may spark other creative efforts.

The proposed transfer of unused development rights of the Christian Heurich Mansion (1892–94) to an office building to be constructed nearby would lessen the financial pressures on the small-scale Washington, D.C., landmark.

RESIDENTIAL STRUCTURES

PRIVATE FUNDING SOURCES

The traditional reluctance of commercial lending institutions to provide loans and mortgage financing for the purchase, renovation, and rehabilitation of older properties is lessening somewhat because of preservationists' educational and lobbying efforts. Some of the nation's largest developers and financial institutions are involved in multi-million-dollar commercial ventures based on historic preservation, yet many banks and lending institutions still have to be convinced that preservation can be a good investment. Some groups therefore have taken the initiative to demonstrate that fact.

Low-interest loan programs to aid rehabilitation have been established in such cities as San Francisco, Norfolk, Va., and Minneapolis. San Francisco's Rehabilitation

Assistance Program (RAP) helps property owners in certain areas of the city renovate their houses; $20 million in municipal bonds was issued and purchased by a commercial bank to be lent to eligible property owners at 5.5 percent interest. The Norfolk Redevelopment and Housing Authority also uses the resources of local banks to provide low-interest rehabilitation loans for owners in so-called conservation areas. The Minneapolis Housing and Redevelopment Authority administers a loan and grant program with interest rates geared to a homeowner's annual gross income.

Enterprising property owners have gotten around the high interest rates on improvement and restoration loans for commercial purposes. In Manhattan, for example, the owner of a brownstone collects a year or two of rent in advance before his tenants move in. This is enough money to pay for customized interior renovation of the apartments they have chosen. The property is thus preserved on what amounts to an interest-free loan.

GOVERNMENT FUNDING SOURCES

The prospective buyer of an old house would do well to investigate various sources of government assistance to aid rehabilitation. A number of government programs, primarily in the U.S. Department of Housing and Urban Development, have been devised to encourage rehabilitation of residential property. One of the most recent is the Urban Reinvestment Task Force, a joint effort of

Sale of the Heurich Mansion's development rights would enable its historical society owner to restore and maintain the house and to protect features such as the copper conservatory (opposite page) and brass stairway (below).

Preservation in San Francisco, like its topography, has ups and downs. Downtown, businesses are trying to erect bigger buildings on landmark sites, while many city residential areas such as this are as yet aloof from such financial pressures.

Unlike many Victorian rows in San Francisco (opposite page), neglected neighborhoods like Baltimore's Otterbein area (above) require government aid. The city is one of those adapting the old homestead system to recycle needed housing and has published rehabilitation guidelines to assist homesteaders.

HUD and the Federal Home Loan Bank Board. The program is aimed at helping revitalize deteriorated neighborhoods through the establishment of Neighborhood Housing Services. The objective of these organizations is to promote cooperation among residents, financial institutions, and local governments in addressing the problem of housing shortages. The Oakland, Calif., Neighborhood Housing Services, Inc., for example, encourages housing rehabilitation by making local financing available for home improvements. The high-risk revolving loan fund program lends at flexible terms and is backed up with technical assistance provided by a task force for development phases of projects.

The Housing and Community Development Act of 1974 also makes funds available to local government units for historic preservation programs. Through the Community Development Block Grant Program, which consolidates such former HUD programs as Historic Preservation, Open Space, Urban Beautification, Code Enforcement, and Urban Renewal grants, assistance is geared in part to conserving the nation's housing supply and rehabilitating and preserving resources of historical, architectural, and aesthetic value. Among the activities eligible for funding are the establishment of revolving funds for the rehabilitation of publicly and privately owned structures and the acquisition, disposition, and moving of properties for preservation. (Further discussion of the act's provisions can be found on page 247.)

The act also continues authorization for the program known as Urban Homesteading. Federally owned urban housing transferred to city governments is disposed of at nominal fees or at no charge to individuals who agree to rehabilitate the structures within certain time limits. In Philadelphia, the program was established in 1973, and as of June 1975 seventy-five properties had been awarded primarily to families in the $6,000 to $10,000 income range. The program also has been used in Wilmington, Del., Baltimore, and Washington, D.C.

REVOLVING FUNDS

In older neighborhoods that are valuable not because of single landmarks but because of their total character,

preservation groups are attempting to save several structures at once. As explained in the book *Revolving Funds for Historic Preservation:*

There are whole neighborhoods of old houses, houses that were once pleasant to see and inhabit, that have been neglected and knocked about, but are not too far gone for redemption. . . . It is in such neighborhoods that the preservationist, aided by good will, clarity of purpose, and money—always money—can work to create and maintain a good environment that continues rather than freezes history. Even if there are no architectural gems, merely competent builder's houses of a century or so past, the rejuvenation of such a neighborhood, if within the preservationist's means, may have a reward equal to or greater than the opening of a house museum. If museums are part of the good communal life, so, all the more, are homes and streets—places to shelter people and form a setting for their activities, conveniently and with style and character.

Because controlling such large areas generally calls for far more financial resources than a group can muster, many have instituted revolving funds for preservation, whereby the same dollars can be used repeatedly to save as many structures and sites as possible. The revolving fund can be cash, equities, lines of credit, or any combination of these, and is used to buy properties in the active real estate market. Purchased properties are then resold as soon as possible to private individuals (with certain restrictions to provide for the property's restoration and preservation). The money from those sales is returned to the fund for loans to purchase or restore other properties. The most valuable aspect of such funds is that they buy time until sympathetic owners can be found.

A revolving fund has been used to revitalize Lafayette Square in St. Louis, a twenty-five-block residential area near the central business district composed of mid-to-late-nineteenth-century town houses and mansions. In the late 1960s several families purchased houses in the square and began renovating them. The Lafayette Square Restoration Committee was formed to promote preservation and restoration efforts in the area. The section's Northeast Quadrant, which contained nearly a third of the structures, was threatened with demolition for a highway, however. LSRC proposed to use a revolving fund to try to spur preservation efforts. After making a survey, LSRC decided to concentrate the fund's work in the Northeast Quadrant to act as a catalyst. Seven of the most dilapidated properties were purchased. The exteriors of the buildings were renovated and they were made as watertight as possible. The group then marketed the houses aggressively and sold them with certain restrictive covenants to assure future preservation. Within three years, the LSRC revolving fund contributed markedly to the revitalization of this in-town residential area. Now, 85 percent of the 400 houses are under restoration.

In Galveston, Tex., the Galveston Historical Foundation established a revolving fund for a different purpose, to revitalize an area of predominantly nineteenth-century commercial structures known as the Strand. Although the foundation used a funding method similar to the Lafayette Square group's, it found that the problems of preserving a commercial area were quite different from those involved in a residential neighborhood. The buildings are much larger, at least 15,000 square feet overall, and the question whether to restore a building was no longer one that could be viewed in terms of personal desire; rather, it centered on whether enough rents could be generated to make the building economical. Because of the use of the revolving fund, coupled with public support for the area, efforts are beginning to show that the Strand can become a vital and active area once again.

Other groups around the country also have been using the revolving fund tool to help conserve buildings. Historic Savannah, Historic Charleston, and Historic Annapolis all use revolving funds to conserve buildings in their downtown areas. The Pittsburgh History & Landmarks Foundation has employed a revolving fund technique to make older residential buildings functional for several income groups, changing the interiors as well as exteriors to make run-down structures into livable and attractive dwellings. These are then rented at a variety of rates, with low-income residents renting under a leased housing program of the local housing authority.

Since 1971 the National Trust for Historic Preservation has administered a revolving fund, the National Historic Preservation Fund, to assist its nonprofit member organizations in establishing their own local revolving funds. One such loan to the Historic Fredericksburg Foundation of Fredericksburg, Va., aided in the preservation of structures in its eighteenth-century historic district. Another was awarded to the Lafayette Square Restoration Committee for its fund, and another to the Heritage Hill Foundation in Grand Rapids, Mich., to assist with the preservation of a historic district of nineteenth- and twentieth-century properties. A grant from the National Trust's fund helped in the refinement of an estab-

Once known as the "Wall Street of the Southwest," Galveston's Strand is now putting elegance back into the marketplace through a revolving fund used to purchase and resell properties with protective deed restrictions.

lished revolving fund administered by Greater Portland Landmarks in Maine. A loan to Historic Ithaca in Ithaca, N.Y., was used to continue the renovation and adaptive use of the downtown Clinton House Hotel (1830). The National Trust program awards money in the form of challenge loans for two reasons. First, its preservation fund is based on a limited endowment, so the Trust wants as many member organizations as possible to benefit from the money by saving as many properties as possible. Second, by requiring matching monies, the Trust attempts to develop community interest through local fund-raising efforts.

TAX ROADBLOCKS

The property and income tax problem goes to the heart of preservation. Whenever property is improved, the tax system assumes that an increased economic potential will be realized and that the benefits should be shared with the community. But in a city full of Empire State Buildings or World Trade Centers, in an area where even thirteen or fifty floors of money-making space are permitted, big trouble is obviously looming over a modest construction built B.O.E. (Before Otis Elevator). Property tax emphasis on "highest and best use," or greatest income potential, often means that small old buildings can be taxed as if they were tall modern buildings, depending on the area's zoning; this is so because the land on which the small old building sits could be used for a big building, which is presumed to be the highest and best use of the land. This system is an incentive not to preserve.

Although restored by the Galveston Junior League before the revolving fund started, the Trueheart-Adriance Building (1881–82) has been a pivotal structure in increasing interest in the Strand. On what is now a soup and sandwich shop, the building's polychrome stonework was brought out during restoration.

Several efforts have been undertaken to develop a solution that would help conserve usable older buildings without affecting tax revenues to a great degree. A number of states are studying the effects of changing tax policies and awarding tax abatements and credits to those willing to improve or protect historic properties. In California, for example, a state landmark or one in the National Register of Historic Places may be named by local governments a historic "zone"; if the owner agrees to preserve the building and allow public visual observation for a certain number of years, taxes will be based on actual rather than potential use. A similar provision exists in the District of Columbia. In Puerto Rico, partial restoration of a significant building in the Old San Juan Historic District exempts the owner from real property tax for five years; total restoration provides ten tax-free years. Rents received during the same time are also exempted.

Maryland counties are allowed to give tax credits against local real property tax of up to 10 percent of the cost of restoring a building in a historic district or 5 percent of the cost of constructing a compatible new building in the area. In New York City the rehabilitation of multiresidential dwellings (such as brownstone rooming houses) is encouraged by providing relief from taxes on

Rising from the ashes of its old home, Baltimore's Center Stage reopened in this 1856 school in less time and at less cost than it would have taken to build a new site.

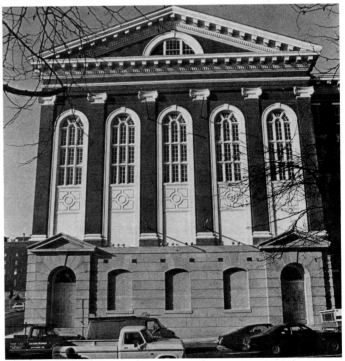

the costs of capital improvements such as renovating interiors or installing new plumbing or electrical systems.

In 1975 the State of Oregon approved four major tax bills as incentives to renovation and preservation. The most comprehensive, declaring it to be state policy to preserve historic architecture, provides for commercial and residential properties included in historic districts listed in the National Register to be individually certified by the state historic preservation officer for assessment at the same value for fifteen years. Thus, the new law makes restoration improvement a virtually tax-free enterprise. Other laws allow single-family residences in industrial, commercial, or high-density residential areas to be taxed at actual rather than potential use; give five-year exemptions on rehabilitation work to non-owner-occupied rental housing of twenty-five years or older; and exempt owner-occupied single-family residences from value-added tax for replacements, repair, or maintenance.

Federal income tax policies, rather than encouraging the conservation of older buildings, provide incentives for their demolition and the construction of new buildings. The Internal Revenue Service Code allows owners to deduct from income the expense of demolition and the unrecovered investment in a building, regardless of its architectural or historical worth; in addition, the federal system permits accelerated tax depreciation on new buildings. From recommendations by the Council on Environmental Quality, the National Trust, and the Advisory Council on Historic Preservation, among others, tax reforms were first proposed to Congress in the President's 1972 environmental program as a step "to encourage preservation of historic buildings and structures." Congress is considering this reform along with others. Legislation also has been introduced to change the evaluation system for historic properties for federal estate tax purposes. In 1976 the National Trust sponsored the first conference to examine the effects of public tax policies on the conservation of the built environment; co-sponsors included the National Park Service, the Advisory Council, and the National Conference of State Historic Preservation Officers.

DOES SUCCESS SPOIL PRESERVATION?

Not always the purpose of preservation, but a good by-product if controlled, tourism usually increases in preserved areas. In every state, tourism is one of the three largest revenue-producing industries; nationally, tourism has increased 350 percent in the past twenty years. Many may think that this happens only if their community is an Annapolis or a Nantucket, but this is not so. Milan, Ohio, draws more than 20,000 visitors a year because of a single site, the birthplace of Thomas Edison.

The town's population is 2,000. Today there are approximately fifty motels in the area surrounding Milan, and tourist dollars are generated throughout the community. But it is not mandatory to boast a famous person's birthplace or the site of a famous event; tourism can develop, if it is desired, on the basis that a place is pleasant to stop in or shop in.

A current success story illustrates how preservation in one area of a town can, like a pebble in a pond, affect and improve the whole community, bringing many fringe benefits. Jacksonville, Ore., boomed to life in 1852 when gold was discovered in nearby Rich Gulch. Eventually the mines ran out, the railroad passed it by, and Jacksonville dwindled to 1,000 people, staying at that level until 1962 (it now numbers about 2,000 people). The residents had few positive ideas about shaping Jacksonville's future. But they knew what they didn't want. They defeated a proposed highway that would have cut across eight city blocks. Then, because they realized they had a historic area, they also refused to go along with a federal plan for urban renewal. Instead, a historic preservation ordinance was enacted to protect their historic properties, and Jacksonville was added to the National Register of Historic Places.

Jacksonville, Ore., businesses helped to reverse the boom town's decline by capitalizing on its old buildings. The ornamental brickwork and bracketed cornice of the Masonic Building (1875) are typical of the restored business district.

A group of business people who also were concerned about saving Jacksonville's integrity persuaded key businesses to forgo new buildings in favor of preserving and restoring their unique properties. This action, which cost roughly $600,000 for interior renovation and exterior restoration of stores, banks, and offices, renewed the physical environment and created a good climate for further investment. Jacksonville, which did not set out to attract tourists, draws 150,000 to 200,000 people annually; based on national averages, visitors spend approximately $600,000 to $800,000 a year in that tiny community.

Through a variety of experimental financial and preservation techniques, including attracting new business ventures, Harrisville, N.H., has been able to remain a living community, saved "not because it is old, but because it is good."

Almost ironically, one of the problems that preservationists now have to face is what happens if or when they succeed. What has happened in a number of places around the country is that preservation has succeeded almost too well. Places such as the Vieux Carré in New Orleans and the Georgetown area of Washington, D.C., have become, because of preservation efforts, exceedingly chic. Sales prices and rents tend to be much higher than in other parts of the city. In such areas, existing residents are either pushed out because they cannot afford the rents or they cash in because of the price their houses can command. Either way the makeup of the people, the central element of any area, changes markedly. The "restored" qualities of the environments are major tourist attractions, and tourism creates its own problems. Because the areas are pre-automobile, the streets are easily clogged with traffic. Because of the desirability of locating in the area, commercial rents are high and stores tend to be high-volume and oriented to the tourist market. These areas have begun to lose some of the amenities that once made them desirable.

Riding on the crest of what appeared to be successful rejuvenation of historic districts, one large eastern city government announced that it was undertaking a major planning effort to revitalize a section of the city using established preservation techniques. Real estate speculators, knowing what had happened to the real estate market in other historic districts, began buying up houses as soon as the city announced its intentions. In all, the preparation of the plan for the area's preservation and revitalization took about two years. When the final document emerged, it called for the government to purchase easements on the buildings in the area as a means of assuring that owners had enough money to upgrade their structures. The idea was that by using easements the city could keep the existing residents and at the same time revitalize the area. However, by the time the plan appeared, few of the residents who had been there two years previously, and at whom the plan was aimed, were still there. They had been bought out by speculators. Today, little more than a document of good intentions has resulted, and the city government is in a quandary.

Fortunately, the problem is being recognized and some attempts are being made to counteract this reverse effect of profitable preservation. A scenic, almost archetypical New England town with mill buildings, white steepled churches, and white frame houses began slowly dying several years ago. By using a variety of preservation devices and economic enticements, new life was breathed into it. Today the town is flourishing and has a solid economic base. But there is a conscious effort among its residents and preservers to avoid too much publicity precisely because many are afraid of just the kind of thing that happened in New Orleans and Georgetown. Without sacrificing the existing residents in the process or destroying the character of the area, other preservation solutions are being sought in order to maintain and enhance the very qualities of the town that made people want to save it in the first place.

This almost archetypical New England town is making a conscious effort to keep its preservation from spoiling its success as a good place to live.

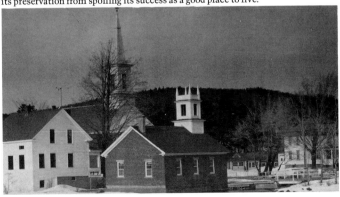

USING OLD BUILDINGS

What do you do with an abandoned piano factory that covers 250,000 square feet and is said to have been the second largest building in America when it was completed in 1853—exceeded in size only by the U.S. Capitol?

The Chickering Piano Company, which built the factory in Boston, manufactured its pianos there until the mid-1930s. After that, the building served several light manufacturing uses, gradually acquiring various small businesses and some artists as tenants. The massive structure was underused, however, and deteriorated rapidly. By 1971 the owners, faced with an investment that gave meager returns, were seriously in arrears in property taxes.

Conversion of Boston's former Chickering Piano Factory (1853) into artists' studio apartments is one example of what can be done with unused commercial and industrial buildings to provide housing at less than it costs to build anew.

The factory's location on Tremont Street in Boston's South End was a good one. The building was structurally sound. Its tower, its Italianate detailing, its 22,500-square-foot courtyard, and its two-story entrance lobby made it aesthetically pleasing. These factors plus excellent natural lighting and the volume of uncluttered space in its manufacturing areas seemed to demand that the building be used.

Architects and planners Gelardin/Bruner/Cott, Inc., called in to redesign a furniture showroom in the building, were intrigued with the old building. After some study they concluded that the factory could be adapted to studio apartments for artists and craftsmen. Coordinated space of this kind was not then available on a large scale in Boston and, happily, there were potential clients, so the decision was made to adapt the factory to new use.

Because the architects liked and understood the building, they decided "not to be precious, but rather to let the building be itself, and not force it into a mold." The two-story entrance lobby was renovated as a gallery and a coffee shop; the bulk of the space was divided into 174 studio apartments. Throughout the building the wooden columns, plumbing pipes, conduits for electrical connections, and brick walls were left exposed. Wooden floors were patched rather than matched. The result was a deliberate contrast of the original with the replacement, making the transition visible.

Because maximum use was made of the space, unit costs were kept to $10.50 a square foot. The architects say they could do the same thing today for about $18.00 a square foot, compared with $30.00 to start over. The Massachusetts Housing Financing Agency backed the project with nearly $3.4 million. Operated by the Piano Craft Guild, the Chickering building is now fully rented, and there's new life in the old piano factory.

Using old buildings for new needs is by no means a phenomenon of recent vintage. As Ogden Nash said:

> As American towns and cities I wander through,
> One landmark is constant everywhere I roam;
> The house that the Banker built in nineteen-two,
> Dim neon tells me is now a funeral home.

It is a curious idea that the old opulence, high ceilings, ornate detail, and spaciousness we find uneconomical for the living are thought appropriate for the dead. But, call it adaptive use, recycling, renovation, rehabilitation, even restoration, with funereal neon or not, such buildings are still around to be used for some purpose, and that is the point of adaptive use—bringing them back alive. The rationale for converting old spaces to new uses is summed up well in a recent study prepared for the National Endowment for the Arts, *Federal Architecture: Adaptive Use Facilities:*

> In the United States, what once seemed an endless supply of land and other resources discouraged any sustained interest in adapting old but sound structures for contemporary needs. Conscious application of this technique was limited to a handful of architects and decision makers, to admirers of aging architectural gems, and to the poor, who adapted from necessity. Since the late 1960s, however, economic and social forces have made adaptive use of existing structures an increasingly promising alternative to new construction.

Urban renewal in the sense of bulldoze-everything-and-start-over-again is no longer the wave of the future. Too many sections of cities still look like pictures of cities bombed in World War II and have waited even longer to be rebuilt. Preservation is now commonly being viewed as a means of renewing cities through intelligent reuse of existing resources. It is difficult if not impossible to define one process or formula for finding new lives for old buildings. It is a creative act, calling for the ingenuity, determination, and sensitivity of a matchmaker. The process is really just that: matching today's needs to yesterday's resources.

In a sense, most of the early historic preservation efforts in the United States were adaptive uses. Homes were turned into museums. Adaptive use, however, need not be limited to the adaptation of architecturally or historically significant buildings. It can take as many forms as it has names. A building also can be adapted to contemporary requirements and continue to serve in the same way it always did. The nineteenth-century church

that has been abandoned by one congregation may easily continue in the same use for another, making room for twentieth-century building requirements such as indoor restrooms, fire exits, and other safety measures. Houses can still be houses. Adaptive use means simply that buildings are modified to some degree to meet contemporary demands.

Old buildings have become all sorts of things. Factories are being developed as shopping centers as well as apartments; an icehouse has been converted to offices, schools to housing, a parking garage to a movie theater, churches to restaurants; a bold plan is under way to open grain elevators to residential use. Even those houses that become funeral parlors sometimes come full circle. In Cleveland, architect Charles Friedrich Schweinfurth's own 1894 home took on the "dim neon" of the William L. Wagner and Son Funeral Home from 1929 to 1969. Cleveland architect R. Van Petten purchased the building in 1970 and turned it back into a residence.

But it must be remembered that not all preservation

Apartments in the Piano Factory were given open plans so that they could double as artists' studios. The building's central entrance, shown here, leads into a gallery where the works of resident artists are displayed.

begins with specific community or individual needs. In the case of some older buildings—perhaps in all—it is just as valid to say that preservation begins with a building's need to be saved. Just as in the case of the Chickering Piano Factory, the aesthetic qualities, spaces, and structural elements seem to demand that they be reused. These buildings deserve continued life, even if a long search is required to find an appropriate use. A case in point is one of the current favorites of the adaptive-use world, railroad stations. From Atchison to Topeka to Santa Fe—almost literally—cities with grand terminals and picturesque depots are seeking and finding a multitude of uses for them.

Nevertheless, adaptive use is still relatively unique in many areas, and new uses often have not been especially imaginative, or new. In fact, one of the pre-eminent restoration architects in the United States, Charles Peterson, once said, "Cautions might be posted against what I call the 'Boutique-Guitar-and-Drippy Candle boom.' There's nothing too wrong about that but it's a fad that next year might quickly turn into a craze for parachute jumping, Chihuahua dogs and Polynesian nose flutes."

Adaptive use has become popular in this country because it seems to many people that it offers positive benefits in economic and social terms. The market for renovation of older structures was expected to reach $10 billion in 1975. Depending on the state of repair in which a building is found, costs of recycling the space and bringing it up to modern codes are often below those of comparable new construction. Architectural critic Sherban Cantacuzino wrote recently in *New Uses for Old Buildings:* "It does not take long to see that in the recent past it has been more often than not substantially cheaper—sometimes ridiculously so—to convert than to build new. The economic argument for rehabilitation or conversion is indeed a powerful one." The engineering, technology, and craftsmanship of many older buildings offer distinctive features that are often not found in modern structures. As everyone knows, "They just don't build them like that any more." In comparison with the unit construction of modern buildings, many prefer the individuality that an old building can offer.

Of course, not everyone likes old buildings, and adaptive use is not always successful in either aesthetic or economic terms. Developers and architects both often shy away from old buildings. For many years, professional ego led architects to create their own monuments, and this usually meant new buildings. Other old buildings have been destroyed by misguided efforts to "restore" them just as surely as if they had been demolished. What an insensitive reuse of an old building can do is strip the building of its character and vitality, the thing that made it valuable in the first place. And incor-

porating merely one wall of an old building in a new structure does not really qualify as adaptive use. There has been something of a shift among architects, however, and many today view the integration of new uses into old buildings as a creative and demanding task no less than designing a new structure, perhaps even more so. From the developer's standpoint, there may be factors in adapting an old building that are not known before construction starts, and these unforeseen problems can sometimes place adaptive-use projects in serious financial trouble. On balance, however, the adaptation of old buildings to new uses has the potential to save part of the past while producing an economically satisfactory use.

"The building itself is the sign," says the owner of the Gandy Dancer Restaurant in Ann Arbor, Mich., in explaining the near-absence of signs on the Richardsonian-style building, which started life in 1886 as a railroad station.

Adaptive use does have some additional advantages that are not readily quantifiable but are nevertheless important. The seniority of old buildings in the community and what is called their "recognition factor," the quality of being known to people, can be a definite economic asset. If a known landmark is in the center of a business community the restorer can count on a predisposed clientele and attract some invaluable good will. It is undeniable that older buildings develop character and that their ambience or historical associations can be used

First as a gospel tabernacle, then as Ryman Auditorium, this 1892 Nashville, Tenn., landmark adapted to changing social and entertainment needs. Until its performers were moved to new quarters, it was best known as the home of the Grand Ole Opry.

for valuable publicity if the owner is so inclined. In Ann Arbor the Gandy Dancer Restaurant, built as a Michigan Central Railroad depot in 1886 and converted to new use in 1971, got its name from the crew of railroad workers who hammered the tracks in rhythm under the supervision of their Irish boss, Gandy. Gandy's "dancers" lend their colorful story to the restaurant's public image.

An important plus factor of adaptive use is that a building already exists; materials are there to be reused. Herbert McLaughlin, a San Francisco architect and developer of adaptive-use projects, maintains that rehabilitation of commercial structures has some economic side benefits that cannot be realized with new construction. Old buildings that are being adapted often can continue functioning during the conversion process. In the rehabilitation of San Francisco's Boldeman Chocolate Factory, for example, tenants stayed in the building during the planning and marketing phases of the rehabilitation. This allowed a cash flow to be maintained during part of the project, McLaughlin pointed out in a recent article in the National Trust magazine, *Historic Preservation*. The new School of Architecture of the University of Tennessee at Knoxville rescued Estabrook Hall, an 1869 classroom building scheduled for demolition. Its design features, solid construction, high ceilings, and light sources provided the character sought by the school. During the six-month period when work was in progress, classes were often held in the midst of construction. Design and construction were carried out by the faculty members of the department and the university maintenance and operating crews. Today the building is in almost twenty-four-hour use by students. If the building is abandoned,

of course, there is no displacement of people. The sheer difference in time spent in getting a new building up and ready for occupancy, along with the costs that proliferate between demolition and new construction, argues for adaptive use of older structures.

Teknor Apex Company of Pawtucket, R.I., created new offices by connecting an old factory and cinder block building with a courtyard repeating the factory's brick arches.

New construction, unless it begins on already cleared land, drains energy in the clearing process: fuel for heavy earth-moving machinery and for demolition bulldozers, the work time of laborers, and the noise and air pollution that accompany such work. If the site is in a crowded urban area, delays or disruptions of traffic and time loss can hardly be calculated. In addition, much of the razed building material ends up as debris, unused except as landfill, representing almost total waste. The manufacture of new materials such as plastics, aluminum, concrete, and steel further depletes natural supplies. Generally, the production of modern materials used in new construction consumes far more energy than that of older materials such as brick, wood, glass, and stone.

Adaptive use also is more energy-efficient than much new construction. Older structures built in the days when technology was limited and common sense prevailed often use less energy and use it more efficiently than do new ones, creating less of a drain on resources and costing less to operate. Many new structures, especially office buildings, are sealed off from the elements, operating more like filing cabinets for humans and making it necessary to produce mechanically a livable climate. The recent federal adaptive-use study noted that "the thick load-bearing masonry walls which characterize older structures delay heat loss and gain and conserve energy more effectively than the glass curtain walls and highly fenestrated shells which enclose more modern structures." Comparisons of total energy consumption in new buildings with that of rehabilitated old buildings must take into account "additional energy costs to society of materials, equipment and transportation fuels expended during the building's lifetime." The report concludes: "When evaluated from this standpoint, adapted buildings offer vastly reduced lifetime energy expenditures. Assuming a soundness of structural elements and shell, the reuse of older buildings substantially reduces demand for energy intensive building materials."

Adaptive-use projects are labor-intensive, that is, the major costs associated with a project are labor-related rather than material-related. "Viewed in the context of the total economy," the government report points out, "this has a positive side. Adaptive-use projects produce more jobs for a given expenditure." While this may be true, the rate of inflation reflected in salaries and wages and the scarcity of competent craftsmen who can sympathetically work with old buildings have increased costs of renovation projects in the last few years. The result, according to *New Uses for Old Buildings*, is that "more recent projects suggest that new uses for old buildings may be economically justified in the future only if the unquantifiable value of age and character is added to the sum." The government report concludes basically the same thing.

But there is no denying that renovated buildings provide variety, interesting spaces, a more human scale, and often profitability. Perhaps the classic example of adaptive use in the United States is Ghirardelli Square in San Francisco. The square was a collection of buildings that once housed a chocolate factory. Beginning in 1962 the buildings were converted to an elaborate shopping complex with many specialty stores. Ghirardelli Square has spawned numerous similar projects in San Francisco and around the country. A profitable venture for the developer, it increased tourism and added to the vitality of San Francisco—and made good use of some nice old buildings.

The invention of the urban, multiuse commercial square ushered in the Preservation Age. Above: The Cannery, near San Francisco's Ghirardelli Square, was created around an old canning factory (c. 1909). Opposite page and below: Canal Square on the historic Chesapeake & Ohio Canal in the Georgetown area of Washington, D.C., mixes old warehouses and new buildings.

The start of the Preservation Age may have come with the invention, not of the wheel, but of the square: Ghirardelli Square, Larimer Square, Trolley Square, Canal Square, Bakery Square, Quaker Square. Tied for glory with the square is the roundhouse, the sheds, the depot, the tracks—anything having to do with railroad stations, the superstars of the recycling galaxy. With the demise of the passenger train as a prime means of transportation, railroad stations have become, to use the British term, redundant structures. Railroad passenger stations once were an expression of civic pride and highly useful

Right: Using a milk-bottling plant and other manufacturing buildings, Brooklyn's Downtown Bedford-Stuyvesant commercial-office-recreational complex is part of a broader restoration effort to make Bed-Stuy "a place to live, not to leave."

With the decline of passenger train travel, many old stations have had to turn to new uses to survive, but some continue to serve railroad needs. Cleveland's B&O Station (1898) is now a freight office.

Creation of the Beverly Depot Restaurant & Saloon in Beverly, Mass., retained not only the town's 1897 train station but its railroading aura as well. The waiting room has become a saloon complete with train clock, and the waiters are dressed in trainmen's clothes.

buildings. Today, however, many that remain are underused or abandoned. Because of their locations in or near the centers of towns and cities and because of the space they provide, they have become excellent candidates for adaptive use, and in some places are even being reused as passenger stations.

In Baltimore, Md., the Mount Clare Station (1831) has been converted to a railroad museum for the B&O/C&O Railroad, while the Mount Royal Station (1896) became the home of the Maryland Institute, College of Art a decade ago. Mt. Vernon, Ohio, has turned its station into a senior citizens' center, and in Yuma, Ariz., the station has become an arts center. In Montgomery, Ala., a civic center flourishes by the tracks. In Menlo Park, Calif., an 1867 station houses the chamber of commerce. In Altamont, N.Y., the small frame train station located on the town green is the home of an insurance agency.

Historic union stations such as the one in Indianapolis, Ind. (1888), provide multi-use space for a variety of functions including public space, offices, shops, and restaurants. The City National Bank of Lincoln, Neb., sought space for a branch office by drawing a circle on a map to get legally outside the radius of the parent bank building; the French Chateauesque-style Rock Island Depot (1893) was found and now serves as the branch. In

Waterbury, Conn., the station with its great tower offered space and the perfect location for a local newspaper plant because it was adjacent to the tracks bringing newsprint. The 1909 Southern Railways Terminal Station in Chattanooga, Tenn., was abandoned in 1970 but was bought by a developer and is now in operation as the Chattanooga Choo-Choo, a hotel/shop/museum/gardens/theater/world's largest model railroad/coffeehouse/and ice cream extravaganza, profiting from the 10 million

A "for sale" sign has replaced the names of the past users of this octagonal frame house in Homer, N.Y. Built about 1902 as a residence, it was adapted as a circus training house, a restaurant and bakery, and, finally, the Circus House Restaurant.

tourists who pass through Tennessee on the interstate from Florida to the Midwest.

Stations in many other parts of the country have found new uses as restaurants. In Boonton, N.J., a local developer has visions of developing a commercial center

While continuing to serve rail passengers, the Spanish Mission–style Santa Fe Railroad Station (1914–15) in San Diego also serves other travelers as part of the move to convert unused train stations to intermodal transportation centers.

called The Station as a means of revitalizing the town, with the railroad depot as the focus. The complex is viewed as an alternative to stores along the highway and the shopping malls around northern New Jersey.

In some places train stations are being reused as passenger stations. Amtrak is studying the possibility of increasing passenger use by rerouting trains once more into and through towns, in the process reopening old stations already conveniently located. In San Diego, Calif., the Santa Fe terminal (1915) will be a transportation center, serving trains, buses, airport ticketing facilities, and connecting transportation.

Because of the care lavished on their design and their central role in a community's life, America's railroad stations of the past century and a half have been likened to Europe's thirteenth-century cathedrals. Shown is a mosaic-lined interior of San Diego's Santa Fe Station, whose construction, paradoxically, caused the demolition of a station built only in 1887. The new depot's Spanish Mission style, in vogue for the 1915 Panama-California Exposition, has endured much longer.

Not all stations fare so well, even registered landmarks. The interior of noted architect Daniel Burnham's Union Station (1903–8) in Washington, D.C., a National Historic Landmark, has been gouged out and a wing demolished to make way for a National Visitor Center, leaving train passengers to fend for themselves. H. H. Richardson's famed Union Station (1885–87) in New London, Conn., barely survived an onslaught of demolition threats, but it is now restored for use as a transportation center, with two floors being leased to Amtrak, as well as a restaurant, shops, and offices. Preservationists also claim that more money has been spent in vacillating on whether or how to save the Cincinnati Union Terminal (1933) than it would have cost to adapt it. The future of the Beaux-Arts Grand Central Station (1913) in New York City has been tied up in the courts for years, and of course, there are those stations—like Grand Central's neighbor, Pennsylvania Station—that simply are not around any more.

Other community needs are being fulfilled through adaptive use.

"There are people, after all, who will never go to see rainbows because their umbrellas might spring leaks," wrote the *Cincinnati Post* when five years of effort to convert the city's Union Terminal for school and transit use were recently aborted.

The escalator between the first and second levels in Minneapolis's old-new Butler Square office and retail complex offers an unparalleled view of the interior atrium created to bring light to tenants and browsers.

HOUSING

It is easy to see that people are using old buildings. Many books and magazine articles in publications ranging from *The New York Times* and *Better Homes and Gardens* to *New Times* attest to the popularity of "restoring" or revitalizing old houses. Neighborhood revitalization is becoming a more common phenomenon in most center cities. Myriad studies and proposals have been made to encourage this work. Last year the U.S. Department of Housing and Urban Development published *Neighborhood Preservation: A Catalog of Local Programs*, listing 100 representative projects from around the country as examples of the approaches that have been used in revitalizing urban areas.

Churches, barns, and shop buildings are popular targets for dwellings. Gatehouses, carriage houses, and other support buildings on old estates are long-time subjects for renovation. Warehouses, factories, and other commercial structures are being altered for residential use. Hotels and department stores are used for apartments and also for needs such as resorts and hospitals.

Showman Billy Rose's forty-room mansion in New York today serves as the Smithers Alcoholism Center and Rehabilitation Unit of Roosevelt Hospital. In Princeton, N.J., the forty-one-room Guernsey Hall was a little large for today's single-family living. An Italianate villa designed in 1849 by architect John Notman, it has been updated for multifamily use. Architect William H. Short divided the house into five condominium apartments and sold four units before the work began, using the income to custom-design all the apartments. The central hallway, circular stairway, and domed skylight, which divided the house naturally, were retained so that four of the mansion's apartments were based on the four major rooms of the house: the living room, dining room, and two master bedrooms. The Italianate tower provides space for a caretaker's apartment.

Large buildings can often be adapted effectively for apartment use. The A. C. Lawrence Leather Company buildings in Peabody, Mass., now provide housing for the elderly. Located on an 8.7-acre site, the complex includes two factory buildings and the three-story Crowninshield Mansion (1814). The large mid-nineteenth-century tannery buildings have kept their identity, walls and façades remain intact, and much of the equipment—vats, tanning wheels, and pumps—is integrated into the landscape of the project. New heating, plumbing, elevators, fire stairs, and insulation provide for the comfort of the residents using the facility in this new way. In New York City, the cast-iron-front McCreery Department Store (1868) in Greenwich Village now houses 144 luxury apartments and because of the building's peculiar layout, no two are exactly alike.

In downtown Philadelphia, in an area near the waterfront known as Old City Center, a number of nineteenth-century commercial and retail buildings are being given new residential life. Young and imaginative architects and planners acting as their own developers have turned such places as an early-twentieth-century paint factory into large, attractive, and unusual apartments. Once an important area of the city, but largely unknown in the twentieth century, Old City Center is again contributing vitality to Philadelphia.

BUSINESS

The 1906 Butler Brothers building in Minneapolis, Minn., for many years the largest mail-order warehouse

Corinthian columns in the middle of the living areas distinguish the apartments in New York's former McCreery Department Store (1868) from their new high-rise counterparts. A fifth floor was added for more space.

in the upper Midwest, has become Butler Square. It is a mixed-use development of more than a half million square feet incorporating office and retail space, and a 300-room hotel is planned. The building has interesting spaces including a large atrium. Because it has a good location, Butler Square has been able to compete effectively with some of the newest office buildings in the city. In Sacramento, Calif., the Sacramento Postal Employees Credit Union is developing the Old Stanford Brothers Warehouse into offices for its own use, together with some shops, restaurants, a branch post office, and space to rent to others. An obsolete complex of buildings in Columbus, Ohio, near the German Village historic district was converted into Court House Square during 1973–74. Only one block from the new county courts complex, the site was acquired by a law firm that planned to demolish the existing buildings, which ranged from the mid-nineteenth century to 1925, and build a new office structure. The original parcel turned out to be too small

for parking as well as a building of the required size, so adjacent land was acquired, a new four-story office building was constructed, and some of the old buildings were renovated at one quarter to one third less than new construction. The mixed office and commercial complex of nearly 50,000 rentable square feet was leased before it was completed.

Houses also have been adapted for use as small offices. A group of mid-nineteenth-century Italianate houses in Wilmington, N.C., serve as offices for the mayor,

Brewer Street in Columbus, Ohio, was converted to a pedestrian walkway as part of the Court House Square project, which used its location near a historic district and new courts complex to successfully recycle good buildings in a rundown area.

city planning department, chamber of commerce, and a church. In Los Angeles, Calif., a 1923 Classic revival bank building has been turned into a combined office and residence for a graphic designer; the bank vault is a guest room. In the lower Queen Anne Hill community of Seattle, Wash., two 1912 houses, a 1906 church, and the 1916 Hansen bakery complex (home of Olympic Bread) have been purchased for use as a retail center, offices, and a restaurant. The bakery flour hopper and other

Not unexpectedly, architects are in the forefront of those recycling old spaces for new offices. Right, above and below: John Hilberry and Associates converted a three-story loft in Detroit's Harmonie Park as part of an area-wide preservation effort. Below: Another Detroit firm, Rossetti Associates, gave this 70-year-old building a skylighted atrium.

equipment are to be retained in the renovation. In Imlaystown, N.J., a landscape architecture firm refurbished the 1695 Salter's Mill as its office. All original milling machinery was left intact and no structural changes were made to the interior.

Space for manufacturing on a small scale and for selling wares—especially arts and crafts—has been found in a number of unusual places. In Alexandria, Va., an abandoned torpedo factory (c. 1917) is now the Torpedo Factory Art Center. There, artists and craftsmen rent space in which to work and to sell their art. Visitors can watch the artists at work, learning techniques of silkscreening, pottery, enameling, harpsichord making, and woodworking, and then can purchase the finished product if they wish. There are obvious advantages here for both customers and artists: monetary profits for the artists and cultural profits for their customers. Such an art

center would, of course, have been possible in a new building. But the vast space, the light, and the building's unusual nature make it one of a kind, a quality highly valued by the tenants. For those who worked on the renovation themselves, the old factory is more than a place to show art—it is itself a work of art.

EDUCATION AND EDIFICATION

Many older structures have been converted to educational uses as museums, libraries, schools, art galleries, training schools, think tanks, and research facilities. One of the most common means of preservation is to convert an old building into a house museum, especially if it is architecturally or historically significant. Most places in the country have at least one old house that has become such a museum; altogether there are so many that the nation is "in danger of strangling in velvet ropes," Helen Duprey Bullock of the National Trust remarked years ago. Rather than bring out more ropes, in many regions that already have their surfeit of house

More than 150 artists and artisans are at work in the studios and retail spaces of the Torpedo Factory Art Center, Alexandria, Va., the left portion of the waterfront munitions plant. Uses for the later portion are under study.

museums, old houses are being used instead as support facilities for tourist industries: as lodgings, as restaurants, or as information centers. In Athens, Ga., the Church-Waddel-Brumby House (c. 1818) is now a welcome center after being saved by the Athens-Clarke Heritage Foundation.

Art galleries and other museums, as protectors of various facets of our cultural patrimony, are frequently equally protective of their museum buildings, making sympathetic additions or being quick to see the value in adapting other old structures. The Brandywine River Museum in Chadds Ford, Pa., is one example. A contemporary circulation core (1971), like a mirror on the valley, wraps around the gallery space in the old Hoffman's Mill (1864), providing an appropriate setting for the works of Howard Pyle and the Wyeths, the artists of the Brandywine.

An unusual educational purpose is being served near Emmaus, Pa., where *Organic Gardening and Farming* magazine has purchased farm acreage and buildings to demonstrate the principles of organic living. Techniques employed before the twentieth century are being tried again, to determine whether they can produce crops as effectively as current methods that depend on chemical pesticides and fertilizers; older varieties of seeds are also being tested.

Since 1966 Baltimore's Mount Royal Station (1896), seen here about 1940, has been home to the Maryland Institute, College of Art, an active adapter of old buildings.

Many colleges have adapted existing structures for new uses. Vincennes University in downtown Vincennes, Ind., renovated and adapted several buildings, including a municipal water purification plant, a fruit and ice storage plant, and a brewery and distillery complex, for classrooms and administrative functions. In Denver, Colo., sixteen late-nineteenth-century residential structures now house part of the state's Auraria Higher Education Center. The residential character of the neighborhood has been maintained by restoration of the exteriors of the structures, but the interiors have been adapted for classrooms. The Virginia Common-

Spacious facilities needed by the art students were easily found in the Mount Royal Station, including a 30,000-volume library (right) and a sculpture studio (below).

wealth University in Richmond has converted two blocks of town houses to similar use. And in Charleston S.C., the College of Charleston convinced state officials that it was more appropriate and more economical to restore than put up new buildings in the college's historic neighborhood. Already some 75 of the college's 120 predominantly nineteenth-century buildings have been renovated for use; designs of new buildings are to be sympathetic to the scale and styles of the old. The State University of New York is renovating the Delaware & Hudson Building in downtown Albany as its central offices. The crescent-shaped structure, built in 1914–18, was designed after the Clothmakers' Guild Hall in Ypres, Belgium.

The former baggage shed in the Renaissance Revival-style Mount Royal Station's left wing now houses the Maryland Institute's sculpture school.

Oakland University in Rochester, Mich., has adapted buildings on a 1,600-acre country estate for educational use. The mansion has become a conference center for continuing education; one barn is a student theater, another a construction trades workshop, and a chicken house was made into a child-care center. When a new chemistry building was constructed at Vanderbilt University in Nashville, Tenn., in 1964, the school decided also to retain the old building, Furman Hall (1907), after determining that renovation was quicker than new construction, that it would cost less, and that there was sentiment in favor of its retention. It now houses the Humanities and Languages Departments.

At the North Dakota State School of Science in Wahpeton, an early-twentieth-century gymnasium serves as a theater, music practice area, and dental hygiene facility. Roosevelt University in Chicago has largely renovated Adler and Sullivan's Auditorium Building (1887), modernizing the Michigan Avenue wing, renovating a long-

unused eight-story tower, and building a "hidden" skyscraper in a former light-and-air court.

RECREATION AND ENTERTAINMENT

The heyday of public entertainment in the nineteenth and early twentieth centuries produced some irreplaceable, lavishly ornamented buildings that can still serve useful functions. The most common approach for theaters, in contrast to other types of old buildings, has been to renovate the structure for a use closely related to the original one, or for the original one itself.

The Ohio Theater in Columbus, built in 1928 as part of the Loew's chain of theaters, is being used again for entertainment purposes. Designed during the height of Art Deco opulence and decorative detail, the theater was saved from demolition by the Columbus Association for the Performing Arts. Today, silent movies with theater organ accompaniment, current motion pictures, stage plays, and the Columbus Symphony season make the theater an important "new" downtown location. After plans were announced to tear down Atlanta's Fox Theater in favor of an office building, Georgia citizens banded together to save the 1929 movie palace, designed in a so-called neo-Mideastern eclectic style with Egyptian and Arabic overtones. Atlanta Landmarks, Inc., borrowed heavily from the banks to purchase the property, and is now continuing fund-raising activities to pay off the mortgage and interest while the theater is continuing its cultural life through orchestra concerts and musicals.

Several communities have found it cheaper to renovate existing halls than to construct new facilities for musical and other performing arts groups. For example, in St. Louis, Mo., the St. Louis Theater was converted during 1966–68 into Powell Symphony Hall, the new home of the St. Louis Symphony Orchestra. Constructed in 1924–25 as a movie palace, the building was completely renovated, including the interior ornamentation and decoration, office space, a new stage shell, and new acoustics. In all, costs were one third to one sixth what would have been necessary to construct a completely new facility. Similarly, in Oakland, Calif., an Art Deco movie house built in 1931 was refurbished and reopened in 1973 as a performing arts center. The cost of reusing the existing structure was $2 million, while construction of new performing arts facilities would have cost an estimated $13 million.

In several places nineteenth-century opera houses have been renovated to provide continuing usefulness as centers of community entertainment. Perhaps the most famous example is the Goodspeed Opera House in East Haddam, Conn. Built at the time of the Centennial in 1876, it has an extremely attractive location on the Connecticut River.

Other types of buildings also lend themselves to reuse as community entertainment centers. In St. Paul, Minn., the Federal Courts Building (1892–1902)—probably not much of a place of entertainment originally—was transferred to the city as surplus federal property. It is being renovated by the St. Paul–Ramsey Arts and Science

"There's no there there," Gertrude Stein said of Oakland, Calif., but now there is at least the Paramount Theatre, a 1931 movie palace resurrected as a performing arts center at a fraction of the cost of a new facility. A new theater also could not have reproduced the 87-foot mosaic façade or the gilt lotus-patterned wall panel in the 3,000-seat auditorium.

Council for the Minnesota Museum of Art, the St. Paul Chamber Orchestra, a theater group, a radio station, and other related uses including a restaurant and public meeting rooms.

Parks, bridges, and canals are being recycled along with buildings. In Vicksburg, Miss., the *Sprague* (1901), said to be the largest sternwheel towboat ever built, served food, river history, and steamboat-era theater under the sponsorship of the Vicksburg Harbor and Port Commission until it burned in 1973; efforts are being made to restore it. In Wisconsin, between Elroy and Sparta, a thirty-two-mile-long bike trail follows the route of an abandoned railway. Developed by the state, this section will join a thousand miles of similar development along other abandoned rail rights-of-way in Wisconsin. These linear parks offer the ultimate in recreational use—architecture is featured in tunnels, bridges, stations, and rail-induced development along the former lines; wildflowers and native trees provide interesting and informative natural landscaping; the bird-watcher and wild-animal enthusiast cannot ride or hike the trail without seeing an interesting specimen. Best of all, the trails lend themselves to active, outdoor, single-person sports.

GOVERNMENTAL STRUCTURES

Around the country governments at all levels are beginning to look at adaptive use of existing structures as a means of satisfying their space needs. In Baltimore, Md., the Old City Hall is being renovated after a study for the city pointed out that this would cost only about half as much as construction of a new building. Careful planning has increased usable space for offices and ceremonial functions by 85 percent. In Marshalltown, Iowa, expanded space was needed for county facilities. Beginning in 1955, the voters of the county repeatedly turned down bond issues that would have provided money for the construction of new courthouse facilities. Finally in 1974 a ballot asking the voters if they would finance rehabilitation of the old courthouse in lieu of a new facility resulted in a vote for renovation. An architect familiar with adaptive use was retained, and today the Marshall County Courthouse (1886) is being restored; inside, the addition of a mezzanine level between two existing floors has helped increase usable space by more than 100 percent, and the county has been able to maintain a visible symbol of its heritage.

Meticulous restoration of the Paramount Theatre's Art Deco grandeur cost $1 million. Scaffolding was erected to regild the auditorium walls to bring out the intricate tropical designs depicting figures in dense foliage.

Even municipal buildings that once housed police are being recycled. In Boston, Mass., the Institute of Contemporary Art recently renovated an 1886 Romanesque-style police station as its new museum. The completely modernized interior allows visitors to see the paintings from various angles, as if in a home, as the director said in a recent interview. What was once a two-story Mansard-style police substation on Lafayette Square in St. Louis has been converted by the city to a visitors' center in an effort to continue to promote the revitalization of the area.

In recent years many efforts have been made to encourage the federal government to take the lead in helping conserve the built environment through the means of adaptive use. It is considering this, for example, in the case of the Old Post Office on Pennsylvania Avenue in Washington, D.C., which has been the subject of extensive adaptive use studies. It is hoped that the building will be converted to offices for the National Endowment for the Arts, with space allowed for exhibitions and other public displays of the activities funded by the Endowment. In Galveston, Tex., the federal government has refurbished an 1861 customhouse, courthouse, and post office for continued use as a courthouse and offices.

What a historic building or site may be used for is generally limited only by the imagination of the preservationist and the needs of the owner and the community. On the perimeter of the Mall in Washington, D.C., an

About 1860 Mathew Brady recorded (below) a lockkeeper's house that was part of the Washington City Canal and Chesapeake & Ohio Canal system. Today, maintained as a public comfort station (above) the house is still there, still being used.

early-nineteenth-century house, originally the residence of a canal lock operator, is used today as a public comfort station. Some may argue that this use is beneath the historical and architectural dignity of the building. But it is there—saved and, for the moment, used. Like any other adaptive use, this one may not be permanent. But the lockkeeper's house remains a useful and interesting part of the contemporary scene and that, after all, is what preservation is all about.

APPENDIXES

APPENDIX A

FEDERAL PROGRAMS

ADVISORY COUNCIL ON HISTORIC
PRESERVATION
1522 K Street, N.W.
Suite 430
Washington, D.C. 20005

U.S. DEPARTMENT OF HOUSING
AND URBAN DEVELOPMENT
Assistant Secretary for Community
Planning and Development
Washington, D.C. 20410

U.S. GENERAL SERVICES
ADMINISTRATION
Historic Preservation Officer
Washington, D.C. 20405

U.S. DEPARTMENT OF THE
INTERIOR
National Park Service
Washington, D.C. 20240
- National Register of Historic Places
- National Historic Landmarks
  Program (National Survey of Historic
  Sites and Buildings)
- Historic American Buildings Survey
- Historic American Engineering
  Record
- Interagency Archaeological Program
- Natural Landmarks Program
- National Environmental Education
  Landmarks Program

SMITHSONIAN INSTITUTION
National Museum Act Program
Washington, D.C. 20560

For information on other federal
programs, see *A Guide to Federal
Programs* and *1976 Supplement*
(Washington, D.C.: National Trust for
Historic Preservation).

STATE HISTORIC PRESERVATION OFFICES

ALABAMA

Director, Alabama Department of
Archives and History, Archives and
History Building, Montgomery, Ala.
36104

ALASKA

Director, Division of Parks, De-
partment of Natural Resources, 323
East Fourth Avenue, Anchorage,
Alaska 99501

ARIZONA

Director, State Parks Board, 1688
West Adams, Phoenix, Ariz. 85007

ARKANSAS

Director, Arkansas Department of
Parks and Tourism, State Capitol,
Room 149, Little Rock, Ark. 72201

CALIFORNIA

Director, Department of Parks and
Recreation, State Resources
Agency, Box 2390, Sacramento,
Calif. 95811

COLORADO

Chairman, State Historical Society,
Colorado State Museum, 200 14th
Avenue, Denver, Colo. 80203

CONNECTICUT

Director, Connecticut Historical
Commission, 59 South Prospect
Street, Hartford, Conn. 06106

DELAWARE

Director, Division of Historical
and Cultural Affairs, Hall of
Records, Dover, Del. 19901

FLORIDA

Director, Division of Archives,
History and Records Management,
Department of State, 401 East
Gaines Street, Tallahassee,
Fla. 32304

GEORGIA

Chief, Historic Preservation
Section, Department of Natural
Resources, 710 Trinity-Washington
Building, 270 Washington Street S.W.,
Atlanta, Ga. 30334

HAWAII

Chairman, Department of Land
and Natural Resources, State of
Hawaii, Box 621, Honolulu,
Hawaii 96809

IDAHO

Director, Idaho Historical Society,
610 North Julia Davis Drive,
Boise, Idaho 83706

ILLINOIS

Director, Department of Conservation,
602 State Office Building,
400 South Spring Street,
Springfield, Ill. 62706

INDIANA

Director, Department of Natural
Resources, 608 State Office Building,
Indianapolis, Ind. 42604

IOWA

Director, State Conservation Department, B-13, MacLean Hall,
Iowa City, Iowa 52242

KANSAS

Executive Director, Kansas State
Historical Society, 120 West 10th,
Topeka, Kans. 66612

KENTUCKY

Director, Kentucky Heritage Commission, 401 Wapping Street,
Frankfort, Ky. 40601

LOUISIANA

Director, Department of Art,
Historical and Cultural Preserva-
tion, Old State Capitol, Baton
Rouge, La. 70801

MAINE

Director, Maine Historic Preservation Commission, 31 Western
Avenue, Augusta, Maine 04330

MARYLAND

Director, Maryland Historical
Trust, 2525 Riva Road, Annapolis,
Md. 21401

MASSACHUSETTS

Executive Director, Massachusetts
Historical Commission, 40 Beacon
Street, Boston, Mass. 02108

MICHIGAN

Director, Michigan History Division,
Department of State, Lansing, Mich.
48918

MINNESOTA

Director, Minnesota Historical Society, 690 Cedar Street, St. Paul,
Minn. 55101

MISSISSIPPI

Director, State of Mississippi
Department of Archives and History,
Box 671, Jackson, Miss. 39205

MISSOURI

Director, Missouri Department of Natural Resources, P.O. Box 176, 1204 Jefferson Building, Jefferson City, Mo. 65101

MONTANA

Administrator, Recreation and Parks Division, Department of Fish and Game, Mitchell Building, Helena, Mont. 59601

NEBRASKA

Director, Nebraska State Historical Society, 1500 R Street, Lincoln, Neb. 68508

NEVADA

Administrator, Division of State Parks, 201 South Fall Street, Carson City, Nev. 89701

NEW HAMPSHIRE

Commissioner, Department of Resources and Economic Development, Box 856, Concord, N.H. 03301

NEW JERSEY

Commissioner, Department of Environmental Protection, Box 1420, Trenton, N.J. 08625

NEW MEXICO

State Planning Officer, State Capitol, 403 Capitol Building, Sante Fe, N. Mex. 87501

NEW YORK

Commissioner, Parks and Recreation, Room 303, South Swan Street Building, Albany, N.Y. 12223

NORTH CAROLINA

Director, Division of Archives and History, and Administrator, Department of Cultural Resources, 109 East Jones Street, Raleigh, N.C. 27611

NORTH DAKOTA

Superintendent, State Historical Society of North Dakota, Liberty Memorial Building, Bismarck, N.D. 58501

OHIO

Director, Ohio Historical Society, Columbus, Ohio 43211

OKLAHOMA

President, Oklahoma Historical Society, 1108 Colcord Building, Oklahoma City, Okla. 73102

OREGON

State Parks Superintendent, 300 State Highway Building, Salem, Ore. 97310

PENNSYLVANIA

Executive Director, Pennsylvania Historical and Museum Commission, Box 1026, Harrisburg, Pa. 17120

RHODE ISLAND

Director, Rhode Island Department of Community Affairs, 150 Washington Street, Providence, R.I. 02903

SOUTH CAROLINA

Director, State Archives Department, 1430 Senate Street, Columbia, S.C. 29211

SOUTH DAKOTA

Director, Office of Cultural Preservation, Department of Education and Cultural Affairs, State Capitol, Pierre, S.D. 57501

TENNESSEE

Executive Director, Tennessee Historical Commission, 170 2nd Avenue North, Suite 100, Nashville, Tenn. 37219

TEXAS

Executive Director, Texas State Historical Survey Committee, Box 12276, Capitol Station, Austin, Tex. 78711

UTAH

Director, Division of State History, 603 E. South Temple, Salt Lake City, Utah 84102

VERMONT

Director, Vermont Division of Historic Sites, Pavilion Building, Montpelier, Vt. 05602

VIRGINIA

Executive Director, Virginia Historic Landmarks Commission, 221 Governor Street, Richmond, Va. 23219

WASHINGTON

Director, Washington State Parks and Recreation Commission, Post Office Box 1128, Olympia, Wash. 98504

WEST VIRGINIA

West Virginia Antiquities Commission, P.O. Box 630, Morgantown, W. Va. 26505

WISCONSIN

Director, State Historical Society of Wisconsin, 816 State Street, Madison, Wis. 53706

WYOMING

Director, Wyoming Recreation Commission, 604 East 25th Street, Box 309, Cheyenne, Wyo. 82001

DISTRICT OF COLUMBIA

Director, Office of Housing and Community Development, Room 112A, District Building, Washington, D.C. 20004

PUERTO RICO

Executive Director, Institute of Puerto Rican Culture, Apartado 4184, San Juan, P.R. 00905

GUAM

Chief, Parks and Recreation Resources Division, Department of Commerce, Government of Guam, P.O. Box 682, Agana, Guam 96910

VIRGIN ISLANDS

Planning Director, Virgin Islands Planning Board, Charlotte Amalie, St. Thomas, V.I. 00801

AMERICAN SAMOA

Territorial Historic Preservation Officer, Department of Public Works, Pago Pago, American Samoa 96799

TRUST TERRITORY OF THE PACIFIC ISLANDS

Chief, Land Resources Branch, Department of Resources and Development, Trust Territory of the Pacific Islands, Saipan, Mariana Islands 96950

For further information, see *A Guide to State Historic Preservation Programs* (Washington, D.C.: National Trust for Historic Preservation).

PRIVATE NATIONAL PRESERVATION AND RELATED ORGANIZATIONS

NATIONAL TRUST FOR HISTORIC PRESERVATION
740–748 Jackson Place, N.W.
Washington, D.C. 20006

Regional offices:

- New England Field Service Office*
141 Cambridge Street
Boston Mass. 02114
*cosponsored with Society for the Preservation of New England Antiquities

- Mid-Atlantic Field Office
740–748 Jackson Place, N.W.
Washington, D.C. 20006

- Midwest Regional Office
407 South Dearborn Street
Suite 710
Chicago, Ill. 60605

- Southwest/Plains Field Office
903 Colcord Building
Oklahoma City, Okla. 73102

- Western Regional Office
802 Montgomery Street
San Francisco, Calif. 94133

For information on new regional offices, write National Trust head-quarters.

AMERICAN ASSOCIATION FOR STATE AND LOCAL HISTORY
1400 Eighth Avenue South
Nashville, Tenn. 37203

AMERICAN ASSOCIATION OF MUSEUMS
2233 Wisconsin Avenue, N.W.
Suite 200
Washington, D.C. 20007

AMERICAN CANAL SOCIETY
809 Rathton Road
York, Pa. 17403

AMERICAN INSTITUTE OF ARCHITECTS
Committee on Historic Resources

1735 New York Avenue, N.W.
Washington, D.C. 20006

AMERICAN INSTITUTE OF PLANNERS
1776 Massachusetts Avenue, N.W.
Washington, D.C. 20036

AMERICAN SOCIETY OF CIVIL ENGINEERS
345 East 47th Street
New York, N.Y. 10017

AMERICAN SOCIETY OF INTERIOR DESIGNERS
730 Fifth Avenue
New York, N.Y. 10019

AMERICAN SOCIETY OF LANDSCAPE ARCHITECTS
1750 Old Meadow Road
McLean, Va. 22101

AMERICAN SOCIETY OF PLANNING OFFICIALS
Planning Advisory Service
1313 East 60th Street
Chicago, Ill. 60637

ARCHAEOLOGICAL INSTITUTE OF AMERICA
260 West Broadway
New York, N.Y. 10013

ASSOCIATION FOR LIVING HISTORICAL FARMS AND AGRI-CULTURAL MUSEUMS
c/o John T. Schlebecker
Room 5032
National Museum of History and Technology
Smithsonian Institution
Washington, D.C. 20560

ASSOCIATION FOR PRESERVATION TECHNOLOGY
Box 2487, Station D
Ottawa, Ontario, Canada K1P 5W6

CLASSICAL AMERICA SOCIETY
10–41 Fifty-first Avenue
Long Island City, N.Y. 11101

THE CONSERVATION FOUNDATION
1717 Massachusetts Avenue, N.W.
Washington, D.C. 20036

COUNCIL ON ABANDONED MILITARY POSTS, U.S.A.
P.O. Box 171
Arlington, Va. 22210

EARLY AMERICAN INDUSTRIES

ASSOCIATION
c/o Old Economy Village
Ambridge, Pa. 15003

FRIENDS OF CAST IRON ARCHITECTURE
44 West 9th Street, Room 20
New York, N.Y. 10011

GARDEN CLUB OF AMERICA
Conservation Committee
598 Madison Avenue
New York, N.Y. 10022

MARINE HISTORICAL ASSOCIATION
Mystic Seaport
Mystic, Conn. 06355

NATIONAL MARITIME HISTORICAL SOCIETY
c/o South Street Seaport Museum
16 Fulton Street
New York, N.Y. 10038

NATIONAL SOCIETY FOR THE PRESERVATION OF COVERED BRIDGES
63 Fairview Avenue
South Peabody, Mass. 01960

THE NATURE CONSERVANCY
1800 North Kent Street
Arlington, Va. 22209

ORGANIZATION OF AMERICAN HISTORIANS
Historic Sites Committee
c/o Indiana University
112 North Bryan Street
Bloomington, Ind. 47401

PIONEER AMERICA SOCIETY
626 South Washington Street
Falls Church, Va. 22046

PRESERVATION ACTION
1225 19th Street, N.W.
Suite 602
Washington, D.C. 20036

SMALL TOWNS INSTITUTE
Box 517
Ellensburg, Wash. 98926

SOCIETY FOR HISTORICAL ARCHAEOLOGY
c/o Department of Sociology/Anthropology
University of Idaho
Moscow, Idaho 83843

SOCIETY FOR INDUSTRIAL ARCHEOLOGY
c/o Robert M. Vogel

Room 5020
National Museum of History and
Technology
Smithsonian Institution
Washington, D.C. 20560

SOCIETY FOR THE PRESERVATION
OF OLD MILLS
P.O. Box 435
Wiscasset, Maine 04578

SOCIETY OF ARCHITECTURAL
HISTORIANS
Historic Preservation Committee
1700 Walnut Street
Room 716
Philadelphia, Pa. 19103

STEAMSHIP HISTORICAL SOCIETY
OF AMERICA
414 Pelton Avenue
Staten Island, N.Y. 10310

THE VICTORIAN SOCIETY IN
AMERICA
Athenaeum of Philadelphia
East Washington Square
Philadelphia, Pa. 19106

**PRIVATE STATE AND LOCAL
PRESERVATION ORGANIZATIONS**

To locate such organizations, contact
state historical societies, state historic
preservation offices, and state and local
chapters of groups listed above. A list
of local landmarks commissions is
available from the National Trust for
Historic Preservation. Reference
sources include *Directory of Historical
Societies and Agencies in the United
States and Canada, 10th ed.*
(Nashville, Tenn.: American
Association for State and Local
History); *Official Museum Directory*
(Skokie, Ill.: National Register
Publishing Co. and American
Association of Museums); and the
forthcoming directory of preservation
organizations being compiled by the
National Trust.

**INTERNATIONAL PRESERVATION
ORGANIZATIONS**

INTERNATIONAL CENTRE FOR
CONSERVATION
Via di San Michele, 13
Rome, Italy 00153

and U.S. Committee:

• International Centre U.S.
  Committee
  1522 K Street, N.W.

Suite 430
Washington, D.C. 20005

INTERNATIONAL COUNCIL OF
MONUMENTS AND SITES
Hotel Saint Aignan
75 rue de Temple
Paris, France 75003

and U.S. Committee:

• U.S. National Committee for
  ICOMOS
  1522 K Street, N.W.
  Suite 430
  Washington, D.C. 20005

INTERNATIONAL FUND FOR
MONUMENTS
15 Gramercy Park
New York, N.Y. 10003

UNITED NATIONS EDUCATIONAL,
SCIENTIFIC AND CULTURAL
ORGANIZATION
Place de Fontenoy
Paris, France 75700

and U.S. Commission:

• U.S. National Commission for
  UNESCO
  Department of State
  Washington, D.C. 20520

PRESERVATION FUNDING SOURCES

APPENDIX B

FEDERAL PROGRAMS

AMERICAN REVOLUTION
BICENTENNIAL ADMINISTRATION
736 Jackson Place, N.W.
Washington, D.C. 20276

U.S. DEPARTMENT OF
AGRICULTURE
Farmers Home Administration
Washington, D.C. 20250

U.S. DEPARTMENT OF COMMERCE
Economic Development Administration
Washington, D.C. 20230

• Office of Business Development
• Office of Public Works

U.S. DEPARTMENT OF HOUSING
AND URBAN DEVELOPMENT
Washington, D.C. 20410
or HUD area or regional offices and
state planning agencies

• Federal Housing Administration
• Housing and Community
  Development (block grant) Program
• Comprehensive Planning Assistance
  Program

U.S. DEPARTMENT OF THE
INTERIOR
Washington, D.C. 20240

• National Park Service
• Bureau of Outdoor Recreation

U.S. DEPARTMENT OF HEALTH,
EDUCATION AND WELFARE
Office of Education
Division of Technology and
Environmental Education
Washington, D.C. 20202

• Environmental Education Grant
  Program

NATIONAL ENDOWMENT FOR THE
ARTS
2401 E Street, N.W.

Washington, D.C. 20506

• Architecture + Environmental Arts
  Program
• Bicentennial Program
• Museum Program

NATIONAL ENDOWMENT FOR THE
HUMANITIES
Museums and Historical Societies
Program
806 15th Street, N.W.
Washington, D.C. 20506

• Interpretive Exhibitions Program
• Community Education Program
• Museum Personnel Development
  Program

SMALL BUSINESS ADMINISTRATION
Economic Development Division
Washington, D.C. 20416

SMITHSONIAN INSTITUTION
Office of Museum Programs
Washington, D.C. 20560

- National Museum Act Program

For complete information on all federal and federally assisted preservation programs, see *A Guide to Federal Programs* and *1976 Supplement* (Washington, D.C.: National Trust for Historic Preservation).

STATE PROGRAMS

- National Register Grant-in-Aid Program
- State Preservation Grant Programs
- Housing Finance Agencies

For complete information on state preservation funding programs, contact state historic preservation offices and see *A Guide to State Historic Preservation Programs* (Washington, D.C.: National Trust for Historic Preservation).

PRIVATE PROGRAMS

AMERICA THE BEAUTIFUL FUND
1501 H Street, N.W.
Washington, D.C. 20005

AMERICAN ASSOCIATION FOR STATE AND LOCAL HISTORY
1400 Eighth Avenue South
Nashville, Tenn. 37203

- Consulting Services Program

NATIONAL TRUST FOR HISTORIC PRESERVATION
740–748 Jackson Place, N.W.
Washington, D.C. 20006

- Consultant Service Grant Program
- National Historic Preservation Fund (revolving fund loans)
- Preservation Education Fund
- Publication Grants Program

FOUNDATIONS

National, state, regional, and local foundations support preservation and related activities. To locate appropriate foundations, consult:

THE FOUNDATION CENTER
888 Seventh Avenue
New York, N.Y. 10019

(A list of regional depository libraries is available from the Center.)

CULTURAL DIRECTORY: GUIDE TO FEDERAL FUNDS AND SERVICES FOR CULTURAL ACTIVITIES
Associated Councils of the Arts
ACA Publications
1564 Broadway
New York, N.Y. 10036

THE FOUNDATION DIRECTORY,
Edition Five
Marianna O. Lewis, Ed.
Columbia University Press
136 South Broadway
Irvington, N.Y. 10533

(Catalogue of private funding available for development programs, grants, etc.)

THE GRANTS REGISTER (1975–77)
Roland Turner, ed.
St. Martin's Press
175 Fifth Avenue
New York, N.Y. 10010

(Current information on worldwide individual award opportunities for teachers, professionals, advanced scholars, etc.)

THE GRANTSMANSHIP CENTER NEWS
The Grantsmanship Center
1015 West Olympic Boulevard
Los Angeles, Calif. 90015

(Newsletter published eight times a year listing private and federal funding programs, plus guidelines on approaching sources, recent publications, etc.)

BIBLIOGRAPHY AND SELECTED READING LIST

General Works: Architectural, Preservation, Planning History

Andrews, Wayne. *Architecture, Ambition and Americans: A Social History of American Architecture.* New York: Free Press, 1964.

Arthur, Eric, and Witney, Dudley. *The Barn: A Vanishing Landmark in North America.* Greenwich, Conn.: New York Graphic Society, 1972.

Chadwick, George F. *The Park and the Town: Public Landscape in the 19th and 20th Centuries.* New York: Praeger Publishers, 1966.

Condit, Carl W. *American Building: Materials and Techniques from the First Colonial Settlements to the Present.* Chicago: University of Chicago Press, 1968.

Crosby, Theo. *The Necessary Monument: Its Future in the Civilized City.* Greenwich, Conn.: New York Graphic Society, 1970.

Cullen, Gordon. *The Concise Townscape.* New York: Van Nostrand Reinhold Co., 1971.

Dober, Richard. *Environmental Design.* New York: Van Nostrand Reinhold Co., 1969.

Feiss, Carl, and Morton, Terry Brust. "True or False: Living Architecture, Old and New." *Historic Preservation,* vol. 20, no. 2 (1968). Reprint. Washington, D.C.: National Trust for Historic Preservation.

Finley, David E. *History of the National Trust for Historic Preservation, 1947–1963.* Washington, D.C.: National Trust for Historic Preservation, 1965.

Fitch, James Marston. *American Building.* Vol. 1, *The Historical Forces That Shaped It.* 2d ed., rev. and enl. Boston: Houghton Mifflin Co., 1966.

————. *American Building.* Vol. 2, *The Environmental Forces That Shaped It.* 2d ed., rev. Boston: Houghton Mifflin Co., 1972.

Garvey, Robert R., and Morton, Terry Brust. "The United States Government in Historic Preservation." *Monumentum,* vol. 2 (1968). Rev. reprint. Washington, D.C.: National Trust for Historic Preservation, 1973.

Gowans, Alan. *Images of American Living.* Philadelphia: J. B. Lippincott Co., 1964.

Greiff, Constance M., ed. *Lost America: From the Atlantic to the Mississippi.* Princeton, N. J.: Pyne Press, 1971.

————. *Lost America: From the Mississippi to the Pacific.* Princeton, N.J.: Pyne Press, 1972.

Gutman, Robert, comp. *People and Buildings.* New York: Basic Books, 1972.

Hamlin, Talbot. *Greek Revival Architecture in America.* New York: Dover Publications, 1964.

Hitchcock, Henry-Russell. *Architecture: Nineteenth and Twentieth Centuries.* 2d ed. The Pelican History of Art. Baltimore: Penguin Books, 1963.

Hosmer, Charles B., Jr. *Presence of the Past: A History of the Preservation Movement in the United States Before Williamsburg.* New York: G. P. Putnam's Sons, 1965.

Jacobs, Jane. *The Death and Life of Great American Cities.* New York: Vintage Books, 1961.

Jordy, William H. *American Buildings and Their Architects: Progressive and Academic Ideals at the Turn of the Twentieth Century.* Garden City, N.Y.: Doubleday & Co., 1972.

————. *American Buildings and Their Architects: The Impact of European Modernism in the Mid-Twentieth Century.* Garden City, N.Y.: Doubleday & Co., 1972.

Kaufmann, E. J., Jr., ed. *The Rise of an American Architecture.* New York: Praeger Publishers, 1970.

Lancaster, Clay. *Architectural Follies in America: or Hammer, Saw-Tooth and Nail.* Rutland, Vt.: Charles E. Tuttle Co., 1960.

Long, Amos, Jr., *Farmsteads and Their Buildings.* Lebanon, Pa.: Applied Art, 1972.

Lynch, Kevin. *The Image of the City.* Cambridge: MIT Press, 1960.

————. *What Time Is This Place?* Cambridge: MIT Press, 1972.

Maass, John. *The Victorian Home in America.* New York: Hawthorn Books, 1972.

Mazmanian, Arthur B. *The Structure of Praise.* Boston: Beacon Press, 1970.

McHarg, Ian L. *Design With Nature.* Garden City, N.Y.: Natural History Press, Doubleday & Co., 1969.

McKee, Harley J. *Introduction to Early American Masonry: Stone, Brick, Mortar and Plaster.* National Trust/Columbia University Series on the Technology of Early American Building. Washington, D.C.: National Trust for Historic Preservation, 1973.

Meeks, Carroll L. V. *The Railroad Station.* New Haven, Conn.: Yale University Press, 1956.

Morrison, Hugh. *Early American Architecture.* New York: Oxford University Press, 1952.

Morton, Terry B., ed. *"I feel I should warn you . . .": Historic Preservation Cartoons.* Washington, D.C.: Preservation Press, 1975.

Mulloy, Elizabeth D. *History of the National Trust for Historic Preservation, 1963–1973.* Washington, D.C.: Preservation Press, 1976.

Mumford, Lewis. *Sticks and Stones: A Study of American Architecture and Civilization.* 2d rev. ed. New York: Dover Publications, 1955.

National Trust for Historic Preservation and Colonial Williamsburg Foundation. *Historic Preservation Today.* Charlottesville: University Press of Virginia, 1966.

————. *Historic Preservation Tomorrow.* Charlottesville: University Press of Virginia, 1967.

Newton, Norman. *Design in the Land: The Development of Landscape Architecture.* Cambridge: Harvard University Press, 1971.

Noel-Hume, Ivor. *Historical Archaeology: A Comprehensive Guide for Both Amateurs and Professionals to the Techniques and Methods of Excavating Historical Sites.* New York: Alfred A. Knopf, 1969.

Pierson, William H., Jr. *American Buildings and Their Architects: The Colonial and Neoclassical Styles.* Garden City, N.Y.: Doubleday & Co., 1970.

Pillsbury, Richard, and Kardos, Andrew. *Field Guide to the Folk Architecture of the Northeastern United States.* Hanover, N. H.: Geography Publications at Portsmouth, 1970.

Rains, Albert, and Henderson, Laurance G. *With Heritage So Rich: A Report of a Special Committee on Historic Preservation, United States Conference of Mayors.* New York: Random House, 1966.

Rasmussen, Steen Eiler. *Experiencing Architecture.* Cambridge: MIT Press, 1962.

Reps, John W. *Town Planning in Frontier America.* Princeton, N. J.: Princeton University Press, 1969.

Scott, Mel. *American City Planning Since 1890: A History Commemorating the Fiftieth Anniversary of the American Institute of Planners.* Berkeley: University of California Press, 1971.

Tidworth, Simon. *Theaters: An Architectural and Cultural History.* New York: Praeger Publishers, 1973.

Venturi, Robert; Brown, Denise Scott; and Izenour, Steven. *Learning from Las Vegas.* Cambridge: MIT Press, 1972.

Whyte, William H. *The Last Landscape.* Garden City, N.Y.: Doubleday & Co., 1968.

Wilson, Forrest. *Structure: The Essence of Architecture.* London: Studio Vista, 1971.

Preservation, Conservation, Adaptive Use Techniques

America the Beautiful Fund. *Old Glory: A Pictorial Report on the Grass Roots History Movement and the First Hometown History Primer.* New York: Warner Paperback Library, 1973.

Architectural Record. Special issue, "Conservation in the Context of Change," vol. 156, no. 8 (December 1974).

Brownstone Revival Committee of New York, Inc. *Back to the City: A*

Guide to Urban Preservation. New York: Author, 1975.

Bullock, Orin M., Jr. *The Restoration Manual: An Illustrated Guide to the Preservation and Restoration of Old Buildings.* Norwalk, Conn.: Silvermine Publishers, 1966.

Cantacuzino, Sherban. *New Uses for Old Buildings.* New York: Watson-Guptill Publications, 1975.

Citizens' Advisory Committee on Environmental Quality. *Citizens Make the Difference: Case Studies of Environmental Action.* Washington, D.C.: Government Printing Office, 1973.

Civic Trust. *Pride of Place: How to Improve Your Surroundings.* London: Author, 1972.

Educational Facilities Laboratories. *Build If You Must, But . . .: Case Studies of Alternatives to New Construction.* New York: Author, 1975.

——————. *Reusing Railroad Stations: A Report.* New York: Author, 1974.

——————. *Reusing Railroad Stations—Book Two.* A report with the National Endowment for the Arts. New York: Author, 1975.

Environmental Protection Agency. *Don't Leave It All to the Experts: The Citizen's Role in Environmental Decision Making.* Washington, D.C.: Government Printing Office, 1972.

Federal Architecture Project. *Federal Architecture: Adaptive-Use Facilities.* Edited by Merrill Ware. Report for the Federal Architecture Task Force. Washington, D.C.: National Endowment for the Arts, 1975.

Harrison, Myra Fraser. *Adaptive Use of Historic Structures: A Series of Case Studies.* Washington, D.C.: National Trust for Historic Preservation, 1971.

Hudson, Kenneth. *Handbook for Industrial Archaeology.* New York: Fernhill House, 1967.

Insall, Donald W. *The Care of Old Buildings Today: A Practical Guide.* London: Architectural Press, 1972.

Miner, Ralph W. *Conservation of Historic and Cultural Resources.* Chicago: American Society of Planning Officials, 1969.

National Trust for Historic Preservation. *A Courthouse Conservation Handbook.* Washington, D.C.: Preservation Press, 1976.

——————. *Economic Benefits of Preserving Old Buildings.* Washington, D.C.: Preservation Press, 1976.

——————. *Preservation & Building Codes.* Washington, D.C.: Preservation Press, 1975.

——————. *Preservation and Conservation: Principles and Practices.* Washington, D.C.: Smithsonian Institution Press for the National Trust, 1976.

——————. *Preservation in Your Town: Annual Meeting Theme Handbook 1.* Washington, D.C.: Author, 1974.

Pyke, John S., Jr. *Landmark Preservation.* New York: Citizens Union Research Foundation, 1972.

Robertson, James, and Lewallen, John, eds. *The Grass Roots Primer.* San Francisco: Sierra Club Books, 1975.

Schlebecker, John T., and Petersen, Gale E. *Living Historical Farms Handbook.* Smithsonian Studies in History and Technology, vol. 16. Washington, D.C.: Smithsonian Institution Press, 1972.

Stanforth, Deirdre, and Stamm, Martha. *Buying and Renovating a House in the City: A Practical Guide.* New York: Alfred A. Knopf, 1972.

Stephen, George. *Remodelling Old Houses Without Destroying Their Character.* New York: Alfred A. Knopf, 1972.

Worksett, Roy. *The Character of Towns: An Approach to Conservation.* London: Architectural Press, 1969.

Ziegler, Arthur P., Jr. *Historic Preservation in Inner City Areas: A Manual of Practice.* Pittsburgh: Allegheny Press, 1971.

Ziegler, Arthur P., Jr.; Adler, Leopold, II; and Kidney, Walter C. *Revolving Funds for Historic Preservation: A Manual of Practice.* With the assistance of the National Trust for Historic Preservation. Pittsburgh: Ober Park Associates, 1975.

Legal Techniques, Historic District Zoning, Land Use

Argan, G. C., and Murtagh, William J. *Historic Districts: Identification, Social Aspects and Preservation.* Washington, D.C.: National Trust for Historic Preservation for the American Committee, International Centre for Conservation, 1975.

Brenneman, Russell L. *Should Easements Be Used to Protect National Historic Landmarks?* A Study for the National Park Service. Washington, D.C.: U.S. Department of the Interior, National Park Service, 1974.

Costonis, John J. *Space Adrift: Landmarks Preservation and the Marketplace.* Urbana: University of Illinois Press for the National Trust for Historic Preservation, 1974.

French and Pickering Creeks Conservation Trust, Inc. *Voluntary Preservation of Open Space.* Proceedings of a conference, March 9, 1974. Pottstown, Pa.: Author, 1975.

Gammage, Grady, Jr.; Jones, Philip N.; and Jones, Stephen L. *Historic Preservation in California: A Legal Handbook.* Stanford, Calif.: Stanford Environmental Law Society and National Trust for Historic Preservation, 1975.

Ipswich Historical Commission. *Something to Preserve.* A Report on Historic Preservation by the Acquisition of Protective Agreements on Buildings in Ipswich, Massachusetts, prepared in cooperation with the Ipswich Heritage Trust and the U.S. Department of Housing and Urban Development. Ipswich: Author, 1975.

Law and Contemporary Problems. Special issue, "Historic Preservation," vol. 36, no. 3 (1971). Durham: Duke University School of Law.

Morrison, Jacob H. *Historic Preservation Law.* 1965. Reprint. Washington, D.C.: National Trust for Historic Preservation, 1974.

——————. *Supplement to Historic Preservation Law.* New Orleans: Author, 1972.

National Trust for Historic Preservation. *A Guide to Delineating Edges of Historic Districts.* Russell Wright, principal consultant. Washington, D.C.: Preservation Press, 1976.

——————. *Legal Techniques in Historic Preservation.* Washington, D.C.: Author, 1972.

Reed, Thomas J. "Land Use Controls in Historic Areas." *Notre Dame Lawyer,* vol. 44 (1969). Reprint. Washington, D.C.: National Trust for Historic Preservation.

Reilly, William K., ed. *The Use of Land: A Citizens' Policy Guide to Urban Growth.* A Task Force Report Sponsored by The Rockefeller Brothers Fund. New York: Thomas Y. Crowell Co., 1973.

Turnbull, H. Rutherford. "Aesthetic Zoning and Property Values." *Wake Forest Law Review,* vol. 7, no. 2 (1971).

Urban Land. Special issue, "Historic Preservation," vol. 34, no. 7 (1975). Washington, D.C.: Urban Land Institute.

Vermont Division of Historic Sites, Agency of Development and Community Affairs. *Historic Preservation Through Land Use Planning.* Montpelier: Author, 1973.

Virginia Historic Landmarks Commission. "Open-Space Easements in Virginia." *Notes on Virginia,* no. 11 (winter 1975). Richmond: Author.

Surveys, Plans, Case Studies

Brown, Gerald, and Griffith, Teddy. *Willard: A Plan for Historic Preservation.* Logan: Utah State University, 1973.

City of San Francisco, Department of City Planning. *The Urban Design Plan for the Comprehensive Plan of San Francisco.* San Francisco: Author, 1971.

City of Sheboygan [Wisconsin]. *Prospects for the Past: A Study of Notable Architecture, Sheboygan Renewal Area—1972.* Washington, D.C.: Government Printing Office, 1973.

Downing, Antoinette F.; MacDougall, Elisabeth; and Pearson, Eleanor. *Survey of Architectural History in Cambridge: Report Two, Mid-Cambridge.* Cambridge, Mass.: Cambridge Historical Commission, 1967.

Dulaney, Paul. *The Architecture of Historic Richmond.* Charlottesville: University Press of Virginia, 1968.

Dunsavage, Lyn, and Talkington, Virginia. *The Making of a Historic District: Swiss Avenue, Dallas, Texas.* Washington, D.C.: Preservation Press, 1975.

Eric Hill Associates, Inc. *Ansley Park Neighborhood Conservation Study.* Atlanta, Ga.: Author, n.d.

Fairfield, California, Department of Environmental Affairs. *The Way It Was: A Program for Historic Preservation.* Fairfield: Author, 1975.

Goeldner, Paul. *Utah Catalogue, Historic American Buildings Survey.* Salt Lake City: Utah Heritage Foundation, 1969.

Green Spring and Worthington Valley Planning Council [Maryland] and Wallace-McHarg Associates. *Plan for the Valleys.* Philadelphia: Authors, n.d.

Hasbrouck, Wilbert R., and Sprague, Paul E. *A Survey of Historic Architecture of the Village of Oak Park, Illinois.* Oak Park: Landmarks Commission, Village of Oak Park, 1974.

Housing Authority of Savannah. *Historic Preservation Plan for the Central Area General Neighborhood Renewal Area, Savannah, Ga.* Washington, D.C.: Government Printing Office, 1966.

John H. Friend, Inc. *Fort Condé Plaza, Mobile, Alabama: Its Development as a Tourist Oriented Historical Attraction.* Washington, D.C.: National Trust for Historic Preservation, 1974.

Johnson, Johnson & Roy, Inc. *Marshall: A Plan for Preservation.* Marshall, Mich.: Marshall Historical Society, 1973.

Land Plans, Inc. *A Plan for Ephraim.* Madison, Wis.: Author, 1973.

Maddex, Diane. *Historic Buildings of Washington, D.C.: A Selection from the Records of the Historic American Buildings Survey.* Pittsburgh: Ober Park Associates, 1973.

Marcou, O'Leary and Associates, Inc. *Historic Cohoes, Cohoes, New York: A Survey of Historic Resources.* Troy, N. Y.: Rensselaer Polytechnic Institute, 1971.

Myers, Denys Peter, comp. *Maine Catalog: Historic American Buildings Survey.* Augusta: Maine State Museum, 1974.

National Capital Planning Commission and District of Columbia Redevelopment Land Agency. *Downtown Urban Renewal Area Landmarks, Washington, D.C.* Washington, D.C.: Government Printing Office, 1970.

New Mexico State Planning Office. *Historic Preservation: A Plan for New Mexico.* Santa Fe: Author, 1971.

New York State Council on the Arts. *Architecture Worth Saving in Onondaga County.* Syracuse, N.Y.: School of Architecture, Syracuse University, 1964.

Newell, Dianne. *The Failure to Preserve the Queen City Hotel, Cumberland, Maryland.* Washington, D.C.: Preservation Press, 1975.

Old Town Restorations, Inc. *Building the Future from Our Past: A Report on the Saint Paul Historic Hill District Planning Program.* St. Paul, Minn.: Author, 1975.

Palmer, Meade. *Green Springs, Louisa County, Va., A Land Use Study.* Warrenton, Va.: Author, 1973.

Pine, Robert H. *Sag Harbor, Past, Present and Future.* Sag Harbor, N.Y.: Sag Harbor Historic Preservation Commission, 1973.

Rolf C. Campbell & Associates, Inc. *Village of Long Grove, Comprehensive Plan.* Lake Bluff, Ill.: Author, 1973.

Rovetti, Paul F.; Haberlen, Richard A.; and Franco, Barbara. *The Park McCullough House, North Bennington, Vermont: A Program of Use.* Washington, D.C.: National Trust for Historic Preservation, 1973.

Schluntz, Roger L.; Erickson, David; Blackwell, John; Shneider, Jeff; and Peterson, Stan. *Design for Downtown.* Lincoln: Urban Research & Development Center, College of Architecture, University of Nebraska, 1973.

Scott, James Allen. *Duluth's Legacy.* Vol. 1, *Architecture.* Duluth, Minn.: City of Duluth, Department of Research & Planning, 1974.

Stephen, George, and Rettig, Robert B., Boston Redevelopment Authority. *Revitalizing Older Houses in Charlestown.* Washington, D.C.: Government Printing Office, 1973.

Stoney, Samuel Gaillard. *This Is Charleston.* 4th rev. ed. Charleston, S.C.: Carolina Art Association, 1970.

Turner Associates, P. C., and Nicholas Satterlee and Associates. *The Logan Circle Historic Preservation Area.* Washington, D.C.: D.C. Redevelopment Land Agency, 1973.

Visnapuu & Gaede, Inc. *Fisher Hall, Miami University, Oxford, Ohio: Its Preservation Potential.* Washington, D.C.: National Trust for Historic Preservation, 1973.

————. *Water Street Study, Chillicothe, Ohio: Suggestions for Rehabilitation.* Washington, D.C.: National Trust for Historic Preservation, 1973.

Walters, Gregory M. *Barrio Historico Tucson.* Tucson: College of Architecture, University of Arizona, 1972.

Wilson, Richard G.; Vaughan, Edward J.; and Downing, Mrs. George E. *Old West Side, Ann Arbor, Michigan.* Ann Arbor: Old West Side Association, 1971.

Wrenn, Tony P. *Woodbury, Connecticut: A New England Townscape.* Washington, D.C.: Preservation Press, 1975.

Wright, Russell J. *The Urban Design Plan: Historic Hill, Newport, Rhode Island.* Newport: Redevelopment Agency of the City of Newport, 1973.

Yguado Association. *Acoma Indian Pueblo, Historic Preservation and Urban Design Plan.* Peralta, N.M.: Author, 1973.

Research and Inventory Manuals

Cumming, John. *A Guide for the Writing of Local History.* Ann Arbor: Michigan American Revolution Bicentennial Commission, 1974.

Georgia State Department of Natural Resources, Office of Planning and Research, Historic Preservation Section, Historic Sites Survey. *Historic Preservation Handbook.* Atlanta: Author, 1974.

Greater Portland Landmarks, Inc., Advisory Service. *Some Notes on Living with Old Houses.* Rev. ed. Portland, Me.: Author, 1974.

Hale, Richard W. *Methods of Research for the Amateur Historian.* Nashville, Tenn.: American Association for State and Local History, 1969.

Harvey, John. *Conservation of Buildings.* Toronto: University of Toronto Press, 1972.

Lord, Clifford L. *Teaching History with Community Resources.* New York: Teachers College Press, Columbia University, 1967.

Maryland Historical Trust. *Photographing Historic Landmarks.* Guides to Historic Preservation Activity, Guide no. 1. Annapolis: Author, n.d.

————. *National Register Nominations: Instructions and Samples.* Guides to Historic Preservation Activity, Guide no. 2. Annapolis: Author, n.d.

————. *Researching Maryland Buildings.* Guides to Historic Preservation Activity, Guide no. 3. Annapolis: Author, n.d.

McKee, Harley J., Historic American Buildings Survey. *Recording Historic Buildings.* Washington, D.C.: Government Printing Office, 1970.

McKerrow, R. B., and Silver, Henry M. "On the Publication of Research." *PMLA,* vol. 55 (1950).

New York State Office of Parks and Recreation, Division for Historic Preservation. *Historic Resources Survey Manual.* Albany: Author, 1974.

U.S. Department of the Interior, National Park Service, Office of Archeology and Historic Preservation. *How to Complete National*

Register Inventory—Nomination Forms. Washington, D.C.: U.S. Government Printing Office, 1972.

Reference Books, Bibliographies, Directories

American Association for State and Local History. *Directory of Historical Societies and Agencies in the United States and Canada.* Edited and compiled by Donna McDonald. 10th ed. Nashville, Tenn. Author, 1975.

Associated Councils of the Arts. *Cultural Directory: Guide to Federal Funds and Services for Cultural Activities,* New York: ACA Publications, 1975.

City of Duluth, Department of Research & Planning. *The Language of Open Space: A Glossary to help you say exactly what you mean.* Duluth, Minn.: Author, 1974.

Ebner, Michael H. *The New Urban History: Bibliography on Methodology and Historiography.* Monticello, Ill.: Council of Planning Librarians, 1973.

Environmental Protection Agency. *Groups That Can Help: A Directory of Environmental Organizations.* Washington, D.C.: Government Printing Office, 1972.

Hitchcock, Henry-Russell. *American Architectural Books: A List of Books, Portfolios, and Pamphlets on Architecture and Related Subjects Published in America Before 1895.* Minneapolis: University of Minnesota Press, 1962.

Jackle, John A. *Past Landscapes: A Bibliography for Historic Preservationists Selected from the Literature of Historical Geography.* Monticello, Ill.: Council of Planning Librarians, 1974.

Lewis, Marianna O., ed. *The Foundation Directory, Edition Five.* New York: Columbia University Press, 1975.

Marsh, John. *Scenery Evaluation and Landscape Perception: A Bibliography.* Monticello, Ill.: Council of Planning Librarians, 1972.

Mazziotti, Donald F. *Neighborhoods and Neighborhood Planning: A Selected Bibliography.* Monticello, Ill.: Council of Planning Librarians, 1974.

McKee, Harley J. *Amateur's Guide to Terms.* Rochester: Landmark Society of Western New York, 1970.

Menges, Gary L. *Historic Preservation: A Bibliography.* Monticello, Ill.: Council of Planning Librarians, 1969.

National Trust for Historic Preservation. *A Guide to Federal Programs: Programs and Activities Related to Historic Preservation.* Washington, D.C.: Author, 1974.

———. *A Guide to Federal Programs: Programs and Activities Related to Historic Preservation. 1976 Supplement.* Washington, D.C.: Preservation Press, 1976.

———. *A Guide to State Historic Preservation Programs.* Washington, D.C.: Preservation Press, 1976.

———. *Historic Preservation Plans: An Annotated Bibliography.* Washington, D.C.: Preservation Press, 1976.

———. *Historical Agency Operation: A Basic Research Bibliography.* Washington, D.C.: Author, 1974.

———. *Historic Preservation Law: An Annotated Bibliography.* Washington, D.C.: Preservation Press, 1976.

Rath, Frederick L., Jr., and O'Connell, Merrilyn Rogers. *Guide to Historic Preservation, Historical Agencies, and Museum Practices: A Selective Bibliography.* Cooperstown: New York State Historical Association, 1970.

———. *Historic Preservation: A Bibliography on Historical Organization Practices.* Nashville, Tenn.: American Association for State and Local History, 1975.

Real Estate Research Corporation. *Neighborhood Preservation: A Catalog of Local Programs.* Washington, D.C.: U.S. Department of Housing and Urban Development, Office of Policy Development and Research, 1975.

Roos, Frank J., Jr. *Bibliography of Early American Architecture: Writings on Architecture Constructed Before 1860 in Eastern and Central United States.* Urbana: University of Illinois Press, 1968.

Saylor, Henry H. *Dictionary of Architecture.* New York: John Wiley & Sons, 1963.

Shillaber, Caroline. *Landscape Architecture/Environmental Planning: A Classified Bibliography.* Monticello, Ill.: Council of Planning Librarians, 1975.

Turner, Roland, ed. *The Grants Register (1975–77).* New York: St. Martin's Press, 1975.

U.S. Department of the Interior, National Park Service, Office of Archeology and Historic Preservation. *The National Register of Historic Places 1972.* Washington, D.C.: Government Printing Office, 1973.

———. *Supplement to the National Register of Historic Places 1974.* Washington, D.C.: Government Printing Office, 1974.

Whiffen, Marcus. *American Architecture Since 1780: A Guide to the Styles.* Cambridge: MIT Press, 1969.

Periodical, Series (National)

AIA Journal. American Institute of Architects, monthly magazine.

AIP Newsletter. American Institute of Planners, monthly.

APT Bulletin. Association for Preservation Technology, quarterly journal.

Architectural Digest. C. T. Knapp, publisher, bimonthly magazine.

Architectural Record. McGraw-Hill, Inc., monthly magazine.

ASPO Planning. American Society of Planning Officials, monthly magazine.

Historic Preservation. National Trust for Historic Preservation, quarterly magazine.

History News. American Association for State and Local History, monthly newsletter.

HUD Challenge. U.S. Department of Housing and Urban Development, monthly magazine.

IA. Society for Industrial Archeology, biannual journal.

"Information" Series. National Trust for Historic Preservation, periodically.

Journal of Housing. National Association of Housing and Redevelopment Officials, monthly magazine.

Journal of the Society of Architectural Historians. Quarterly magazine.

Landscape Architecture. American Society of Landscape Architects, quarterly magazine.

Monumentum. International Council of Monuments and Sites, annual journal.

Museum News. American Association of Museums, monthly magazine.

National Parks & Conservation Magazine. National Parks & Conservation Association, monthly.

The Old-House Journal. Old-House Journal Co., monthly newsletter.

Parks & Recreation. National Recreation and Parks Association, monthly magazine.

Preservation News. National Trust for Historic Preservation, monthly newspaper.

Progressive Architecture. Robert N. Sillars, Jr., publisher, monthly magazine.

SAH Newsletter. Society of Architectural Historians, bimonthly.

SIA Newsletter. Society for Industrial Archeology, bimonthly.

Sierra Club Bulletin. The Sierra Club, monthly magazine.

Small Town Journal. Small Towns Institute, monthly magazine.

Smithsonian Magazine. Smithsonian Institution, monthly.

"Technical Leaflet Series." American Association for State and Local History, periodically.

Urban Land. Urban Land Institute, monthly magazine.

PHOTOGRAPHIC CREDITS

Abbreviations:
National Trust—National Trust for Historic Preservation; HABS—Historic American Buildings Survey; HAER—Historic American Engineering Record

JACKET AND COVER
JAY MAISEL. Landmarks of yesterday and tomorrow: a church in Maine (front), a Texas oil refinery's storage facility (back)

HALF TITLE PAGE
MARK JUNGE, Wyoming Recreation Commission. Barbed-wire fence near Guernsey, Wyo.

TITLE PAGE
CERVIN ROBINSON Cast-iron-front Haughwout Building (1857), New York City

CONTENTS PAGE (facing page)
JACK E. BOUCHER, HABS. Masonic Lodge (1865), Mendocino, Calif.

ACKNOWLEDGMENTS (facing page)
DAVID PLOWDEN. Storefront (1887), Hillsboro, Kans.

FOREWORD
© **PHILLIP MACMILLAN JAMES & ASSOCIATES.** Butler Brothers Building (1906–08), Minneapolis, now recycled as Butler Square

AUTHOR'S PREFACE (facing page)
L. H. DREYER, Gil Amiaga collection. New York State Department of Education Building (1908–12), Albany

PAGE
13 **Balthazar Korab.** Abandoned farmhouse, Monroe, Mich.
14 **Bob Smith,** U.S. Environmental Protection Agency
15 (left) **Balthazar Korab**
(right) **Jack E. Boucher,** HABS
16 (left, above) **Wm. Edmund Barrett**
(left, below) **Carleton Knight III,** National Trust
(right) **Balthazar Korab**
17 (left) **Carleton Knight III,** National Trust
(right) Citizens Federal Savings and Loan Association of San Francisco
18 (above) **Randy Wagner,** Wyoming Travel Commission
(below) **Phil Stitt,** Arizona Architect
19 © **Randolph Langenbach**

20 (left) **Carleton Knight III**
(right) **Wm. Edmund Barrett**
21 **Tony P. Wrenn**
22 **Frances Benjamin Johnston,** Library of Congress
23 (left) **Wm. Edmund Barrett**
(right) Mayor's Office of Lower Manhattan Development, New York City
24 (left) **James Q. Reber**
(right) **Ed Nowak**
25 **Ed Nowak**
26 (left) **Balthazar Korab**
(right) **Wm. Edmund Barrett**
27 (above, left) **Carleton Knight III,** National Trust
(above, right) **Sandra Dallas**
(below) **Lyman E. Nylander,** St. Louis County Historical Society
28 (left) **Carleton Knight III,** National Trust
(right) Pittsburgh History & Landmarks Foundation
29 **Joshua Freiwald**
31 **L. H. Dreyer,** Gil Amiaga collection
32 **Carleton Knight III**
33 **Mark Junge,** Wyoming Recreation Commission
35 **Cervin Robinson.** Chrysler Building (1929–30), New York, N.Y.
36 **Jack E. Boucher,** HABS
37 (both photos) **Carleton Knight III**
38 (left) **Jack E. Boucher,** National Park Service
(right, above) **Jack E. Boucher,** HABS
(right, below) **Cervin Robinson**
39 (left, above) **Cervin Robinson,** HABS
(left, below) **Jack E. Boucher,** HABS
(right) **Hans Padelt,** Landmark Society of Western New York
40 (left) National Trust collection
(right, above) **Jack E. Boucher,** HABS
(right, below) © **Randolph Langenbach**
41 (left) **George Eisenman,** HABS
(right, above) **Louis S. Wall,** National Trust
(right, below) **Jack E. Boucher,** HABS
42 **Tony P. Wrenn,** Old Woodbury Historical Society
43 (all photos) **A. Pierce Bounds**
44 (left) **Carleton Knight III**
(right, above) **James Q. Reber**
(right, below) **Jack Fahnestock,** Mayor's Office of Lower Manhattan Development, New York City

45 (left photos) **Jack E. Boucher,** HABS
(right, above) **Tony P. Wrenn**
(right, below) Utah Power & Light Company
47 (left) **John P. Conron,** New Mexico State Planning Office and Cultural Properties Review Committee
(right, above) **John P. Conron**
(right, below) **Balthazar Korab**
48 (left) **Arthur Haskell,** Society for the Preservation of New England Antiquities
(right, above) **Claire K. Tholl,** HABS
(right, below) **Ned Goode,** HABS
49 (left, above) National Trust
(left, below) **John J. G. Blumenson,** National Trust
(right) **Jack E. Boucher,** HABS
50 (left) **Jack E. Boucher,** HABS
(right, above) Pittsburgh History & Landmarks Foundation—Pennsylvania Historical and Museum Commission
(right, below) Utah Heritage Foundation
51 (left) **Gil Amiaga**
(right) University of Texas
52 (left, above) National Trust collection
(left, below) **Cervin Robinson**
(right) **Allen Stross,** HABS
53 (left, above) **Jeffrey K. Ochsner**
(left, below) **Balthazar Korab**
(right) **Carleton Knight III,** National Trust
54 (left, above) **Tony P. Wrenn,** Old Woodbury Historical Society
(left, below) Historic Charleston Foundation
(right, above) © **Randolph Langenbach**
(right, below) **Ronald Comedy,** HABS
55 (left) **B. Clarkson Schoettle**
(right) **Thomas R. Tucker,** National Trust
56 (left, above) **Cervin Robinson,** HABS
(left, below) **Piaget,** HABS
(right, above) **Cervin Robinson,** HABS
(right, below) **Marvin Rand,** University of Southern California
57 (left, above) Historical collection, Title Insurance and Trust Company of San Diego
(left, below) **Cervin Robinson**
(right, above) Indiana Architectural Foundation, from Indianapolis Architecture
(right, below) **Erol Akyavas,** Marcel Breuer and Associates

PHOTOGRAPHIC CREDITS

58 (above) © **Robert S. Oakes**,
National Geographic Society
(below) U.S. Department of
Transportation
59 (left) **Carleton Knight III**, National
Trust
(right) **Bill Hedrich**, Hedrich-
Blessing
60 **L. H. Dreyer**, Gil Amiaga
collection
61 **Fred Mang, Jr.**, National Park
Service
62 **Jack E. Boucher**, HABS
63 (above) **Wm. Edmund Barrett**
(below) **Cervin Robinson**, HABS
64 (left) **P. Kent Fairbanks**, HABS
(right) **Wm. Edmund Barrett**
65 (above) Nebraska State Historical
Society
(below, both photos) **Wm. Edmund
Barrett**
66 (left) **Thigpen Photography**,
National Register of Historic
Places
(right) **Wm. Edmund Barrett**
67 (above) **Wm. Edmund Barrett**
(below) **B. Clarkson Schoettle**
68 (above) **Jerry Thompson**
(below) **David J. Kaminsky**,
National Register of Historic
Places
69 (left) **Carleton Knight III**
(right) **Jack E. Boucher**, HABS
70 **Prime Beaudoin**, HABS
71 **Fred Mang, Jr.**, National Park
Service
72 (left, top) **P. Kent Fairbanks**, HABS
(left, middle) **MacFall Photo**,
Sleepy Hollow Restorations
(left, bottom) **H. G. Hamekamp**
(right) **Jack E. Boucher**, HABS
73 **Carleton Knight III**, National Trust
74 (left, top) **Tony P. Wrenn**
(left, middle) **Jack E. Boucher**, HABS
(left, bottom) Idaho State
Historical Society
(right) **B. Clarkson Schoettle**
75 **L. H. Dreyer**, Gil Amiaga collection
76 (both photos) **Marvin Rand**,
University of Southern California
77 (left photos) **Balthazar Korab**
(right, above) **Marvin Rand**, HABS
(right, below) National Register of
Historic Places
78 **Gil Amiaga**
79 (left photos) **Lester Jones**, HABS
(right photos) **Wm. Edmund Barrett**

80 (left, above) Virginia Historic
Landmarks Commission
(left, below) **Wm. Edmund Barrett**
(right) **B. Clarkson Schoettle**
81 (both photos) Historical collection,
Title Insurance and Trust
Company of San Diego
82 (left) **Balthazar Korab**
(right) **Jack E. Boucher**, HABS
83 **Wm. Edmund Barrett**
84 **Mark Junge**, Wyoming Recreation
Commission
85 **Balthazar Korab**
86 **Balthazar Korab**
87 (left, above) **Randall Page**, North
Carolina Department of Archives
and History
(left, below) **Balthazar Korab**
(right, above) Kansas State
Historical Society
(right, below) Maine Historic
Preservation Commission
88 (left) **Mark Junge**, Wyoming
Recreation Commission
(right) National Park Service
89 (left, above) **Chester H. Liebs**,
National Register of Historic Places
(left, below) Kansas State Historical
Society
(right, top) **Cervin Robinson**, HABS
(right, middle) **Wm. Edmund Barrett**
(right, bottom) **Wm. Edmund
Barrett**, National Trust
90 (left) **Robert Hatch**, National
Register of Historic Places
(right) Wyoming Recreation
Commission
91 (above) **Wm. Edmund Barrett**
(below) **Mark Junge**, Wyoming
Recreation Commission
92 (left) **Mary Randlett**
(right, above) **Wm. Edmund Barrett**
(right, below) **Tony P. Wrenn**
93 (left and above) **Tony P. Wrenn**
(right, below) **Wm. Edmund Barrett**
94 **Balthazar Korab**
95 (left, above) **Balthazar Korab**
(left, below) **Wm. Edmund Barrett**
(right) **Carleton Knight III**
96 (left) National Register of Historic
Places
(right, above) **Wm. Edmund Barrett**
(right, below) **Catherine Cockshutt**,
North Carolina Department of
Archives and History
97 (above, left) Pennsylvania
Historical and Museum
Commission

(above, right) Tri-County
Conservancy of the Brandywine,
National Register of Historic Places
(below) **Cervin Robinson**, HABS
98 (above) **Richard Federici**, New
Mexico State Planning Office and
Cultural Properties Review
Committee
(below) **Wm. Edmund Barrett**,
Roanoke River Museum—
Prestwould Foundation
99 Arkansas Historic Preservation
Program
100 New Mexico State Planning Office
and Cultural Properties Review
Committee
101 (above) **Randall Page**, North
Carolina Department of Archives
and History
(below) **Balthazar Korab**
102 **Cervin Robinson**
103 **Cervin Robinson**
104 (left) **Wm. Edmund Barrett**
(right) **B. Clarkson Schoettle**
105 **Wm. Edmund Barrett**
106 (above) **Jack E. Boucher**, HABS
(below) **B. Clarkson Schoettle**
107 University of Texas
108 (all photos) **Jack E. Boucher**, HABS
109 **Cervin Robinson**
110 (left) **Wm. Edmund Barrett**
(right) **Jack E. Boucher**, HABS
111 (above) **Buerki & Becker**, State
Historical Society of Wisconsin
(below) Central City Opera House
Association
112 (above, left) HABS
(above, right) Texas State Historical
Survey Committee
(below) Library of Congress
113 National Park Service
114 (above photos) **Jack E. Boucher**,
HABS
(below) **Thomas R. Tucker**
115 **Jack E. Boucher**, HABS
116 Mitchell (S.D.) Area Chamber of
Commerce
117 Los Angeles State and County
Arboretum
118 (above) **Jack E. Boucher**, HABS
(below) **Rhoda Baer**
119 **Marvin Rand**, HABS
120 **B. Clarkson Schoettle**
121 **Wm. Edmund Barrett**
122 (left) **Cortland V. D. Hubbard**,
HABS
(right) © **Bettye Lane**, *The
National Observer*

123 **Stuart C. Schwartz**
124 (both photos) **Balthazar Korab**
125 **Jack E. Boucher**, HABS
126 National Park Service
127 (above, left) **Karl Kernberger**, New Mexico State Planning Office
(above, right) **Jack E. Boucher**, HABS
(below) National Park Service
128 **Cortland V. D. Hubbard**, HABS
129 **Lanny Miyamoto**, HABS
130 (left) **Mark Junge**, Wyoming Recreation Commission
(right) **Jack E. Boucher**, HAER
131 (left) **Arthur Steelhorne**, HABS
(right photos) **Wm. Edmund Barrett**
132 (left) **Steven Zane**, HAER
(right, above) **George Eisenman**, HABS
(right, below) **Wm. Edmund Barrett**
133 © **Randolph Langenbach**
134 **Wm. Edmund Barrett**
135 © **Randolph Langenbach**
136 (left) **Carleton Knight III**, National Trust
(right) **Jack E. Boucher**, HAER
137 (above) **Wm. Edmund Barrett**
(below) **Wm. Edmund Barrett**, HAER
138 **J. F. Brooks**, HABS
139 (above) **Carleton Knight III**
(below) National Park Service
140 (above) **Wm. Edmund Barrett**
(below) **Balthazar Korab**
141 (above) **James L. Dillon & Company**, Pennsylvania Historical and Museum Commission
(below) **Neil Pearson**, North Carolina Department of Archives and History
142 (left, above) **Jack E. Boucher**, HABS
(left, below) **Jack E. Boucher**, National Park Service
(right, above) **Janet Seapker**, North Carolina Department of Archives and History
(right, below) **Jack E. Boucher**, HABS
143 **Herbert C. Darbee**, Connecticut Historical Commission
144 (left) **Gil Amiaga**
(right) **Wm. Edmund Barrett**
145 (above) Utah Heritage Foundation
(below) **L. H. Dreyer**, Gil Amiaga collection
146 **L. H. Dreyer**, Gil Amiaga collection

147 (both photos) **L. Y. Dreyer**, Gil Amiaga collection
148 (above, left) **Al Honeycutt**, North Carolina Department of Archives and History
(above, right) **Wm. Edmund Barrett**
(below) **B. Clarkson Schoettle**
149 (above, left) **Wm. Edmund Barrett**, HAER
(above, right) **Wm. Edmund Barrett**
(below) **Wm. Edmund Barrett**
150 © **Randolph Langenbach**
151 (left) **David Plowden**, U.S. Department of Transportation
(right photos) **Balthazar Korab**
152 (above) Goodyear Aerospace Corporation, National Register of Historic Places
(below) General Dynamics
153 (both photos) **Steven Zane**, HAER
154 **Jack E. Boucher**, HAER
155 **Balthazar Korab**
156 **Balthazar Korab**
157 (above, left) **Jack E. Boucher**, HAER
(above, right) Idaho State Historical Society
(below) **Wm. Edmund Barrett**
158 (left) **William F. Winter, Jr.**, HABS
(right) **Wm. Edmund Barrett**, HAER
159 (above) HABS
(below) **Stuart C. Schwartz**, North Carolina Department of Archives and History
160 © **Randolph Langenbach**
161 © **Randolph Langenbach**
162 (both photos) **Wm. Edmund Barrett**, HAER
163 (above) **Paul Vanderbilt**, State Historical Society of Wisconsin
(below) Idaho State Historical Society
164 (left) **Carleton Knight III**, National Trust
(right, above) **Richard Nickel**, National Register of Historic Places
(right, below) **Thomas R. Tucker**, National Trust
165 **Wm. Edmund Barrett**, Virginia Historic Landmarks Commission
166 **Wm. Edmund Barrett**
167 (above) **Wm. Edmund Barrett**
(below) **George Newschafer**, HABS
168 Indiana Architectural Foundation, from *Indianapolis Architecture*
169 **L. H. Dreyer**, Gil Amiaga collection
170 **Wm. Edmund Barrett**
171 (left) **Jack E. Boucher**, HABS

(right) HABS
172 **Leonard C. Rennie**
173 **Leonard C. Rennie**
174 **Carleton Knight III**, National Trust
175 (left, above) **Wm. Edmund Barrett**
(left, below) **Jack E. Boucher**, HABS
(right, above) Merchants National Bank of Winona, Minn.
(right, below) **Jack E. Boucher**, HABS
176 **Clover Vail**, Friends of Cast Iron Architecture
177 (above) **Carleton Knight III**, National Trust
(below) **Jack E. Boucher**, HABS
178 **Carleton Knight III**
179 (above photos) **Thomas R. Tucker**, National Trust
(below) Ohio Historical Society, National Register of Historic Places
180 Niagara Mohawk Power Corporation, Cultural Resources Council of Syracuse and Onondaga County, Inc.
181 **Cervin Robinson**
182 National Park Service
183 **David Plowden**
184 (above) **Wm. Edmund Barrett**
(below) **George A. Grant**, National Park Service
185 **Jack E. Boucher**, National Park Service
186 (left) **Thomas R. Tucker**, National Trust
(right) **James Butters**, HABS
187 **David Plowden**
188 (left) **Balthazar Korab**
(right) **Carl Purcell**, ACTION/Peace Corps
189 (both photos) National Park Service
190 (left) **Balthazar Korab**
(right, above) **Michael Richman**
(right, below) National Park Service
191 (both photos) **Wm. Edmund Barrett**
192 (above) **Harry W. Doust**, National Park Service
(below) **David Plowden**
193 **David Plowden**
194 **Jack E. Boucher**, HABS
195 National Trust collection
196 **Stuart C. Schwartz**, North Carolina Department of Archives and History
197 (above) **Richard Federici**, New Mexico State Planning Office
(below) **Jack E. Boucher**, HABS
198 (above) **Wm. Edmund Barrett**
(below) **Douglas Armsden**
199 **Wm. Edmund Barrett**, HAER

PHOTOGRAPHIC CREDITS

200 **William H. Pierson, Jr.**
201 (above) **Jack E. Boucher**, HABS (below) **William H. Pierson, Jr.**
202 **Balthazar Korab**
203 (all photos) **Jack E. Boucher**, HABS
205 **William H. Pierson, Jr.** The mill town of Harrisville, N.H.
206 © **Randolph Langenbach**
207 © **Randolph Langenbach**
208 (left) **Balthazar Korab** (right) **A. Pierce Bounds**
209 (all photos) **Victor M. Andrade**
210 **Balthazar Korab**
211 (above) City of Philadelphia Records Department (below) National Park Service
212 Plimoth Plantation
213 **Carleton Knight III**
214 (left) **Robert Nugent** (right) **George Cserna**, Ulrich Franzen & Associates, Architects
215 **Robert S. Oakes**
217 **Turner Associates**, HABS. Row in the Logan Circle Historic District, Washington, D.C.
218 **Tom Lutz**, Old Town Restorations
219 Minnesota Historical Society
220 (all photos) **Paul Sprague**
221 (left) Bucks County Planning Commission—Doylestown Borough Planning Commission (right) Chamber of Commerce—Historic Savannah Foundation
222 (above) National Trust (below) **Jack E. Boucher**, HABS
223 **Wm. Edmund Barrett**, HAER
224 **N. Jane Iseley**
225 **Frances Benjamin Johnston**, Library of Congress
226 Marshall Historical Society
227 (all photos) **John Ulven**, City of Duluth Department of Research & Planning
228 **Richard Federici**, New Mexico State Planning Office
229 (left) **Hoyt E. Carrier II**, *The Grand Rapids Press* (right) Vision, Inc.
231 **Gil Amiaga**. Jackson Place on Lafayette Square, Washington, D.C.
232 Jack Daniel Distillery
233 **Jack E. Boucher**, HABS
234 **George Creed**, Mayor's Office of Lower Manhattan Development, New York City
235 **Richard Nickel**, Richard Nickel Committee
236 Chamber of Commerce—Historic Charleston Foundation

237 (left) **Richard Nickel**, Commission on Chicago Historical and Architectural Landmarks (right, above) **M. Hamilton Morton, Jr.** (right, below) Nantucket Information Bureau
238 (both photos) **Bruce M. Krivisky**, Historic Walker's Point
239 (above) Old West Side Association, from *Old West Side* (below) **Bruce M. Krivisky**, Historic Walker's Point
240 Old West Side Association, from *Old West Side*
241 **John J. G. Blumenson**, National Trust
242 **Balthazar Korab**
243 **George Cserna**
244 (left photos) **Balthazar Korab** (right) **Joe Rosen**, Pittsburgh History & Landmarks Foundation
245 **Joe Rosen**, Pittsburgh History & Landmarks Foundation
246 (left) **Joe Rosen**, Pittsburgh History & Landmarks Foundations (right) **John Beckman**
247 (left) **George McCue** (right) **Robert Pettus**, HABS
249 Historical collection, Title Insurance and Trust Company of San Diego. Hotel del Coronado, San Diego, open yet not completed in 1887.
250 (left) **Robert Thall**, University of Illinois Press (right) **Jim Ball**
251 National Trust collection
252 **Richard Nickel**, Richard Nickel Committee
253 © **Steve Rosenthal**
254 **Richard Nickel**, Commission on Chicago Historical and Architectural Landmarks
255 (both photos) © **James O. Milmoe**, State Historical Society of Colorado Library
256 (both photos) Trolley Square Associates
257 **Carleton Knight III**, National Trust
258 **Day Walters**
259 **Ron Linek**, Community Design Committee
260 **Jack E. Boucher**, HABS
261 (left) **Jack E. Boucher**, HABS (right) **Joshua Freiwald**
262 **Joshua Freiwald**

263 Land Design/Research, from *Otterbein Homestead Area: Guidelines for Exterior Restoration*
264 Galveston Historical Foundation
265 (left) **Richard Tichich** (right) Center Stage
266 **Jack E. Boucher**, HABS
267 (both photos) **William H. Pierson, Jr.**
269 **Delmar Lipp**. Waiting room of Union Terminal (1933), Cincinnati, Ohio
270 © **Greg Heins**
271 © **Greg Heins**
272 **Balthazar Korab**
273 (left) **Jack E. Boucher**, HABS (right) © **Ezra Stoller**/ESTO
274 (above) **Joshua Freiwald** (below) **Norman McGrath**, Arthur Cotton Moore Associates
275 (above) Arthur Cotton Moore Associates (below) **Norman McGrath**, Arthur Cotton Moore Associates
276 (left) **Thomas R. Tucker**, National Trust (right, above) Anderson Notter Associates (right, below) **Jack E. Boucher**, HABS
277 (both photos) **Marvin Rand**, HABS
278 **Marvin Rand**, HABS
279 **Delmar Lipp**
280 © **Phillip MacMillan James & Associates**
281 (left) **James Brett** (right) Urban Land Institute
282 (all photos) **Balthazar Korab**
283 **Wm. Edmund Barrett**
284 Maryland Institute, College of Art collection
285 (above) **Ken Houston** (below) **George Cserna**
286 Maryland Institute, College of Art collection
287 (both photos) Paramount Theatre of the Arts
288 **Cathe Centorbe**
289 (above) **Carleton Knight III** (below) Brady-Handy collection, Library of Congress
291 **William H. Pierson, Jr.** Looking across Harrisville Pond to the upper town of Harrisville, N. H.
296 **Paul Sprague**. Preserved information and funding sources: Charles Cloud House (1881), now a library, and the Cloud Street Bank (1883–84), McLeansboro, Ill.

INDEX

INDEX

THE NATIONAL TRUST

The National Trust for Historic Preservation is a nonprofit educational organization working to save America's forgotten heritage of buildings, sites, objects, and neighborhoods of character and significance in the history and culture of the United States. Chartered by Congress in 1949, the National Trust is a private organization with a membership of 100,000 individuals and associated groups. From its headquarters in Washington, D.C., and five regional and field services offices serving every state and U.S. Territory, the National Trust provides assistance in such preservation-related areas as architectural restoration, law, planning, preservation financing, historic property management and museum development. It also maintains historic properties, administers grant and loan funds, sponsors educational and technical conferences and student intern programs, provides reference and research services in the field of preservation and coordinates a speakers bureau. The Preservation Press of the National Trust, which directed the preparation of **America's Forgotten Architecture**, publishes books in preservation as well as a monthly newspaper, **Preservation News,** and a quarterly magazine, **Historic Preservation,** both of which are privileges of membership in the National Trust. Its programs and publications are made possible by membership dues, contributions and matching grants from the U.S. Department of Interior, National Park Service, under provisions of the National Historic Preservation Act of 1966. Information on National Trust programs and addresses of its regional offices are available by writing the National Trust for Historic Preservation, 740-748 Jackson Place, N.W., Washington, D.C. 20006.

GRAPHIC CREDITS

The text type for this book, Trump Medieval, is a film version of the original linotype face designed by George Trump in 1959. All secondary typefaces within the book, as well as the display type, have also been set in film, using various versions of the Trump family typeface. This book was photocomposed in film by *The Clarinda Company*. The halftone reproductions were also made by *The Clarinda Company*, and the printing was executed by *Kingsport Press*.
Production and manufacturing coordination was directed by Constance Mellon. Graphics were directed by R. D. Scudellari. Book design concept and graphics were styled by Janet Odgis.